A Primer on Industrial Environmental Impact

A Primer on Industrial Environmental Impact

Michael R. Greenberg and Glen Belnay,
William Cesanek, Nancy Neuman,
George Shepherd

THE CENTER FOR URBAN POLICY RESEARCH
RUTGERS UNIVERSITY
P.O. BOX 489
PISCATAWAY, NEW JERSEY 08854

TD
194.6
.G73
a.2

Cover design by Francis G. Mullen
Graphics by Frank Gradilone
Copyright 1979, Rutgers—The State University of New Jersey
Published in the United States of America
by the Center for Urban Policy Research
New Brunswick, New Jersey
Library of Congress Cataloging in Publication Data
Greenberg, Michael R.
  A Primer on industrial environmental impact

  Bibliography: p.
  Includes index.
  1. Environmental impact analysis. 2. Industries, Location of—Environmental aspects. I. Title.
  TD194.6.G73   333.7'7   78-11642
  ISBN 0-88285-050-4

to Josh

Contents

Acknowledgments

This book has grown out of my attempts to teach graduate students and conduct research about the impact of industrial development. The literature is voluminous, but terribly diffuse. The four co-authors and eight other graduate students studied these specialized literatures and collaborated on a case study which is used as an illustration in some of the chapters.

While we met as a group at least weekly for a year and shared information, the following major contributions were made. Glen Belnay and Nancy Neuman prepared major portions of the air resources chapter. Wayne Thompson also contributed to this chapter. William Cesanek and George Shepherd prepared an initial draft of the noise chapter. Michael Greenberg prepared the introductory, checklist, water resources, and solid waste chapters and pulled together and added to the noise and air chapters.

The authors would like to thank the following members of the group who contributed their efforts to the overall project: John Janoski, Beth Krugman, Robert Kull, James Marchetti, Paul Peterson, Nils Stolpe, and Nicholas Valente:

Funds for this publication were provided by the Center for Urban Policy Research at Rutgers University. The checklist questions presented in chapter two were originally prepared for an environmental mediation project conducted by the American Arbitration Association in New Jersey and funded by the Rockefeller Foundation.

I would like to thank the following colleagues and students who read and commented upon specific portions of the text: Professors George Carey, Robert Hordon, and Jerome Rose of Rutgers University and students Ken Gallagher, William Page and Daniel Travers. Special thanks are tendered to the staff members of the United States Environmental Protection Agency who were responsive to our many, many questions.

Michael R. Greenberg

A Primer on Industrial Environmental Impact

Chapter 1
Introduction

THERE ARE MANY REASONS why an industry may choose to locate in a place and equally many reasons why a community, region or state may support or oppose an industry's siting decision. From the industry's perspective, management would like to be close to its market and raw materials, in a place that provides an inexpensive and reliable labor force, and amid flexible and inexpensive transportation and communication networks. In addition, management will be attracted to a site that provides inexpensive and plentiful supplies of energy and water. Industrial management will look favorably at a community that provides financial incentives such as low and/or deferred taxes, local financial backing, and large plots of flat and inexpensive land having proper drainage and soil characteristics. Those of us who studied location theory during the early 1960s mastered these classical site selection factors.

Increasingly during the late 1960s and into the 1970s, amenity and environmental factors have become important considerations to the company. Industrial managers want to locate in places where the lives of their

1

families and those of their workers and their families are perceived to be attractive. The catch-all *attractive* includes meeting increasingly high aspirations for quality housing, shopping, entertainment, education, outdoor recreation, medical, legal, and security services.

Environmental considerations eliminate many otherwise attractive sites. If the state, regional, county, and local governments have a history of insisting on lengthy environmental assessments which are not assured of a positive evaluation, industry may go to a place that offers more opportunity for externalizing effluent emissions. Industries have also become increasingly sensitive to citizen opposition. Sites which may be opposed by an active environmental group and/or by a group which opposes the disruption of existing neighborhoods may be perceived by industry as a site they can reject. Overall, today site selection from an industry's perspective involves trade-offs among economic return, amenity benefits, and environmental costs.

The citizen/government perspective has received much less attention in the literature. The perspective is diverse. Some segments strongly favor and will only consider income and employment benefits. Other public/government participants will only consider environmental impacts.

The direct economic benefits to the region begin with increased employment during the construction and operating periods at the facility and at related industries. The jobs produce increased regional income which in turn leads to more purchases by local residents. More income and purchases lead to increasing tax revenues from income, property, sales, and other taxable items. More tax revenue and community wealth may lead to expansion of community services, recreational opportunities, and other favorable amenities.

The facility, however, implies some costs to the region. Some are short-term such as the displacement and relocation of some residents, increased traffic during construction, and the need for additional housing, school space, and other public services. Long-term costs include the loss of land for other more beneficial uses and the loss of regional attractiveness due to environmental degradation.

The environmental impacts of industrial location from the perspective of the public/government are the focus of this primer. The volume is called a primer because the impacts of industrial developments and methods of making assessments are many. Frankly, a full treatment is beyond the scope of a single volume. We chose to introduce the usual major impacts with a check list and to focus on those impacts which we consider to be most important. The check list (chapter 2) is relatively comprehensive without being an encyclopedic review. It should be used as a means of quickly flagging probable serious negative impacts.

Chapters are devoted to four impacts of major concern: noise, water, air, and solid waste. Each of these chapters focuses predominantly on impacts in urban, suburban, and exurban areas.

A second similarity among the four chapters is their organization. Assuming that the reader has little background, each chapter begins by identifying the harmful pollutants, their impacts and sources, and legal and technical control procedures. The overview is followed by specific information on industry, establishing the ambient environment, and measuring the impact of industrial development. Finally, each of the four chapters concludes with a summary and a report of additional sources of information.

The chapter organization may, at first, be confusing to the reader who expects to see impact analysis methods discussed before management techniques. Since this book is concerned with measuring the extent of industrial impact, we have reviewed management prior to impact analysis. The extent of the impact is frequently tied to laws and regulations. By discussing management first, we can rapidly zero in on the need for particular ambient data sets and impact methods.

Beyond the above two similarities, the noise, air, water, and solid waste chapters are quite different in approach. Published ambient noise surveys are rare. A careful person can make an acceptable noise survey. Accordingly, one of the purposes of the noise chapter survey is to review procedures. Other goals are to estimate the impact of industrial facilities and related activities, such as transportation and construction. In comparison to water and air quality, there has been relatively little work in noise pollution. Federal and state noise regulations and economics are, therefore, not as complex as the water and air counterparts. Accordingly, the chapter emphasizes monitoring and impact analysis, while legal and economic aspects are only touched on.

A similar focused approach was taken in the solid waste chapter. In terms of volume and weight, industrial solid waste and residential/commercial/institutional solid waste are insignificant when compared with agricultural and mining wastes. We believe that the most important industrial solid waste question is how to identify, treat, dispose of, and learn to live with hazardous industries, waste treatment, and disposal facilities. After review of the problems caused by conventional industrial solid waste and methods of solving these problems, additional information is provided about hazardous wastes.

The water and air programs, in contrast to the noise and solid waste management fields, have been built on relatively well-funded federal programs. The results of these strong programs are impact assessments and a literature which tends to be comprehensive. Our air and water chapters reflect major funded research efforts in the science, law, and economics of these fields. The two chapters present detailed reviews of the legal/administrative and economic aspects of air and water resources. Monitoring and impact methods are considered insofar as we judge that the methods are capable of being used by a nonexpert without access to a computer.

Summarizing, the air and water chapters attempt to deal with the spectrum of information, methods, and policies involved in evaluating the environmental impact of industry. The noise and solid waste chapters are much more focused on particular issues.

This volume is intended for the citizen, government employee, and student who does not have an extensive science, engineering, and math background but who has to respond to or wishes to learn about the impacts of industrial location. It assumes no previous knowledge. The few mathematical models that are presented are introductory. The text tries to provide the reader with the background necessary to recognize a probable environmental impact, a review of the basic legal and technical studies which should be done to evaluate the impact, and references to quickly determine whom to contact for technical and legal help.

Chapter 2
Screening Questions For Industrial Environmental Impact Analysis

THIS CHAPTER PRESENTS a check list which may be used to indicate probable, major adverse impacts of industrial development during the construction and operation of an industrial facility and related activities. The check list consists of two sets of questions which address the most general air, noise, odor, water quality and supply, solid waste, and land quality impacts.

The first set of twenty-two general questions aids the user in determining whether any cause for concern exists. For example, does the facility discharge oxygen-demanding wastes? If the answer is negative, then no further concern for direct pollution from processes and on-site domestic waste is necessary. If the facility will discharge oxygen-demanding wastes, then concern followed by research is appropriate.

A second set of thirty-eight follow-up questions helps the users determine if their concern should be minor or if major concern for a possible serious negative impact should exist. For example, on the one hand, a small amount of a domestic waste from an industrial facility can be handled by many techniques including septic systems, an EPA-approved treatment plant, or a connection to a municipal system. On the other hand, a large process discharge may have a serious impact and must be carefully reviewed with state and federal officials.

The user will note that we deliberately did not assign weights to different levels of concern. While people may agree that a particular impact is of concern, they assign different priorities to different impacts. One region may be more concerned with air, a second with solid waste, a third equally concerned with both or another combination. If users can achieve consensus about their levels of concern over different environmental characteristics, then the questions can be weighed and a quantitative score developed for every proposed project.

In developing these questions the senior author has been influenced by many other check lists which have been reviewed elsewhere.[1] Of special note is the work of Moore and others for the state of Delaware.[2] Like other check lists, this one is necessarily confined to ubiquitous problems and is intended to serve as a guide. Some of the thresholds in the check list are tied to legal standards; others are the senior author's best judgments. In order to understand all the questions, the untrained reader will probably have to read the noise, air, water, and solid waste chapters.

NOTES

1. See M. Greenberg, "Beyond the Checklist Approaches—Specific Problems of EIS Inquiry," pp. 215-31 in *The Environmental Impact Handbook*, eds. R. Burchell and D. Listokin (New Brunswick, N.J.: Center for Urban Policy Research, Rutgers University, 1975), for a brief review and list of some of these.

2. J.L. Moore *et al.*, *A Methodology for Evaluating Manufacturing Environmental Impact Statements for Delaware's Coastal Zone* (Columbus, Ohio: Battelle-Columbus, 1973).

AIR QUALITY

General Question	Answer		Follow-up Question	Answer	
	No concern if answer is no	Some concern if answer is yes		Some concern if answer is no	Major concern for possible serious negative impact if answer is yes
1. Will discharges directly from the facility be different from the conditions of the ambient environment?			1a. Will the discharges lead to the violation of an air quality standard in the case of: carbon monoxide nonmethane hydrocarbons nitrogen dioxide photochemical oxidants particulate matter sulfur dioxide?		
			1b. Will the discharge include the following: toxic organics toxic inorganics (too many of these to list; would include lead, asbestos, etc.)?		

AIR QUALITY (Continued)

General Question	Answer		Follow-up Question	Answer	
	No concern if answer is no	Some concern if answer is yes		Some concern if answer is no	Major concern for possible serious negative impact if answer is yes
2. Will traffic in and out of the plant or from the workers commuting to the facility produce serious traffic congestion?			2a. Will the discharges lead to localized carbon monoxide, nitrogen oxide, and/or photochemical oxidant air quality standard violations?		
			2b. Will the discharges lead to a concentrated discharge of lead within 200 feet of a major residential development?		
3. Will construction of the facility, its operation, and/or attendant transportation activities produce a noise level above the ambient?			3a. Will this level exceed 55 dB(A) outdoors near or 45 dB(A) inside of residential		

developments, schools, hospitals, libraries, recreation areas?

3b. Will this level exceed 70 dB(A) during the night and 80 dB(A) during the day?

4a. Will the odor be apparent in a residential neighborhood or a shopping area?

5a. Will the stack be visible for more than ½ mile?

---

4. Will the facility and attendant activities produce an odor?

5. Will the facility contain a stack and emissions?

SOLID WASTE MANAGEMENT

General Question	Answer		Follow-up Question	Answer	
	No concern if answer is no	Some concern if answer is yes		Some concern if answer is no	Major concern for possible serious negative impact if answer is yes
6. Will the solid waste stream be different from residential waste?			6a. Are these nonresidential wastes hazardous (e.g. toxic, flammable, carcinogenic, etc.)?		
			6b. Are any of these wastes not readily degradable in the environment (e.g., plastics, glass, ferrous and nonferrous metals)?		
			6c. If the waste is being disposed of by landfill, is the landfill near a source of water used for fishing, public potable supply, or contact recreation?		

7a. Will a new landfill site presently inhabited by rare or economically important species be filled to meet the demands of this facility?

8a. Will these vehicles lead to or contribute to the violation of an air quality standard or raise the decibel level to greater than 55dB in a major residential area?

8b. Will the changes cited in 8a occur during the night?

9a. Same as follow-up questions in 7a, 8a, 8b.

7. Will the volume of the waste exceed the current capacity of existing landfills or hasten the filling of the landfills?

8. Will the trucks removing the waste pass through a residential or institutional area, or add additional traffic to an already crowded thoroughfare?

9. Will the population added to the region by the facility and secondary activities lead to the impacts as in 7 and 8 above?

WATER RESOURCES

General Question	Answer		Follow-up Question	Answer	
	No concern if answer is no	Some concern if answer is yes		Some concern if answer is no	Major concern for possible serious negative impact if answer is yes
10. Will the discharges contain waste which will exert an oxygen demand?			10a. Will the discharge lead to the violation of a dissolved oxygen standard?		
11. Will the discharges contain solids at a concentration exceeding that of the receiving water?			11a. Will these discharges reduce light penetration, lead to eutrophication, or discolor the water?		
			11b. Will these discharges contain substances which will severely alter the pH and/or salinity of the water and lead to a violation of a water quality standard?		

12. Will the temperature of the discharges be the same as that of the receiving body of water?

12a. Will the water temperature change lead to the violation of a water quality standard?

13. Will the discharges contain hazardous substances?

13a. A long list as in air quality would be used here.

14. Will the discharges contain substances with high coliform counts?

14a. Will these discharges contribute to a violation of a water quality standard?

15. Will the facility's construction cause the course of bodies of water to be changed?

15a. Will this change last longer than the construction period?

16. Will the impervious cover of the facility and attendant parking areas lead to any of the impacts as in 10, 11, 13, and 14 above?

16a. Same as follow-up questions in 10, 11, 13, and 14.

17. Will nearby sources of water be affected in quality or quantity by the facility, by its

17a. Will a new water supply source be needed?

General Question	Answer		Follow-up Question	Answer
secondary industries, and by additional residents brought into the community?	No concern if answer is no	Some concern if answer is yes	17b. Will this new source require heavy chemical treatment? 17c. Will interagency transfers be required to meet these demands?	Some concern if answer is no / Major concern for possible serious negative impact if answer is yes

LAND QUALITY

General Question	Answer		Follow-up Question	Answer
18. Will the facility be constructed on hilly or other sensitive terrain?	No concern if answer is no	Some concern if answer is yes	18a. Is this slope greater than 15 percent? 18b. Are the soils and bedrock easily eroded? 18c. Will a portion of the floodplain be occupied?	Some concern if answer is no / Major concern for possible serious negative impact if answer is yes

19. Are the facility and attendant activities incompatible with existing land uses?

19a. Will the facility raise the value of the land and force out nearby less intensive uses?

19b. Will the facility change the existing economic base by competing for local labor and other, man-made resources or through environmental degradation of farms, resorts, etc.?

19c. Are any of these structures of historic value?

19d. Will the facility be visible from parklands, beaches, or other preserves or areas of recreation or block the view of scenic sites?

LAND QUALITY (Continued)

General Question	Answer		Follow-up Question	Answer	
	No concern if answer is no	Some concern if answer is yes		Some concern if answer is no	Major concern for possible serious negative impact if answer is yes
20. Will the facility and its secondary impacts require the expansion of community infrastructure?			20a. Will the facility and its secondary impacts require additions to the following local government infrastructure components: schools highways electric utility recreation fire social services health services water/sewer?		
			20b. Will these facilities pass through relatively		

undeveloped areas and act as undesirable development paths?

21. Will the facility and its attendant industries threaten the safety of people?

21a. Will the facility contain the following hazards?

  hazardous substances

  hazardous fixed equipment

  hazardous mobile equipment

21b. Will the hazards be confined within the boundary of the facility?

22. Will terrestrial plants or animals and associated aquatic species be affected by the facility?

22a. Will species biomass be reduced?

22b. Will species diversity be reduced?

22c. Will rare or endangered species be affected?

Chapter 3
Noise Impacts of
Industrial Development

As a result of the Noise Control Act of 1972, the din which disturbs sleep, interrupts conversation, causes anxiety and stress, and damages hearing is a federal criterion for determining the acceptability of a site for varying land uses. This chapter reviews noise pollution in three parts: (1) the creation and impacts of noise; (2) establishing the ambient environment; and (3) estimating the impact of major new noise sources on the ambient environment. The focus of this review is noise produced by the construction of plants, by industries, and by trucks which transport products to and from plants. Other sources of noise normally associated with urban industrial development will be briefly reviewed here. The chapter is not concerned with protecting workers exposed to noise where they work; rather its focus is the surrounding environment developed or zoned for residential and noise-sensitive institutional uses.

The Creation and Impacts of Noise

Sound and Its Measurement

Sound results from the transfer of mechanical vibrations through the air. The vibrations produce disturbances in the form of atmospheric pressure variations. Sound comes in waves which are characterized by amplitude, frequency, and duration. Amplitude is a measure of the magnitude of the pressure vibrations. It is measured in terms of the unit *microbar* which is one-millionth of the normal atmospheric pressure, or in newtons/meter^2 (which equals ten microbars). In noise measurement, amplitude is stated in terms of decibels (dB), partially because decibels are keyed to the human ear. One decibel is about the level of the weakest sound a human can discern in a quiet listening environment.

Decibels are measured on a logarithmic scale. A ten-decibel increase is associated with a tenfold increase in energy. A 10-decibel reading is 10 times more intense than 1 decibel; a 20-decibel reading is 100 times more intense than 1 decibel. Present noise sources can produce a range from one to about two hundred decibels. A very soft whisper is about 30 decibels (Exhibit 1). In contrast, a blaring radio is close to 110 decibels, and a Saturn rocket is close to 200 decibels. Conversational speech level is normally between 60 and 65 decibels. Levels above 120 dB can cause severe pain, and levels above 180 dB, if sustained, can cause death.

In order to properly understand the impacts of noise, one must characterize not only the amplitude measured in dB, but also the frequency of the vibrations. Frequency is the number of atmospheric pressure variations (vibrations) that occur in a second; the unit is called hertz (Hz). The human ear can sense between 20 and 20,000 vibrations per second.

Harmonics are tones that are multiples of the basic frequency. For example, the middle note on a piano is a tone composed of frequencies of 440 cycles (the fundamental frequency), and 880, 1,760, 3,520, and 7,040 cycles (the overtones, or harmonics). The lowest frequency in a sound is called the fundamental. The tone of a sound is the frequency of the fundamental and the various harmonics. A one-octave increase in the tone means that the frequency level of the fundamental has been doubled. Thus all octaves above and below a fundamental are also considered harmonics.

Loudness is the human physical response to both sound energy and frequency. The apparent loudness that people attribute to a sound does not vary directly with energy and frequency. At both very high and low frequencies human perception of loudness is not as keen as for the mid-range frequencies. This nonlinear change in perception is taken into account electronically on an instrument called the sound level meter, which is designed to measure the sound pressure level. Depending upon the specific meter, it will contain weighting networks which imitate different perceptions of sound. The current American national standard specification for sound level meters (ANSI S1.4-1971) requires that four weighting networks be provided in instruments for general use. The four alternate

EXHIBIT 1
ACOUSTIC POWER OF VARIOUS SOURCES

POWER (WATTS)	DECIBELS	SOURCE	EFFECT
100,000	170		
		TURBO-JET ENGINE WITH AFTERBURNER	
10,000	160	TURBO-JET ENGINE	
1,000	150		
		PROPELLER AIRLINER	
100	140	AIR RAID SIREN	PAINFULLY LOUD
10	130	75-PIECE ORCHESTRA	
		SMALL AIRCRAFT ENGINE	
1	120	PIANO, DISCOTHEQUE, THUNDER	PEAK VOCAL EFFORT
0.1	110	BLARING RADIO, PILE DRIVERS	
0.01	100	CHAIN SAW	
0.001	90	HEAVY TRUCK VOICE-SHOUTING	VERY ANNOYING, HEARING DAMAGE
0.0001	80	HAIR DRYER	
0.00001	70	FREEWAY TRAFFIC VOICE-CONVERSATION LEVEL	PHONE CONVERSATION DIFFICULT
0.000001	60	AIR CONDITIONING	
0.0000001	50	LIGHT AUTO TRAFFIC	QUIET
0.000,000,01	40	QUIET OFFICE	
0.000,000,001	30	VOICE-VERY SOFT WHISPER	VERY QUIET

frequency-response characteristics are obtained by weighting networks designated A, B, C, and D. The A weighting network is legally required by the United States Environmental Protection Agency (U.S. EPA) because it is the one most closely approximating the human ear's loudness reactions to the midrange sounds. The C scale is a better indicator of the response to low frequency noises (e.g., diesel locomotives). A fourth scale, D, has been developed for monitoring jet aircraft noises. This chapter focuses on the A weighting network. Additional information on U.S. EPA-approved meters will be presented later in the chapter.

Meters allow noise sources to be classified on the basis of frequency and amplitude. However, relating a decibel reading from a meter to human reaction is not straightforward. Impact criteria such as speech interference, sleep interruption, and annoyance depend on both physical characteristics of noise such as level, frequency, and fluctuation as well as nonphysical aspects such as information content and/or human interpretation of the noise. For example, rattles and noises in automobiles are often disturbing not because of the noise level but rather because the noise indicates a possible expensive malfunction.

While the dB(A) is normally used to measure impact, it can produce misleading results. The dB(A) embodies the human ear's sensitivities to certain frequencies; but a dB(A) measurement does not indicate all of the primary offending frequencies. The focus on selective information may hide the true source of the noise pollution. For example, a truck produces several different kinds of noise: engine vibration, exhaust system, tires and horns. Frequency analysis has shown that the major offending noise is often the exhaust noise, which is characterized by low frequencies and therefore not necessarily accurately described by the A weighting network.

Noise spectra (octave analysis) are far more valuable than a single number rating in characterizing the noise levels. An octave analysis requires equipment which is usually owned by consulting firms. Octave analysis is normally performed on an octave band analyser connected to the sound level information which has been recorded on magnetic tape. An electronic filter separates the noise into one-third octaves, which a digital processor converts into sound pressure levels measured in dB in one-third octaves from 25 to 20,000 Hz. This processor also has the potential of adding A, B, or C weighting networks to the dB output. It is possible to generate a number of statistical values from this sophisticated electronic process, including the following: maximum and minimum dB levels; number of noise occurrences; the mean and standard deviation; and the tenth (L_{10}) (ambient), fiftieth (L_{50}) (median), and ninetieth (L_{90}) (intrusive) percentile noise levels for each one-third octave.

These statistical summaries are normally presented in a histogram format. Each dB level found in the noise emission is a variable on the horizontal axis of the histogram, and the number of occurrences is indicated usually by asterisks. Exhibit 2 is one example of a computer-generated histogram. The modal dB(A) level for both daytime and nighttime is 56

EXHIBIT 2
SAMPLE HISTOGRAM OF DAY AND
NIGHT NOISE READINGS

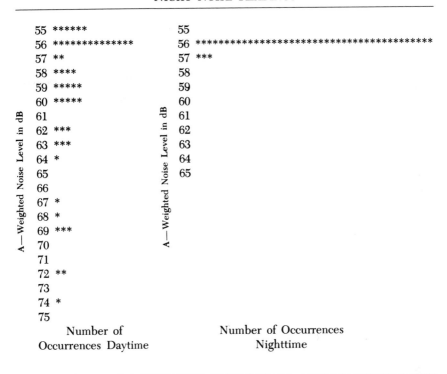

| Number of
Occurrences Daytime | Number of Occurrences
Nighttime |

SOURCE: U.S.EPA, *Noise from Industrial Plants,* (*Washington, D.C.: EPA, 1971,*
pp. 191-199.

dB(A). Note, however, that the daytime is punctuated by frequent higher readings, indicating a louder environment. Histograms such as the one pictured in Exhibit 2 can also be done by hand. This one was done with the Environmental Protection Agency methodology developed in Waco, Texas (examined in depth later in this chapter).

Given the limitations of a single dB(A) reading and the great expense and complexity of octave analysis, the U.S.EPA has derived measurements which fall between the dB(A) and octave analysis in complexity. The dichotomy between working and sleeping hours is recognized by EPA. The federal agency recommends the use of two measurements, Leq and Ldn, in assessing noise. These two indicators produce decibel measurements which take into account the duration, the frequency, and, in the case of Ldn, the time of the day. Sample Leq and Ldn calculations are made later in the chapter. Therefore, at this point, the reader need not closely study the formulas. The Leq measurement is generated from the data on the histograms. Leq is expressed as:

$$Leq = 10 \log_{10}(\tfrac{1}{n}) \sum (n_1 \times 10^{(dB/10)} + n_2 \times 10^{(dB/10)} + \ldots + n_m \times 10^{(dB/10)})$$

where n equals the total number of samples in the histogram; $n = 1, 2 \ldots m$ is the number of samples (occurrences) for each dB level in the histogram; and dB is the decibel level for the entire range of dB levels generated, beginning with the smallest and progressing to the highest.

The Ldn (sound level, day and night) measurement does not require a histogram but instead the ambient day and night dB levels.

$$Ldn = 10 \log_{10} (1/24) (15 \times 10^{Ld/10} + 9 \times 10^{(Ln + 10/10)})$$

where Ld is the Leq obtained between 7 a.m. and 10 p.m. and Ln is the Leq obtained between 10 p.m. and 7 a.m.

Both of these measurements can be programmed into a computer and be presented as part of the octave analysis explained earlier. They can also be done by hand provided an electronic calculator which handles logarithms is available.

As the formulas above indicate, decibels are logarithmic ratios of two sound pressures. Therefore, one cannot simply add together decibels to arrive at a single figure. The higher decibels mask the lower levels. In general, adding together two equal sounds increases the level by 3 decibels. If one sound is 10 decibels louder than a second sound, the impact of the lower sound is minimal. One of the implications of sound masking is that a sound between 70 and 80 dB can prevent normal conversations. This rule-of-thumb and others will be elaborated upon later in the chapter by referring to recommended sound levels for different activities.

The noise descriptions presented to this point are the basis of evaluating the physical impact of noise. They do not touch on the interpretative aspects of noise such as information content and annoyance. These non-physical parameters are less frequently covered than the physical parameters in the noise literature because they are cultural and thus subjective. These nonphysical parameters are usually integrated with more easily quantifiable physical parameters during the impact analysis. The impacts of the physical and nonphysical parameters will be discussed in the next section on impact identification and evaluation.

THE IMPACTS OF NOISE

This section reviews the physiological and psychological responses of people to disturbing sound. The three major harmful impacts of sound are

EXHIBIT 3
ESTIMATES OF MAGNITUDES OF NOISE EFFECTS
[in dB(A)]

Effect	Moderate Level	Appreciable Level
[Direct]		
Hearing Damage Risk	70	90
Speech Interference	45	60
Sleep Interference	40	70
[Indirect]		
Physiological Stress	—	90
Startle	—	110
Annoyance	40	60
Task Interference	55	75

SOURCE: U.S.EPA, *Noise from Construction Equipment,* NTID300.1 (Washington D.C.: EPA, 1971) p. 63.

hearing damage, speech interference, and sleep interruption. These three direct effects are most frequently mentioned in the noise literature and by the public in complaints. The complaints have led to extensive research which has contributed to more knowledge about direct effects than about secondary effects. The secondary effects are stress, startle, annoyance, and task interference. These reactions to noise are not well researched and are difficult to quantify. Exhibit 3 indicates what the U.S.EPA considers moderate and appreciable levels of reactions to noise.

Hearing damage is the easiest, legally determinable effect of noise exposure. The Walsh-Healey Public Contracts Act specifies allowable, permanent threshold shifts at various frequencies.[1] A threshold shift describes a change in the ability of a person to detect specific frequency ranges. The law permits permanent threshold shifts up to 10 dB at frequencies below 1,000 Hz, up to 15 dB shifts below 2,000 Hz, and up to a 20 dB shift at frequencies above 3,000 Hz. This hearing damage threshold has been criticized.[2] The criticisms are that both the Walsh-Healey and the Occupational Safety and Health acts permit amplitudes and frequencies considerably higher than what many noise experts would term acceptable.

Speech interference is a key criterion for the planner. The criterion for speech interference is based on verbal communication in the home. Criteria of 98 percent comprehension of all sentences and 85 percent comprehension of all standard, phonetically balanced words at a distance of five meters requires a vocal effort of about 65 dB(A). Five meters is the maximum distance at which conversation at normal levels might be achieved in a quiet environment. A 60 dB(A) background noise level is assumed to preclude conversation at nominal levels of vocal effort at distances greater than one meter. For television watchers and radio listeners, indoor levels of 35 to 51 dB(A) are recommended.[3]

There are two ways that noise exposure might interfere with sleep. The first is to delay the onset of sleep and the second is to shift sleep stages. It has been generally accepted that the initial time necessary for an individual to fall asleep increases with exposure to increasing noise levels. Also, prolonged exposure to high noise levels can cause tinnitus (ringing in the ears), which many subjects claim delayed the onset of sleep. The aftereffects of noise exposure, even in the absence of any immediate noise, can interfere with sleep. It has also been shown in various experiments that noise levels as low as 35 dB(A) can induce shifts from deeper to lighter levels of sleep, or even awaken many people.

The criterion level of 70 dB(A) is recognized as the level at which sleep interference effects are felt by a considerable portion of the population. More than half the population may be awakened by exposure to noise levels of 70 dB(A), while about half of the population will find difficulty in falling asleep when exposed to this noise level. Beranek puts indoor sleeping requirements at between 25 and 56 dB(A) with additional adjustments of 10 to 20 dB(A) for open windows.[4]

The secondary effects of harmful noises are psychological stress, startle, annoyance, and task interference. These are all reactions that at low noise levels depend primarily on the information content contained within the noise. A sound in a dark room, a growling animal, or a harsh voice may trigger these reactions because of the subjective meaning of the noise and not the level. In short, the stress potential of many noises is caused by acculturated and instinctive associations.

Accordingly, no minimum level of effect can be specified. At high noise levels, stress becomes evident. Physiological studies correlate high noise levels [90 dB(A)] with pupillary dilation, increased pulse and heart rate, and greater blood pressure. These studies signify that at higher noise levels stress occurs in and of itself, rather than being a function of meaning.

The interrelationship between meaning and stress reactions may also be applied to the startle reaction. Again, however, there is no minimal level of effect that can be quantified. The phenomenon of habituation causes most people to experience a marked decrease in their degree of sensitivity to repeated exposure to startle noises. Expectation, regularity, familiarity, and numerous other individual idiosyncrasies strongly mitigate startle reactions. Even high noise levels are affected by high ambient noise conditions that can mask or reduce the startle effect. This area of noise impact needs much research to make it predictable and useful for planning.

The levels indicated in Exhibit 3 are, in reality, not independent of one another and are intended to reflect the range at which any of the effects can occur. The research available on noise impacts on task performance is highly contradictory. It is agreed that loud, random, and intermittent noise impedes efficient task performance. Some studies show that low level noise is actually better for task performance than none at all.[5] One research problem is that in many experiments the subjects are aware their task performance is being measured, and in spite of the noise, they actually improve efficiency through greater concentration. This area of impacts also needs much additional research to achieve a more useful status.

Noise-induced distraction has the potential of causing strong and generalized psychophysical stress, emotional response, and direct autonomic responses. Some typical effects are changes in skin temperature, blood pressure, pulse rate, and other indicators of autonomic changes in the nervous system. These changes in the nervous system may occur without conscious knowledge by the individual. The obvious manifestation may be entirely physical; however, it also may precipitate a strong psychophysical response leading to emotional disturbances. One commonly referred to and unfortunate example is the New York City resident who shot his garbageman for banging the lids on the trashcans.

The physical-autonomic reaction to noise is greatly complicated by the socioeconomic response to noise exposure in both its informational and level characteristics. For example, some community noise measurement methodologies allow up to 10 dB(A) more noise if it is directly related to the economic welfare of the community (e.g., the town factory).

Overall, the variability of human response to noise makes anything other than a physical description of the noise environment subjective. Much more is known about physical noise parameters than about psychological human responses. Thus far, the most effective approach has been to measure the noise source as comprehensively as possible with known physical parameters, and then later include specific community or individual response characteristics in the noise evaluation. Questions concerning the impacts of noise are being investigated by many countries with results that, so far, are inconclusive.[6]

While research is not conclusive, the U.S. EPA has developed information on levels considered to be requisite to protect public health with a margin of safety.[7] At the present time, EPA's working ambient numbers are 45 dB for indoor activity and 55 dB for outdoor activity. The 45 dB sound level is given as the requisite to protect against indoor activity interference in residences, hospitals, and schools. The 55 dB threshold is the goal to protect against outdoor activity interference.

Given some residual ambient noise, some habituation of the population, and some open windows, the EPA indicates that as the dB levels rise, community reaction will increase. At noise levels between 50 and 60 dB the noise becomes noticeable. There may be a few complaints; however, general citizen reaction should not be expected. When the offending noise is between 60 and 70 dB, widespread complaints and a threat of legal action is likely to occur. If the intruding noise is between 70 and 80 dB, several threats of legal action should be expected as well as appeals to local officials to intervene. At levels above 80 dB, vigorous community actions should be expected. Overall, the 45, 55, and 70-80 dB numbers are the critical ones for most impact studies. They were used in the check list.

Summarizing, this initial section of the noise chapter has defined sound, described how sound is measured, and reviewed the harmful impacts of sound. The key information to remember is that loudness, which is the perception of sound, is composed of a combination of sound frequency, duration and amplitude. Second, dB(A) is used in most studies to characterize sound. However, dB(A) is an imperfect indicator and therefore it may be necessary to use Leq or Ldn measurements and octave analysis in some studies. Third, the major harmful impacts of sound include hearing damage and speech and sleep interference. Other impacts are stress, startle, annoyance, and task interference. Recent EPA studies have set 45 and 55 dB(A) as indoor and outdoor impact levels.

Whereas the EPA has established dB levels, the cost and legal/administrative implications of realizing the desired levels are not well known.[8] In its 1971 report to the EPA, the National Bureau of Standards concluded that "data available on the entire subject of noise and its abatement are so rudimentary that they do not lend themselves to even the most primitive economic analyses." The National Bureau report prepared crude estimates for cost of equipment redesign and replacement, right-of-way, and receiver insulation. Few data were available on the impact of noise and its abatement on wages, prices, productivity, production costs, employment, balance of payments, real property value, and health.

Economic data have improved in recent years in response to EPA's efforts to develop a national noise strategy. In April 1977, the EPA published a document called *Toward a National Strategy for Noise Control.* The document and supplements are seen as stepping stones toward the formulation of a comprehensive national noise strategy. The documents set forth five operational goals to achieve the general goal of "an environment for all Americans, free from noise that jeopardizes their health or welfare."

1. Take all practical steps to eliminate hearing loss resulting from noise exposure.
2. Immediately reduce outdoor Ldn to 75 dB.
3. Eventually reduce Ldn to 65 dB by vigorous regulatory and planning actions.
4. Ultimately reduce Ldn to 55 dB.
5. Encourage and assist other federal, state, and local agencies in the development of noise control policies.

Three main tools are to be used to implement the goals:

1. Federal noise emission regulations for new products.
2. State and local controls.
3. Federal regulations requiring the labeling of products.

The first tool has already been used in regulating interstate motor and rail carriers, air compressors, medium and heavy trucks, motorcycles, buses, and truck-mounted solid waste compactors, among others. A current issue is the effectiveness of a new product standard after the product has left the factory. Enforcement of anti-tampering regulations, warranty, and useful life of product provisions are seen as essentials.

State and local agencies can greatly assist in the task of bringing the national strategy to fruition. Besides helping in the enforcement of federal regulations, they can develop their own controls and cooperate with EPA in implementing two new EPA programs: Quiet Communities and the ECHO (Each Community Helps Others) program. Quiet Communities would select demonstration communities in which model noise control programs would be developed. These and other communities which have independently developed successful noise control programs would be assisted by EPA under ECHO to provide help to other communities with similar problems.

Finally, labeling may prove to be as effective as new product standards. EPA assumes that given a choice the consumer will purchase quieter shop tools, garden equipment, vacuum cleaners, auto equipment, air conditioners, dishwashers, food blenders, refrigerators, chain saws, and other products.

Overall, while the EPA has begun to move toward a national noise strategy, the legal/administrative tools are not well developed and tested, and the economic implications are not well known.

Establishing Ambient Noise Levels

Before a project is constructed, the background noise levels should be established for the pre-impact record. This section reviews site description and four methods of establishing background noise levels. A good deal of detail is presented because monitoring is usually left to the community or consultant representing the community. We will draw upon a case study to help illustrate the process. The case study is a new industrial park which is proposed to contain industrial facilities drawing upon the solid waste stream for most of their raw materials. The case study is probably more complicated than a normal industrial park from the noise perspective because it contains many relatively noisy industrial operations and will generate a good deal of truck traffic.

SITE DESCRIPTION

It is important that the rationale for selecting ambient monitoring stations be carefully presented. For example, the project site is in an industrial park far removed from any residential area. The closest residence is an inn located about four thousand feet from the northwest extremity of the project site. The next closest residential area includes a schoolhouse and single family housing located about six thousand feet away from the northwest corner of the project site. The project site is mainly filled marsh with a few abandoned ammunition sheds, some offices, and one industrial plant. Overall, a minimum impact to people should be expected from noise generated by on-site processes.

MAJOR SOURCES OF NOISE

The major noises one hears at the proposed site should always be described. At the sample site noise comes from four sources: (1) distant road noises; (2) minimal noise produced by one nearby plant and by some distant industrial facilities; (3) occasional airplane noise; and (4) noise produced by the local wildlife.

The project is expected to generate a great deal of vehicular traffic, notably refuse disposal trucks. Therefore, we assumed that the most significant noise impact of the project, if any, would be from solid waste trucks.

Since we decided to orient the study to highway transportation noise, most of the measurement sites were located along expected routes of the refuse disposal trucks, near noise sensitive residential areas. Only a few sites were chosen around the site itself to document existing conditions.

We cannot say precisely how many monitoring stations are necessary for a specific project. However, we offer the following guidelines. First, from one to three monitors should be located at the site: one near the likely noisiest source at the site; and, if necessary, a second and a third at the boundary of the site as close as possible to the nearest noise sensitive residences or establishments. Next, noise sensitive locations should be monitored including groups of homes, hospitals, schools, and recreation and commercial facilities within 1/4 to 1/2 mile of the site. Finally, if the facility is going to generate a good deal of truck and automobile traffic, locations along the route should be monitored. For example, the main entrance to the site is an obvious place to monitor, at traffic lights and along hills which trucks will pass, and at points along roads at which many trucks will exit.

The 1/4 to 1/2-mile monitoring radius noted above reflects the fact that the dB level of sound decreases with increased distance between the source and the listener. Assuming a reference distance of 100-200 feet, the rate may be approximated by this rule-of-thumb: the doubling of distance between a point source (a factory whistle) and a listener results in a 6 dB decrease in sound level; the doubling of distance between a line source (a roadway) and a listener results in an approximately 3 dB decrease in the sound level. A line source has more than one point of origin, and therefore the distance decay function is not as rapid as in the case of a single point of origin. This distance decay function assumes that the sound can radiate in any compass direction uniformly, without obstructions from barriers which can reflect or dampen noise. Additional information will be provided on the distance decay of noise later in the chapter.

Summarizing, the important off-site places to locate monitors are at noise sensitive land uses and at places where vehicles must stop, turn, and climb.

DETAILED SITE DESCRIPTIONS

The measurement sites should be described in detail. Such descriptions should always be included as part of an impact analysis. Three of the nine sites (4, 7, and 9) which were part of our case study will be used throughout the chapter. They are described below for illustrative purposes.

Measurement Site 4. Data were obtained at the property line of the parking lot of a small nursery school which is now the location of the county department of parks and recreation. The primary reasons for choosing this site were: it is a noise sensitive facility; it enabled us to compare a site without a traffic light with another site with a traffic light, and a site far from the road with another site close to the road. Opportunities for making such comparisons should be sought. The road at this point is primarily used by industry. The nearest residential area is a couple hundred feet north of the school.

Measurement Site 7. Measurements were taken at the intersection of some of the railway lines that cross the industrial park, several hundred feet away from any roadway and near some offices. The area is generally quiet, with occasional noise coming from nearby roadways. Gunshots were occasionally heard. When such unusual sounds are heard they should be eliminated from the meter readings. We measured near the railway to document the noise environment near the offices and for future reference.

Measurement Site 9. Site 9 is in an undeveloped part of the industrial park. There are no major noise sources, with the exception of a road that is traveled infrequently. The contribution of sound to the existing environment is made up of a combination of minor sources such as birds, airplanes, a distant roadway, and one industrial plant which releases stack gases. This site is relatively quiet, and accordingly the construction and the operation of the project should have a major noise impact on this environment.

Monitoring Procedures

This section describes four monitoring procedures: (1) the British Standard; (2) state of New Jersey; (3) EPA-Waco composite, and (4) computer. The British Standard is presented as a long-standing method which is relatively easy to use, but is not recommended in the United States. The New Jersey method demonstrates the fact that the user should determine if the state has specific requirements. The EPA-Waco method is recommended to the American user. The computer methodology is what a consultant is likely to do. The British Standard, New Jersey, and computer methods are overviewed. The EPA-Waco composite method is presented in greater detail because it is the procedure we recommend to the user who will not be able to use a consulting firm.

THE BRITISH STANDARD—4142

An effective method of rating industrial noise affecting mixed residential and industrial areas is the British Standard—4142. It is a simple and useful method of determining whether or not a complaint is justified. Duerden indicates that the standard is so important in industrial noise control in Great Britain that it is suggested that a copy should be available at all public health departments.[9]

The British Standard rating procedure consists of three separate tasks: (1) the measurement of the noise in question; (2) the measurement of the background noise into which the noise in question intrudes; and (3) a comparison of the intruding noise corrected for certain characteristics with the background noise corrected for local circumstances. These are called the corrected noise levels and the corrected criterion, respectively. With the aid of a good sound level meter, one can determine whether or not the intruding noise is a nuisance in comparison with recommended levels and with noise rating curves.

The meter used in the analysis must comply with British Standard —3489 (industrial grade) or British Standard—4197 (precision). The battery voltage must be checked immediately before and after each series of measurements. The meter must be checked with a calibrator. If the change is more than 4 dB the meter should be returned to the manufacturer and completely recalibrated. It should be recalibrated at least every six months. A windscreen should be used if considered necessary. Frankly, in our opinion, a windscreen is always a good idea.

The base measure is the A-weighted sound level. A full octave analysis is recommended to identify the annoying components in the noise. Meter readings are taken outdoors with the sound level meter set to the slow response position at a measurement location chosen to give results representative of the noise outside the building from which complaints have risen or are likely to arise. The microphone is to be at a height of about 1.2 meters (4 feet) and at least 3.6 meters (12 feet) from any reflecting surface, if possible. Positions in front of windows are preferred as most noise enters a building through windows.

Measuring and Correcting the Noise Readings with the Intruding Noise Present. The logic behind the corrections is that the single, long burst of noise will cause a more severe startle reaction than the more frequent, shorter bursts. After the appropriate corrections are applied, the measured levels plus the corrections are now referred to as the corrected noise levels.

When the intruding noise is steady, its general level (L_1) should be measured in dBA. If it fluctuates within about a 10 dB range, the meter readings should be averaged. If there are periods of significantly louder and/or more disturbing levels in addition to a continuous noise, the higher level (L_2) should be recorded. The durations of L_1 and L_2 should also be recorded. Corrections are added to the measured level according to the character of the noise in question. The ambient level should be increased by 5 dBA for a continuous, distinguishable sound or a significant, impulsive, irregular sound. If both types are present, 10 dBA should be added. If the noise is not continuous, the sum of the occurrences in an eight-hour period should be determined and given as a percentage of the total time. Appropriate corrections will be made from Graph 1 for daytime and from Graph 2 for nighttime (Exhibit 4). (Night is from 10 p.m. to 7 a.m.) The following are examples of this correction which can be followed on Exhibit 4.

EXHIBIT 4
WORKING CHARTS FOR BRITISH STANDARD SYSTEM

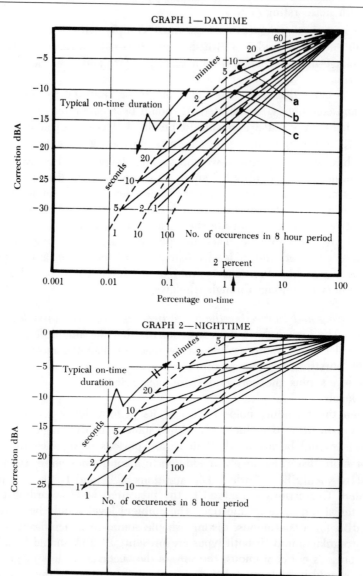

SOURCE: C. Duerden, *Noise Abatement*, (London: Butterworth 1970), p. 65.

Daytime - Graph 1

600 seconds (or 1/6 hour in an 8-hour period) = 2 percent of the time.

1 occurrence of 600 seconds—deduct 6 dBA (point *a* on Graph 1)

10 occurrences of 60 seconds—deduct 10 dBA (point *b* on Graph 1)

100 occurrences of 6 seconds—deduct 13 dBA (point *c* on Graph 1)

Measurement of Background Noise. The background noise is to be determined at the same location during the same period, but without the source of intrusive noise operating. The value to be recorded should be a typical low value, and no corrections are to be added for character or intermittency. When measurement of the background noise is impractical, an acceptable ambient criterion should be determined. The ambient criterion consists of a basic number plus corrections. The basic number for an area with new factories, or existing factories with structure alterations, or existing factories with new processes is 50 dBA. The basic number for established factories not typical of the area is 55 dBA. For old, established factories that are typical of the area the basic number is 60 dBA.

Corrective Criteria for Different Local Environments. The following corrections should be made to determine the corrected criterion. For rural residential areas, deduct 5 dBA. For a suburban area with little traffic, there is no correction. For an urban residential area, add 5 dBA. For an urban residential area with some light industry or main roads, add 10 dBA. For a general industrial area, add 15 dBA. For a predominantly industrial area, add 20 dBA. Only one of the preceding should be used. When the noise occurs only on weekdays, add 5 dBA. The measured ambient noise level should be obtained whenever possible and should be used in preference to the ambient criterion. For purposes of comparison, it is valuable to determine the ambient criterion even if the measured ambient is available.

Overall, the British Standard method is acceptable for rating noise affecting mixed residential and industrial areas. A basic fault of the method is the lack of technical support for the corrections. The intermittency allowances and other adjustments have no direct foundation in experimentation. If possible, more sophisticated methods should be used.

METHOD RECOMMENDED BY THE STATE OF NEW JERSEY [10]

Given the fact that the case study occurs in New Jersey, we examined that state's regulations, the Noise Control Regulations for the State of

Octave Band Center Frequency	Octave Band Sound Pressure Level 7 a.m. to 10 p.m.	Octave Band Sound Pressure Level 10 p.m. to 7 a.m.
31.5	96 dB	86 dB
63	82	71
125	74	61
250	67	53
500	63	48
1,000	60	45
2,000	57	42
4,000	55	40
8,000	53	38

New Jersey, which became effective on January 23, 1974, and were revised January 1, 1976.[11] They include the following provisions. No person is allowed to cause, suffer from, allow, or permit sound from any *commercial* operation which when measured at any *residential* property line is in excess of any of the following: continuous sound with a level higher than 65 dBA from 7 a.m. to 10 p.m., and continuous sound that exceeds 50 dBA from 10 p.m. to 7 a.m. Next, a continuous sound that has an octave band sound level that exceeds the following values in one or more octave bands is not permitted.

Noise readings should be taken with an approved sound level meter and an octave band analyzer. The readings should be taken every 15 seconds for 3 minutes. The information should be recorded as a maximum and a minimum for each site.

A graphical representation of the readings is prepared. Next, time graphs of the three-minute readings should be superimposed. The time graphs should include the following representative levels: (1) an ambient residual level, which represents the background noise level and is to be recorded at a time when ambient noise is at a minimum; (2) a reference level, which represents a level falling between the ambient residual and impact levels; and (3) the impact level, which represents the worst case and is taken at a time when noise levels are at a maximum. All three measurements must be taken on the same day. Any comparative analysis should be made only when readings have been taken at the same time on the same day. All measurements should be in dBA.

The accuracy of the readings depends upon the sophistication of the equipment and the amount of subjectivity entering the measurement process. For a Type II meter, the recommended equipment, the accuracy is usually at least plus or minus 2 dB. When presented as evidence in court, the readings are generally accepted to be accurate within 3 dB.[12]

EPA-WACO COMPOSITE METHODOLOGY BASED PRIMARILY
ON A NOISE ASSESSMENT OF WACO, TEXAS [13]

The composite methodology is structured in part on a study done in
Waco, Texas, in 1973. Modifications of the assessment procedure came
about as a result of talks with officials and through experimentation. First,
the methodology as presented in the assessment of Waco, Texas will be
presented. Then the composite methodology will be reviewed.

Noise Assessment of Waco, Texas. The Waco, Texas, study was funded
by the Office of Noise Abatement and Control of the U.S. Environmental
Protection Agency. The objectives of the project were four. The first was
to measure environmental *noise levels in noise sensitive land use areas* in
order to obtain an environmental noise assessment of the area for land use
planning and zoning. Second, they sought to focus on the impacts of aircraft, surface transportation, and construction activities in the area. Third,
they sought to orient and train local and EPA personnel in noise measurement methodology and techniques. Fourth, of greatest significance
from a general perspective, was that the study was aimed at evaluating a
noise measurement methodology developed by the Region VI Environmental Protection Agency Noise Program personnel whereby the *least expensive equipment could be manned by interested persons after only a
minimal amount of training.*

The data that were collected in this assessment with a Type II sound
level meter were compared to data obtained using a more sophisticated
tape recorder and noise classifier technology. The results of the comparisons demonstrated that the simpler methodology is sufficient for the purpose of community noise surveys to assist local planners. Unskilled personnel using less expensive equipment can successfully make the necessary sound level measurements.

The major pieces of equipment used in this methodology are: a Type II
sound level meter; a stopwatch; a tripod and an inexpensive weather station; and a cassette recorder to be used for comparisons. A Type II sound
level meter and calibrator which are approved by the U.S.EPA can be
purchased for about $750, or often one can be borrowed from a regional
U.S.EPA office or nearby university. Readings from the sound level
meter were made every 10 seconds by students and other personnel who
had received only a minimal amount of training. An hour of data collection was recorded on data sheets specifically designed for the project
(Exhibit 5). At the beginning of each hour of data collection, the sound
level meter was calibrated and the condition of the batteries for the meter
was checked. Then, A-weighted noise levels were recorded manually on
the sheets. At 5-minute intervals, the cassette recorder was turned on for

EXHIBIT 5
COMMUNITY NOISE ASSESSMENT DATA SHEET

STATION NUMBER:_____
OPERATOR:_____
DAY OF WEEK: _____ DATE: _____ SKY: _____ WIND: _____
TIME_____
CHECK BATTERY: _____ TIME: BEGIN_____ FINISH_____
METER ON "FAST" POSITION: __ CAL. BEGIN_____ FINISH_____
METER ON A-WEIGHTING: _____
Leq _____

WET BULB TEMPERATURE
TEMPERATURE
RELATIVE HUMIDITY
WIND SPEED (MPH)
WIND DIRECTION (N-1, E-2, S-3, W-4)
BAROMETRIC PRESSURE (mm Hg)

VARIATION AND BACKGROUND	OVERALL DESCRIPTION
LOW BACKGROUND _____	QUIET & PEACEFUL _____
MED. BACKGROUND _____	SOME NOISE BUT PLEASANT_____
HIGH BACKGROUND _____	NOT ALWAYS PLEASANT NOTICEABLE NOISE _____
VERY FEW VARIATIONS_____	NOISY BUT PLEASANT _____
SOME VARIATIONS _____	NOISY BUT UNPLEASANT _____
MANY VARIATIONS _____	I WOULD NOT MIND LIVING IN SUCH A SOUND ENVIRONMENT _____
SOFT VARIATIONS _____	I WOULD MIND LIVING IN SUCH A SOUND ENVIRONMENT _____
MEDIUM VARIATIONS _____	
LOUD VARIATIONS _____	

SOURCE DESCRIPTIONS

EMERGENCY VEHICLE	_____	INDUSTRIAL	_____
LIGHT AIRCRAFT	_____	COMMERCIAL	_____
LARGE AIRCRAFT	_____	RESIDENTIAL	_____
RAILROAD	_____	MUSIC	_____
TRUCK	_____	INSECTS	_____
CONSTRUCTION	_____	BIRDS	_____
AUTOMOBILE	_____	DOGS	_____
MOTORCYCLE	_____	RECREATIONAL	_____
BOAT	_____	OTHER	_____

EXHIBIT 5 (Continued)
COMMUNITY NOISE ASSESSMENT DATA SHEET

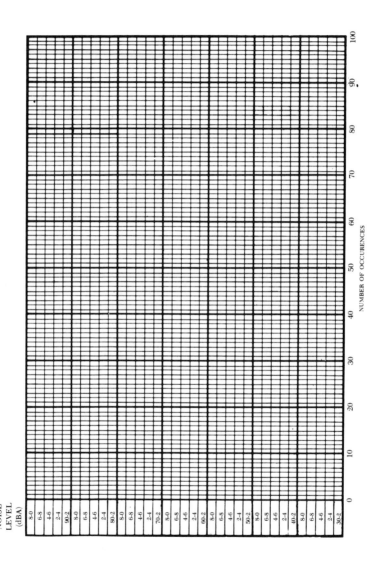

SOURCE: Adopted from H. Watson, Jr.; G. Putnicki; and C. Riddel, *An Environmental Noise Assessment of the Waco, Texas Metropolitan Area with a Low Cost Methodology* (Dallas: Region 6, U.S.EPA, 1973).

about 20 seconds to document the types of noise sources. After 20 minutes, data collection was stopped to record the weather conditions. A sling psychrometer was used to determine the temperature, and wind speed and direction were determined with a low cost flow meter and compass, and the sky condition was noted. After a 10-minute pause, the data collection was continued for another 20 minutes. The last 10 minutes were used to recalibrate the meter and answer the questions on the data sheet.

Site selection was subjective. Most of the sites chosen in the Waco study represented noise sensitive land uses. An effort was also made to choose residential and school sampling sites that are representative of other residential and school areas in the city. A fixed number of sites was not suggested.

Two of the primary concerns of the study were to substantiate the assumption that each of sixteen sampling sites was representative of a *homogeneous area* and that the data collected at the particular sampling site would be similar to data obtained at other points within that homogeneous area. To test these assumptions, a special sampling study of one of the sites was done.

Data were collected simultaneously at four locations 1/2 mile away from the original site, and at four locations 1/4 mile away. Site descriptions included population counts, land use, traffic, major and minor noise source types, overall street and housing maps, aerial photographs, and detailed maps and photographs of microphone locations. A total of 442 hourly data sheets were collected in the Waco assessment. Pertinent information was recorded on computer cards and processed. Outputs computed included L_{max}, L_{01}, L_{10}, L_{50}, L_{90}, L_{99}, L_{min}, L_{np}, L_{dn}, L_{eq}, and the traffic noise index (TNI). Correlation coefficients were computed for L_{10}, L_{50}, and L_{eq} to determine the interdependence of these statistics.

Validating the data obtained with the Type II sound level meter was done this way. Two roving monitoring stations visited each of the sixteen fixed stations. These roving stations consisted of a vehicle equipped with precision tape recording systems and environmental noise classifiers. The tape recorders used in noise monitoring are specifically developed to include all important sounds. They are therefore extremely expensive and are normally available only to consultants.

The tape noise level statistics L_{10}, L_{50}, and L_{eq} were compared with those obtained from the data of the Type II meter. The data compared were taken at the same times. The results showed that within reasonable statistical and experimental accuracy the Type II meter method is sufficient for measurement of the statistics studied.

Composite Methodology

This methodology of noise assessment differs from the one used in the Waco study in that some of the measuring parameters are more clearly defined, some are modified, and others are completely eliminated because of resource and time constraints. If a Type II sound level meter is available for a limited amount of time or if personnel to use it are limited, then the amount of data that can be collected will be limited.

When working subject to resource constraints, the following composite methodology is suggested with this equipment: A Type II sound level meter, a windscreen, a watch, and a tripod. The tripod is not essential; however, it is useful because it acts to steady the meter and makes the recording of data less tiresome. It also allows the person recording the readings to have hands free and not shield the microphone.

Before and after each period of data collection, the meter should be calibrated and the battery should be tested. The meter should be allowed to warm up for at least five minutes. Readings from the sound level meter are made every 10 seconds, or every 15 seconds if the site experiences small changes in sound pressure levels. Data are recorded on the same type of sheet used in the Waco study. Coding can be incorporated so that data can be recorded in 1-decibel intervals instead of the 2-decibel intervals allotted on the Waco study sheet. Meter readings should be made instantaneously—individual readings should not be subjectively averaged. Readings should be taken during at least three separate periods of time. One reading period should record the residual level, a time when the sound level is at a minimum (night, Sunday, holidays). A second should be a representative level, a time when the sound level is between the residual and impact levels (Saturday, weekday after hours). Finally, a third reading period should include an impact level, a time when the sound level is at a maximum (weekday 8:30 a.m.–5 p.m.). If readings cannot be made simultaneously, as will be the case with a limited number of meters and/or limited number of personnel, they should be made as close to each other in time as possible.

The meter should be at least 4 feet off of the ground. It should be at least 25 feet from any reflecting surface, if possible. Measurements should be taken at the property line, if the measuring site is located in a residential area. If a distinguishable noise source exists, the meter should be directed perpendicular to it. A windscreen should be used for winds greater than 4 miles per hour. Readings should not be taken in the rain. Certain readings can be eliminated if it is felt that the particular sound emission is not representative (e.g., backfiring of autos, firecrackers). Weather can be documented by obtaining information from the nearest station.

Many of the statistics computed in the Waco study can be hand calculated or calculated with an electronic calculator using the data obtained from this methodology. Conclusions will not be as broadly based as in the Waco study, but will be significant in assessing the baseline noise at each site. The methodology (illustrated by the case study) is about the best that can be hoped for, given limited resources. Exhibit 6 is the data recorded

EXHIBIT 6a
Monitoring Site 9 Ambient Data

STATION NUMBER: __9__
OPERATOR:_____
DAY OF WEEK: __FRI.__ DATE: 11/21/75 SKY: CLOUDY WIND: HIGH   *DRIZZLE*
TIME __10:00 - 10:20__
CHECK BATTERY: _____ TIME: BEGIN____ FINISH____
METER ON "FAST" POSITION: __ CAL. BEGIN____ FINISH____
METER ON A-WEIGHTING: ____
Leq. __59.6__

				WET BULB TEMPERATURE
				TEMPERATURE
				RELATIVE HUMIDITY
				WIND SPEED (MPH)
				WIND DIRECTION (N-1, E-2, S-3, W-4)
2	9	7	6	BAROMETRIC PRESSURE (mm Hg)

EXHIBIT 6b
MONITORING SITE 9 AMBIENT DATA

STATION NUMBER: _9_
OPERATOR:_____
DAY OF WEEK: _SAT._ DATE: _11|22|75_ SKY: _FAIR_ WIND: ____
TIME _3:50 - 4:00_
CHECK BATTERY: _____ TIME: BEGIN____ FINISH____
METER ON "FAST" POSITION: __ CAL. BEGIN____ FINISH____
METER ON A-WEIGHTING: ____
Leq _54.8_

				WET BULB TEMPERATURE
				TEMPERATURE
				RELATIVE HUMIDITY
				WIND SPEED (MPH)
				WIND DIRECTION (N-1, E-2, S-3, W-4)
3	0	0	8	BAROMETRIC PRESSURE (mm Hg)

NOISE
LEVEL
(dBA)

EXHIBIT 6c
MONITORING SITE 9 AMBIENT DATA

STATION NUMBER: _9_
OPERATOR: _____
DAY OF WEEK: _SUN._ DATE: _11/23/75_ SKY: _CLEAR_ WIND: _____
TIME _5:40 - 5:50_
CHECK BATTERY: _____ TIME: BEGIN___ FINISH___
METER ON "FAST" POSITION: __ CAL BEGIN___ FINISH___
METER ON A-WEIGHTING: _____
L eq _56.5_

3	0	1	0

WET BULB TEMPERATURE
TEMPERATURE
RELATIVE HUMIDITY
WIND SPEED (MPH)
WIND DIRECTION (N-1, E-2, S-3, W-4)
BAROMETRIC PRESSURE (mm Hg)

NOISE
LEVEL
(dBA)

for site 9 and a sample L_{eq} calculation. The first chart (for day) represents the impact level, the second is the representative (Saturday), and the third, the residual (Sunday). Note that due to traffic patterns, the residual sample produced some higher readings than the representative sample and thereby affected the Leq. An Leq calculation will be done later in the chapter.

ESTABLISHING THE AMBIENT ENVIRONMENT
WITH THE COMPOSITE METHODOLOGY

Exhibit 7 summarizes the ambient environment at the three sites (4,7, and 9). The first L_{eq} represents the reading period when sound levels were at a maximum or impact level. The second shows a representative level for each site. The third is a residual level. Note that one of the three sites already exceeds the N.J. noise control regulation standards, and all three exceed the U.S.EPA 55 dBA outdoor level. These figures suggest that site 4 already has a high level of noise; and because of that, it is going to take a great deal of additional noise to make a significant impact. It is expected that sites 7 and 9 will be affected. But these sites are located so far from any residential areas that impacts of these types will not infringe upon the rights of people. Local and migrating wildlife could, however, be seriously affected.

COMPUTER METHODOLOGY

Comprehensiveness and accuracy are goals of noise impact analysis. Given the large number of numerical calculations involved in source characterization and the technical complexity of these calculations, the most advanced assessment methodology utilizes computer analysis. Computer techniques take many of the subjective decisions about data acquisition, reduction, and analysis out of the hands of people and perform the calculations so that the results may be obtained quickly.

The U.S.EPA has recommended a methodology for baseline studies which requires a specific data acquisition and analysis procedure. An overview of the methodology is presented so that the reader will derive a sense of the relative strengths and weaknesses of the four ambient monitoring methods and the high degree of subjectivity involved in the process.

Data are gathered with an approved sound level meter and a magnetic tape recorder. The output sound levels are recorded so that the noise environment may be preserved for data reduction. The tape recording is fed into a multifilter and then into a real time analyzer which is controlled by a mini-computer. The magnetic tape recording is sampled by the

EXHIBIT 7
BASELINE AMBIENT NOISE ENVIRONMENT

Measurement Site	Noise Level	Date	Day	Time	Value
4	Maximum	11/21/75	Friday	8:10 am	73.8
	Representa-tive	11/22/75	Saturday	2:20 pm	67.8
	Residual	11/23/75	Sunday	4:20 pm	62.4
7	Maximum	11/21/75	Friday	9:40 am	55.5
	Representa-tive	11/22/75	Saturday	3:30 pm	53.6
	Residual	11/23/75	Sunday	5:15 pm	48.9
9	Maximum	11/21/75	Friday	10:10 am	59.6
	Representa-tive	11/22/75	Saturday	3:50 pm	54.8
	Residual	11/23/75	Sunday	5:40 pm	56.5

mini-computer which analyzes the data and produces a histogram, cumulative distribution, L_{eq} and L_{dn} noise levels, and usually L(10), L(50), and L(90) levels.

Siting the meter is an important step in the process. Topographic and aerial maps and site visits are recommended to determine the predominant sources of ambient noise. Usually the sources are human activities in places such as factories, roads, or recreation areas. Secondary sources of ambient noise should also be identified. These include meteorological factors such as winds and fauna such as birds and insects.

The number of measurement locations is not specified, but the number should be adequate to analyze the site effectively. Too many locations become impossible to cope with logistically. Usually between five and ten locations are used. Each collection methodology should be site specific. New Jersey state law, for example, specifies that residential boundary lines are mandatory measurement locations because the home owner should expect reasonable enjoyment of property. It is also usually recommended that a measurement be taken on the proposed site and near any principal roadways, if the traffic volume might increase.

Measurement times are usually dictated by the geographic location of the proposed site. For example, state projects in New York must be sampled (according to Article VIII, Part 75 of the New York State Public Service Laws of 1972, Chapter 385) during winter and summer, during weekend and weekday, during daytime (7 a.m. to 7 p.m.), evening (7 p.m. to 10 p.m.), and nighttime (10 p.m. to 7 a.m.) for utilities. In general, the New York State Department of Environmental Conservation divides the day into two periods: 7 a.m. to 11 p.m. and 11 p.m. to 7 a.m.[14] The U.S.EPA, for federal projects, divides the day into two periods: 7 a.m. to 10 p.m. and 10 p.m. to 7 a.m. Measurements must be made during both periods. The reason for winter and summer sampling is to account for foliage differences and their effects on the noise environment.

Meteorological conditions for sampling are strict. It is not recommended that ambient sound levels be sampled in rain or snow or when winds are greater than 6 m.p.h. Wind-induced microphone noise and sound from precipitation serve to distort analysis. In addition, to support the reliability of the data, most states and the EPA require meteorological measurements such as wet and dry bulb temperature, barometric pressure, wind speed and direction, and relative humidity.

Once the locations have been determined, the next step is to record the ambient sound through the sound level meter and the magnetic tape recorder. The amount of measurement time can vary from site to site, but once established it must be maintained consistently on all measurement locations. The measurement periods are usually between 10 and 20 minutes.

Data reduction can occur once the recordings have been obtained for all locations and at all measurement times. The recorded acoustic data are fed into a multifilter equalizer, which has a calibrated attenuator in each of its 1/3 octave filters to correct transducer (microphone) and tape recorder frequency response nonlinearities. The output of the multifilter is then fed into a real time analyzer controlled by a digital mini-computer.

The major components of the analyzer are a multifilter (discussed above) and a multichannel root-mean-square (rms) detector. The detector samples the multifilter outputs and converts these data into digital binary form. These binary data are then used to compute *rms* levels for each of the 1/3 octaves. These outputs, 1/3 octave band pressure levels for 25 Hz to 20,000 Hz, usually A-weighted, are then stored in a mini-computer for further computation or eventual printout. The EPA utilizes the Digital Equipment Corporation PDP-8/I digital computer with FORTRAN IV language. Each ambient noise sample yields a sound level histogram and a cumulative distribution through the computer for analysis. During sampling, any intrusive noise which occurs that is not representative of the noise environment is deleted from the data fed to the computer.

The analog signals from the multifilter may be sampled for integration periods from 1/8 second to 30 seconds by the real time analyzer before *rms* levels are computed. The usual time period utilized is 1 second. The *rms* detector finds the average of all analog acoustic data for that second in all 1/3 octaves separately before this information is stored in the processor. This process occurs repetitively until the end of the tape recording. In one sample 15-minute tape there are 900 one-second integration periods. The logarithmic sum of these sound pressure level data forms a sampled data set for each measurement. The EPA utilizes a statistical data analysis program to generate the necessary statistical values (histogram, L_{eq}, L_{dn}) and percentile values (cumulative distribution, L(10), L(50), and L(90)). The mean, median, and standard deviation are computed for the sound pressure levels. A sample computer printout is found in Exhibit 8.

EXHIBIT 8
Sample Cumulative Distribution[a]

```
53 **        8
54 *******        31
55 ******************        78
56 ******************************************        160
57 *******************************        134
58 ******************************        130
59 ************************        100
60 ***********************        95
61 **********************        90
62 *****************        71
63 **********        40
64 *****        21
65 *****        23
66 **        11
67 *        6
68 *        2
```

Octave Band	L10	L50	L90
31.5	64	60	56
63	65	61	58
125	69	63	59
250	63	58	53
500	59	53	49
1,000	57	52	49
2,000	53	49	46
4,000	45	41	37
8,000	36	29	26

NOTE: a. Each asterisk represents four readings.
SOURCE: F. Kessler, Dames & Moore, Cranford, New Jersey.
         Obtained in interview 10/10/75.

The computer also has the ability to produce a graph of 1/3 octave band sound pressure levels (frequency by decibel). These data can be used to more accurately characterize the type and source of noises produced on the tape recording. The graph indicates the dominant (greatest dBA) tones in the noise spectrum and is invaluable in identifying the offending noise.

Overall, the computer based methodology is to be preferred because of the accuracy of the readings and the comprehensive analysis of ambient sound. However, only a consulting firm and an occasional university possess the equipment. Given financial resource constraints, the researcher may utilize the composite method to establish the ambient environment. Be sure to find out if your state and/or local agency has specific requirements.

Estimating the Impact of Major New Noise Sources

This section overviews the contribution of major sources of noise— transportation, construction, and manufacturing.

TRANSPORTATION

The most important noise sources and the ones that are most difficult to avoid are from transportation systems. By far the most significant contributions are made by trucks and automobiles (Exhibits 9 and 10). These contributions are likely to continue. The second most important transportation noise sources are aircraft takeoffs and landings. Projections into the future indicate that by 1985 there will be more than 430 million aircraft

EXHIBIT 9

PERCENT CONTRIBUTION OF EACH SOURCE IDENTIFIED BY RESPONDENTS CLASSIFYING THEIR NEIGHBORHOOD AS NOISY

(72% of 1,200 Respondents)

Source	Percentage
Motor Vehicles	55
Aircraft	15
Voices	12
Radio & TV Sets	2
Home Maintenance Equipment	2
Construction	1
Industrial	1
Other Noises	6
Not Ascertained	8

SOURCE: U.S.EPA, *Information on Levels of Environmental Noise Requisite to Protect Public Health and Welfare with an Adequate Margin of Safety* (Washington, D.C.: EPA, 1974), p. B-3.

EXHIBIT 10
ESTIMATED CUMULATIVE NUMBER OF PEOPLE IN MILLIONS
IN THE UNITED STATES RESIDING IN URBAN AREAS
WHICH ARE EXPOSED TO VARIOUS LEVELS OF
OUTDOOR DAY/NIGHT AVERAGE SOUND LEVEL

Outdoor L_{dn} Exceeds	Urban Traffic	Freeway Traffic	Aircraft Operations	Total
60	59.0	3.1	16.0	78.1
65	24.3	2.5	7.5	34.3
70	6.9	1.9	3.4	12.2
75	1.3	0.9	1.5	3.7
80	0.1	0.3	0.2	0.6

SOURCE: U.S.EPA, *Information on Levels of Environmental Noise Requisite to Protect Public Health and Welfare with an Adequate Margin of Safety* (Washington, D.C.: EPA, 1974), p. B-3.

operations per year in the United States, more than about five times the 1972 total. Even if this projection is revised downward due to fuel costs, aircraft will play a more crucial role in noise pollution and control, especially if supersonic aircraft are introduced.[15]   The least amount of attention has been paid to rail systems as sources of noise. Railroad passenger traffic has steadily declined by 67 percent from 1950 to 1970. However, in the same period movement of freight by rail has substantially increased. On the whole, though, the total number of vehicles used in the rail system has been decreasing.[16]

The following presentation will characterize each of these noise sources:

Trucks and Automobiles. Trucks and autos are two major categories of surface vehicles that are acoustically significant. Automobiles, although relatively quiet on a unit basis, exist in such numbers as to make their total noise contribution significant. Automobiles average between 70 and 80 dB, buses 80-90 dB, large and medium trucks 82-85 dB, and motorcycles 90-110 dB.

Traffic control is a fundamental means of noise control. Though traffic can bypass populated areas via limited access highways, almost every highway must affect some people. Highways often attract residential and semi-residential developments, and therefore it must be expected that highways in nonpopulated areas may eventually cause environmental noise problems.[17]

The Noise Control Act of 1972 established a national policy "to promote an environment for all Americans free from noise that jeopardizes their health and welfare." Subsection 5(b)(1) requires the administrator of EPA, after consultation with appropriate federal agencies, to publish a report or series of reports "identifying products which in his judgment are major sources of noise." Finally, the administrator is required to publish proposed regulations for each product.[18] The "Background Document for Proposed Medium and Heavy Truck Regulations" was published in the *Federal Register* of October 30, 1972. The standards are summarized as follows:[19]

Low Speed Standard

January 1977	83 dB(A) Standard in Force
January 1981	80 dB(A) Standard in Force
January 1983	75 dB(A) Standard in Force

The 1977 standard was set for trucks produced in 1975; 75 dB(A) is the eventual goal. More than 30 percent of present trucks have noise levels less than 83 dB(A).[20] One percent are now at 80 dB(A). Engine noise is a prime target for meeting the standards.[21] However, there is a trend toward increased use of diesel engines for heavy duty trucks.[22] Since diesel trucks are generally 8 to 10 dB noisier than gasoline powered trucks and 12 to 18 dB noisier than automobiles,[23] it is going to be more difficult to bring diesel trucks in conformity with the standards, and therefore probably more costly. As propulsion noise of trucks is reduced by new truck regulations, tire noise will constitute an increasingly larger share of a truck's highway noise.[24] Additional research will have to be done in the area of tire and tread design. In the near future, more background documents will be presented and standards promulgated for other sources of noise including light duty trucks, automobiles, and other surface transportation vehicles. Garbage compactors are particularly noisy and are receiving special attention as noted earlier in the chapter.

Impact Methodologies. Three methods of measuring traffic noise will be presented. The first two will be discussed in detail because the readers of this volume should be able to use them. The last, entitled "A Design Guide for Highway Engineers," will be summarized. (The last is also the precursor for the HUSH computer model.) All three methodologies can determine existing noise levels and predict future noise levels.

1. Evaluation of site exposure to roadway noise: HUD method.[25] To evaluate a site's exposure to roadway noise, all major roads within 1,000 feet of the site should be considered. The following information is required: (1) distances from the site to the centerlines of the nearest and furthest lanes of traffic, (2) the peak hourly automobile traffic flow in both directions, (3) the peak hourly truck traffic flow in both directions, (4) the gradients, (5) traffic control mechanisms, (6) mean speed, and (7) the presence or absence of a barrier. To help explain the HUD approach, we have applied it to site 4.

EXHIBIT 11
Effective Roadway distance Chart: Site 4

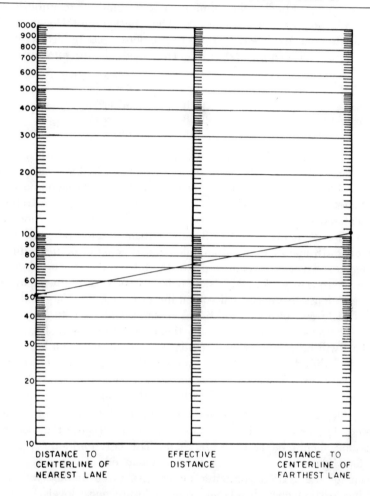

SOURCE: T.J. Schultz and N.M. McMahon, *Noise Assessment Guidelines*, (Washington, D.C.: HUD, 1971, Figure 1.

First, the effective distance from the site to each road must be determined. This is done by locating (on Exhibit 11) the distances from the site to the centerlines of the nearest and furthest lanes of traffic of each roadway, drawing a line through each pair of points, and locating the effective distance on the center scale. With respect to site 4, the centerline of the nearest lane was 52 feet. The centerline of the furthest lane was 106 feet.

The effective distance obtained from Exhibit 9 is 76 feet. These values should be recorded along with all other required information on the worksheet developed by HUD (Exhibit 12). On Exhibit 12, road 1 is the present traffic conditions, road 2 the impact condition.

Traffic surveys demonstrate that the level of roadway noise depends on the percentage of trucks in the total traffic volume. To account for this effect, these guidelines provide for separate evaluation of automobile and truck traffic. Site 4 hourly truck and automobile flows were required. The only data that were available were average daily flows which did not give the truck and automobile mix. Data were therefore derived from a combination of other sources (Exhibit 13).

The percentage of truck traffic varies from 14 to 24. Peak hour data were not available. The maximum hourly flows derived from special surveys of the Hackensack Meadowlands solid waste study of 18.75 percent and 12.5 percent were used. Worst mixes and preferred case mixes were derived from these data and assumptions. The total daily flow of 6,000 vehicles passing by Woodbridge Avenue and Mill Road was assumed for existing conditions at Site 4. Case A represents a combination of a 14 percent truck mix and 18.75 percent of the daily flow during the peak hour. Case B represents a 24 percent truck mix and a peak hour of 2.5 percent of the daily flow. Case D represents a 24 percent truck mix and a maximum hour of 12.5 percent of the daily flow. Case C represents about the best case mix because it contains the fewest trucks.

To illustrate the HUD methodology, the best and worst of existing and impacted auto and truck conditions are used (underlined in Exhibit 14). They are recorded in the appropriate necessary information categories of the HUD worksheets (Exhibit 12). The only difference between the existing conditions (road 1) and the expected impact conditions (road 2) is in the number of trucks.

Multipliers are used to make automobile and truck traffic adjustments take into account different speeds, grades, barriers, and stops. The following discussion covers auto traffic.

No adjustments in decibels for automobiles are necessary if all three of the following conditions are met: (1) no traffic signal or stop sign is within 800 feet of the site, (2) mean speed is 60 mph, and (3) no barrier exists to effectively shield the site from the road. If these three conditions are met, the noise evaluation for automobiles for that particular road can be obtained by plotting the hourly automobile flow and the effective distance on Exhibit 15. Note that the use of a sound level meter is not required for this evaluation and the results are given in terms of whether the roadway noise is clearly acceptable, normally acceptable, normally unac-

EXHIBIT 12

WORKSHEET C—ROADWAY NOISE: MEASUREMENT SITE 4

List all major roads
within 1000 ft of the site:

| | Acceptability Category: | |
	Automobiles	Trucks
1. Woodbridge Ave.-Existing conditions	NORMALLY UNACCEPT.	NORMALLY UNACCEPT.
2. Woodbridge Ave.-Expected conditions	NORMALLY UNACCEPT.	NORMALLY UNACCEPT.
3.		
4.		

Necessary Information:

	Road #1	Road #2	Road #3	Road #4
1. The distance in feet from the site to the centerline of				
a. nearest lane:	52	52		
b. furthest lane:	106	106		
2. The total number of automobiles per hour in both directions:	A.968	A.968		
	D.570	D.570		
3. The number of trucks per hour				
a. uphill direction:				
b. downhill direction:				
c. both directions:	B.270,C.105	B.304,C.128		
4. Effective distance from site to road:	76	76		
Adjustments for Automobile Traffic				
5. Stop-and-go:				

6. Mean speed: 50, multiply flow by .7   A.678   A.678
                                                  D.399   D.399

Adjustments for Truck Traffic
7. Road gradient:
8. Stop-and-go: B.170   B.192
9. Mean speed: 50, multiply flow by .63   C.66   C.81

Barrier Adjustment
10. Distance from site to barrier:
11. Distance from center of road to barrier:
12. Effective elevation of road:
13. Effective elevation of site:
14. Effective elevation of barrier:
15. Difference in elevation between site and road:
16. Difference in elevation between barrier and road:
17. Adjusted distance:

Date: 5/12/76
Signature: George Shepherd

SOURCE: T.J. Schultz and N.M. McMahon, Noise Assessment Guidelines, (Washington, D.C.: HUD, 1971), worksheet c.

acceptable, or clearly unacceptable. These categories are summarized as follows.

a. Clearly acceptable—the noise exposure is such that both the indoor and outdoor environments are pleasant.
b. Normally acceptable—the noise exposure is great enough to be of some concern, but common building constructions will make the indoor environment acceptable, even for sleeping, and the outdoor environment will be reasonable for recreation and play.
c. Normally unacceptable—the noise exposure is significantly severe that costly building constructions are necessary to make the indoor environ-

EXHIBIT 13

TRAFFIC DATA FOR SITE 4 CASE STUDY

Measuring Location	Daily Average Flow of Vehicles	Truck Mix (percent)
Route 18 at Spotswood	35,800	14
Route 1 at Route 18	77,000	17
Plainfield Ave. at Rt. 27	21,000	
Woodbridge Ave. at Mill Rd.	6,000	
Woodbridge Ave. at Old Post Rd.	5,000	
Route 35 at the Raritan River	18,500	14
Route 9 at Route 440	61,100	
Route 440 at Outerbridge Crossing	14,300	
N.J. Turnpike near Carteret	115,100	
N.J. Turnpike near Rt. 440	82,300	
Route 287 near New Durham Rd.	47,700	24
Route 9 at Smith St.	63,800	23

SOURCE: Data without the truck mixes were obtained from the Department of Transportation, Middlesex County, 1973 figures. All data with the truck mixes are 1974 figures and were obtained from Mr. Whitely of the New Jersey Department of Transportation, Data Resources section.

EXHIBIT 14

VEHICULAR FLOW FOR SITE 4 CASE STUDY

Case	Existing Conditions		Expected Impact Conditions	
	No. of Autos	No. of Trucks	No. of Autos	No. of Trucks
(A)	968	157	968	191
(B)	855	270	855	304
(C)	645	105	645	128
(D)	570	180	570	203

ment acceptable, and barriers must be built between the site and the major noise sources to make the outdoor environment acceptable.

d. Clearly unacceptable—the noise exposure is such that both the indoor and outdoor environments are totally unacceptable and almost impossible to be modified to make them tolerable.

The site's exposure to noise is evaluated according to the least favorable category found for that source after all of the roads have been evaluated. If any of the three conditions for auto traffic is not met, the following adjustments should be made before using Exhibit 15. When cars stop they make less noise. If there is a traffic signal or stop sign within 800 feet of the site, multiply the total number of automobiles per hour by 0.1. Record this figure on line five of the worksheet (Exhibit 12).

If there is not a traffic signal or stop sign within 800 feet of the site *and* the mean automobile speed is other than 60 mph, multiply the total number of automobiles by the following appropriate adjustment factor.

Mean Traffic Speed (mph)	Adjustment Factor
20	0.12
25	0.18
30	0.25
35	0.32
40	0.40
45	0.55
50	0.70
55	0.85
60	1.00
65	1.20
70	1.40

In the case study, the mean speed was 50 mph. Accordingly, the auto flow was multiplied by 0.7 (see line 6, Exhibit 12).

If there is a barrier, use the instructions for this adjustment found in the truck traffic evaluation, as it is the same for autos. The barrier calculations will be reviewed later in this section.

Assuming no further adjustments, plot the mean auto flow and effective distance (76 feet) on Exhibit 15. Under the best conditions (399 equivalent cars), the traffic barely falls into normally unacceptable. The 678 equivalent auto flow is further into the normally unacceptable category.

The following discussion covers truck traffic.

No adjustments for trucks are necessary if all four of the following conditions are met: (1) there is a road gradient of less than 3 percent, (2) no traffic signal or stop sign is within 800 feet of the site, (3) the mean truck

EXHIBIT 15
JUDGING THE ACCEPTABILITY OF A ROAD
DESIGN FOR AUTOMOBILE NOISE

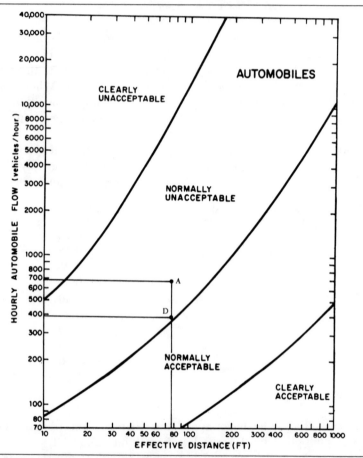

SOURCE: T.J. Schultz and N.M. McMahon, *Noise Assessment Guidelines*
(Washington, D.C.: HUD, 1971), Figure 2.

traffic speed is 30 mph, and (4) there is no barrier which effectively
shields the site from the road. If all four of these conditions are met the
noise evaluation for trucks for that particular road can be obtained by
plotting the hourly truck flow and the effective distance on Exhibits 16
and 17.

If any of the above conditions is not met, the following adjustments
should be made before using Exhibits 16 and 17. If there is a gradient of
3 percent or more, multiply the number of trucks per hour *in the uphill*

direction by the appropriate adjustment factor. Note the enormous impact on noise of even a slight gradient.

Gradient (%)	Adjustment Factor
3-4	1.4
5-6	1.7
More than 6	2.5

Add this figure to the number of trucks per hour in the downhill direction and record this figure on line seven of the worksheet (Exhibit 12).

When trucks stop they create more noises. If there is a traffic signal or stop sign within 800 feet of the site, multiply the number of trucks by 5 and record this number on line 8 of the HUD worksheet (Exhibit 12). If the number of trucks has been adjusted for gradient, use the adjusted figure in this adjustment. If there is no traffic signal or stop sign within 800 feet of the site and the mean speed is not 30 mph, the following steps are to be taken. If the mean truck speed differs with direction or inclination, multiply each speed by the appropriate adjustment factor below. Use the uphill adjusted figure if the truck traffic was adjusted for gradient in the uphill direction.

Mean Traffic Speed (mph)	Adjustment Factor
20	1.60
25	1.20
30	1.00
35	0.88
40	0.75
45	0.69
50	0.63
55	0.57
60	0.50
65	0.46
70	0.43

Record this figure on line nine of the worksheet.

The final step is to plot the results on Exhibits 16 and 17. Exhibits 16 and 17 demonstrate that the existing and impacted truck flows are both normally unacceptable. The impacted traffic case makes the noise level more unacceptable.

In the case of autos or trucks, an adjustment must be made for existing barriers between the road and the site. A barrier can be formed by the

EXHIBIT 16
Judging the Acceptability of a Road Design
for Truck Noise: Site 4 Existing Truck Flow

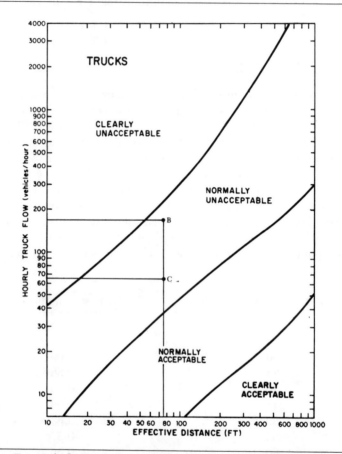

SOURCE: T.J. Schultz and N.M. McMahon, *Noise Assessment Guidelines*
(Washington, D.C.: HUD, 1971), Figure 3.

road profile, a solid wall or embankment, a continuous row of buildings, or by the nature of the terrain. To be an effective shield the barrier must block all residential levels of all buildings from the *line-of-sight* of the road, and it must not have any gaps that would allow the noise to leak through. This adjustment is only necessary when the site's exposure to noise has been found normally or clearly unacceptable.

The first step to adjust for a barrier is to record the distances between the site and the barrier and between the center of the road and the barrier (lines ten and eleven of the worksheet). Next, the differences in effective elevation between the road and the site and the road and the barrier must be determined. The effective elevation of the road is determined by finding out the actual elevation above or below the natural terrain. Five feet should be added to this figure and recorded on line twelve (Exhibit 12). The effective site elevation is determined by first obtaining the ground elevation of the site and the number of stories of the proposed or already existing facility. Multiply the number of stories by 10 feet. Add the site elevation and then subtract five feet from this total. Record this figure on line 13 (Exhibit 12). The effective barrier elevation is determined by obtaining the elevation of the terrain where the barrier is located. The actual height of the barrier is added to obtain the effective barrier elevation. Record this figure on line fourteen of the worksheet. On line fifteen the difference in effective elevation between the site and road should be recorded. On line sixteen the difference in effective elevation between the barrier and the road should be recorded.

Exhibit 18 is used to find the adjustment factor for a barrier. First, the distance between the center of the road and the barrier is plotted against the distance between the site and the barrier on graph 1. Second, a vertical line is drawn from the point found on graph 1 to a point on graph 2 which indicates the difference in elevation between the site and the roadway. Third, a horizontal line should be drawn from the point on graph 2 to a point on graph 3 which indicates the difference in elevation between barrier and roadway. If the line from graph 2 does not meet the appropriate curve on graph 3, then the barrier is not an effective shield and there is no barrier adjustment.

If it does, the fourth step is a line drawn from the point found on graph 3 to a point on graph 4 which indicates the number intersected by the line going from graph 1 to graph 2. Fifth, a horizontal line is then drawn from the point found on graph 4 to a point on graph 5 which indicates the distance between the site and the barrier. Finally, a vertical line is drawn from graph 5 down to the line indicating the barrier adjustment factor. Using this multiplier, the effective distance is adjusted by multiplying the normal effective distance by this adjustment factor. The site's exposure is determined now by whichever of Exhibits 15, 16, or 17 is applicable, by using the adjusted effective distance and the adjusted hourly automobile or adjusted hourly truck flows.

Summarizing, the HUD methodology, like the British Standard, works by making empirical adjustments to a measurement base. The HUD method has the advantage of requiring no monitoring data and of being acceptable to one of the major government agencies. The disadvantages are that the method is far more subjective than methods which begin with

EXHIBIT 17
JUDGING THE ACCEPTABILITY OF A ROAD DESIGN
FOR TRUCK NOISE: SITE 4 IMPACT CASE

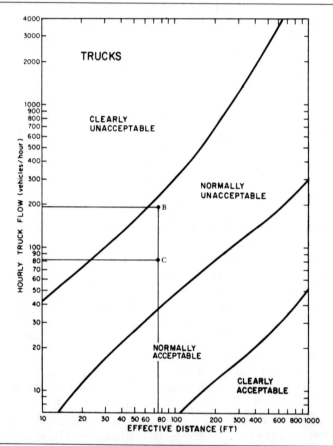

SOURCE: T.J. Schultz and N.M. McMahon, *Noise Assessment Guidelines*,
(Washington, D.C.: HUD, 1971, Figure 3.

ambient monitoring. The HUD method begins with one of four subjective
evaluations of the site. It ends with another categorization of relative acceptability. The methods which follow are much more rigorous. They
begin with ambient monitoring and end with impact dB numbers which
may be compared to the EPA guideline number.

2. *Method for determining population impacted due to highway noise:
use of the composite method.*[26]   Three components comprise population
noise impact analysis: assessment of background noise, estimation of noise

impact after the projected change occurs, and the relationship between any specified noise environment and expected human impact.

The first two components of the assessment require either measurement or estimates of the environmental noise before and after the action being considered. The third component, the relationships of noise to human response, is measured in terms of the number of people in occupied areas exposed to noise of a specified level. It is assumed that the average response of groups of people is related to cumulative noise exposure. The cumulative response is assumed to be a combination of such physiological and psychological impacts as speech interference, sleep interference, and the desire for a peaceful environment. The measure of this response is related to the proportion of people in a population that would be expected to indicate a high annoyance to a specified level of noise.

EPA has chosen the A-weighted sound level as the noise measure. Specifically, the two measures that have been chosen to describe the noise environment are Leq and Ldn. Leq is the equivalent noise level over a specific amount of time. Ldn is the day-night equivalent level describing the noise level of a site over a 24-hour period. Recapitulating the previous presentation (Exhibit 6), Leq is expressed as:

$$Leq = 10 \, \log_{10}(\tfrac{1}{n}) \sum (n_1 \times 10^{(dB/10)} + n_2 \times 10^{(dB/10)} + \ldots + n_m \times 10^{(dB/10)})$$

where N equals the total number of samples over a specified time, usually one hour, N^m is the number of samples that have a unique dB(A) level. L_{dn} is expressed as:

$$Ldn = 10 \, \log_{10} (1/24) (15 \times 10^{Ld/10} + 9 \times 10^{(Ln + 10/10)})$$

where Ld is the level obtained from 7 a.m. to 10 p.m. and Ln is the equivalent level obtained from 10 p.m. to 7 a.m.

Using these measures one can determine the environmental noise before and after the action being considered. To determine population impacted, an impact threshold must first be derived from EPA studies in the literature. The indoor threshold of 45 dB is the base level. When the dB level reaches 64, the intelligibility of sentences to listeners drops to 90 percent. Intelligibility drops to 50 percent when the level is increased to 69 dB. The intelligibility for sentences known to listeners drops to 90 percent when the level is increased to 67 dB. It drops to 50 percent when the level is increased by 26 dB above the threshold to 71 dB. EPA concluded that when the level of environmental noise is increased by more

EXHIBIT 18
BARRIER ADJUSTMENTS

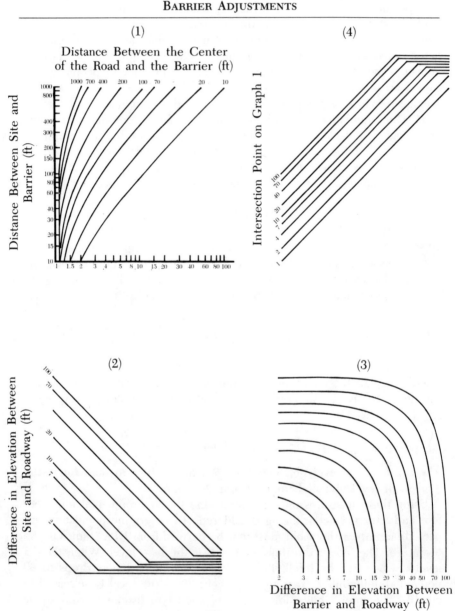

EXHIBIT 18 (Continued)
BARRIER ADJUSTMENTS

(5)
Distance Between Site and
Barrier (ft)

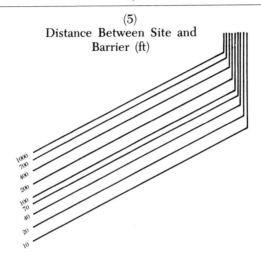

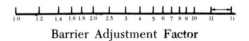

Barrier Adjustment Factor

than 20 dB above the threshold level, the intelligibility of conversational speech deteriorates rapidly with each decibel increase. For this reason, the agency considers 20 dB above the 45 dB threshold as having a 100 percent impact on the people who are exposed. Furthermore, for levels between 0 and 20 dB above the specified level, the impact is assumed to be linearly related. For example, a 17 dB excess is taken to imply an 85 percent impact (17/20 = 0.85).

The EPA assumes that as Ldn changes from 5 dB below the background level to 19.5 dB above it, reactions to a noise source change from none to vigorous. This relationship may be expressed as the following equations:

$$FI = .05 \ (L\text{-}Lc) \ for \ L \ greater \ than \ Lc; \ and$$
$$FI = 0 \ for \ L = Lc$$

where *FI* is the fractional impact; *L* is the Leq or Ldn for the specific site; *Lc* is the appropriate identified criterion level (for example, 45 dBA); and an FI of 1 represents an impact of 100 percent.

The final step in determining population impacted is to multiply the number of people exposed to the particular level of environmental noise by the FI associated with this level of noise:

$$Peq = (FI)P$$

where *Peq* is the magnitude of the impact on the population and *P* is the number of people who can all be impacted if FI = 1.

The concept can be refined by taking into account multiple sources, the distance between sources and receivers, and whether a person is behind a barrier or inside a structure. These considerations will be reviewed in the construction impact section.

The population equivalent methodology is applicable to a large range of situations. Care must be taken in selecting the appropriate criterion level. Good judgment must be used in selecting intervals for differing levels in determining the fractional impacts. On the whole, the fractional impact methodology serves a useful purpose. However, we believe that more evidence is necessary to substantiate the linear relationship assumed in regard to differing fractional impacts.

To illustrate the use of the composite methodology in the case of transportation, we present the impact potential of truck noise on sites 4, 7, and 9. The impact methodology has four steps: (1) determine the number and frequency of trucks passing the sites, (2) estimate the noise levels of the vehicles, (3) superimpose the noise levels of the trucks on the existing condition histograms, and (4) recompute the Leq levels. These levels will be presented only for the impact level histogram for each of the three sites.

Three vehicle mix cases were developed for two operating levels to determine the number of incoming vehicles. Six combinations result, of which the worst plausible case is used for an illustration. The worst plausible case is based on the assumption that the site will receive 6,000 tons per day of solid waste and that all of the waste will be hauled to the site by five-ton compactors. We selected routes for these trucks based on information about truck speed and maneuverability and information about which route drivers preferred. Next, we derived a schedule of truck arrivals from local sources. Then for each site we determined the worst plausible case: site 4—17 arrivals per hour or 34 trucks passing by each hour; site 7—210 arrivals per hour or 420 trucks passing each hour; and site 9—refuse disposal vehicles are not expected to pass this site; the major sources affecting this site will be considered later in the chapter.

At this point, an intuitive estimate may be made of the potential impact of the solid waste truck noise. Keeping in mind that garbage compactors generate in excess of 82 dBA,[27] one could guess that site 7 would be seriously affected by the truck noise. The grounds for the intuitive conclusion are summarized in Exhibit 19.

Site 4 already has a very high ambient level, site 9 will not have a truck impact, but site 7 which has a relatively low ambient noise level is bound to be impacted.

Intuitive judgment, however, is less satisfactory than quantification. Accordingly, the next step was to determine the impact of truck noise at the three noise sensitive sites. Truck noise impact was estimated by segregating noise readings into truck and nontruck noises. Specifically, additional readings were taken at three sites. The readings were not put directly into the histograph, but instead were categorized into readings which did not include trucks and readings which were influenced by the

EXHIBIT 19

COMPARISON OF MAXIMUM AMBIENT NOISE
LEVELS AND NUMBER OF PASSING
SOLID WASTE TRUCKS

Site	Maximum Noise Level, dB(A) (Exhibit 7)	Worst Plausible Truck Schedule Per Hour
4	73.8	34
7	55.5	420
9	59.6	0

passing of trucks. The three sites selected were intended to be representative of the varying distances away from the significant noise sources. Exhibit 20 shows the final form of this work for site 4.

EXHIBIT 20
METER READINGS WITH AND WITHOUT
TRUCK NOISE AT SITE 4 (IN dB(A))

Without		With	
63	57	75	75
60	52	82	73
57	68	74	85
73	71	80	73
70	75	85	71
68	60	73	78
67	57	73	72
75	59	72	73
64	60	79	74
52	57	86	76
57	59	78	75
68	60	73	85
72	67	74	73
71	68	74	75
69	69		
60	69		
59	57		
52	70		
68			

Total Leq = 75.3
Without Leq = 67.8
With Leq = 78.5
11/24/75, Monday
8:05 a.m.

The total Leq at site 4 is 75.3, which is comparable to the baseline Leq, 73.8. The impact of the truck readings on the ambient noise environment is substantial. The difference between the with and without Leqs is about 11 dBA. At other sites the differences were between 11 and 18 dBA.

The truck Leqs which we monitored in the street are similar to U.S. EPA estimates of garbage compactor noise. The truck Leqs were factored into the ambient Leqs in the following manner. If twelve trucks passed during the hour, then two truck Leqs assuming a 10-minute measuring time ($\frac{1}{6} \times 12 = 2$) were substituted for two existing readings. The two readings that are removed are chosen randomly. Next, the ambient Leqs were recalculated with the truck Leqs added. A simple illustration should help.

At this point, suppose the pre-impact dB(A) readings were the following and yielded an Leq of:

Step 1	dB(A)	# of events
	70	2
	60	6
	50	2
	Total	10

Step 2—

$$2 \times 10^{(70/10)} = 20,000,000$$
$$6 \times 10^{(60/10)} = 6,000,000$$
$$2 \times 10^{(50/10)} = 200,000$$

$$26,200,000$$

Step 3—Divide by n: $26,200,000/10 = 2,620,000$

Step 4—Compute $\log_{10} 2,620,000 = 6.42$

Step 5—Multiply by 10: 64.2

Step 6—Report Leq as 64.2

The truck noise Leq is 80. We substitute two truck Leq readings for two 60 dB readings (randomly selected) and recompute the Leq.

Step 1	db(A)	# of events
	80	2
	70	2
	60	4
	50	2
	Total	10

Step 2—

$$2 \times 10^{(80/10)} = 2 \times 10^8 = 200,000,000$$
$$2 \times 10^{(70/10)} = 2 \times 10^7 = 20,000,000$$
$$4 \times 10^{(60/10)} = 4 \times 10^6 = 4,000,000$$
$$2 \times 10^{(50/10)} = 2 \times 10^5 = 200,000$$
$$224,200,000$$

Step 3—divide by n: 224,200,000/10 = 22,420,000

Step 4—compute $\log_{10}$: 22,420,000 = 7.35

Step 5—multiply by 10: 73.5

Step 6—report Leq as 73.5

In this illustrative case, the baseline Leq is 64.2, the impact Leq 73.5. The truck Leqs were computed for each of the monitoring sites. Exhibit 21 presents the worst plausible case results for sites 4, 7, and 9.

Exhibit 21 confirms the intuitive analysis that site 9 has no impact, site 4 an insignificant impact, and site 7 a major impact.

EXHIBIT 21
Truck Impact Leqs

Site	Ambient Maximum Noise Level	Truck Impact Level	Judgment
4	73.8	74.6	Minor or No Impact
7	55.5	78.8	Major Impact
9	59.6	No trucks	No Impact

Overall, the composite methodology derived from the EPA-Waco study is by no means the perfect way to paint a completely accurate picture of ambient sound environments and noise impacts. However, it is the simplest methodology that can be executed with a minimum amount of time and money while producing a completely quantitative determination of the sound environment.

3. *Methodology of traffic noise prediction: "A Design Guide for Highway Engineers."* [28] The previous subsections reviewed in detail HUD and EPA methods for estimating highway impacts. This subsection overviews a third procedure which led to the computerized HUSH model. The model considers three variables: traffic, roadway, and observer characteristics.

Traffic variables describe traffic situations simplified for ease of calculation. For example, *vehicle volume* defines the total number of vehicles that pass a certain point on the road during one hour. *Vehicle mix* describes the proportion of heavy trucks in the traffic volume. *Average speed* describes the difference between truck and auto noise impacts at the same speeds.

Roadway characteristics include the following: the distance across the roadway; the roadway elevation or depression when compared to the surrounding topography; flow interruption imposed by roadway design; the percentage of gradient of the roadway; and the roughness of the pavement.

Observer characteristics describe the location of the roadway with respect to the observer and take into account any distance related attenuation. *Observer distance* defines the shortest distance between the road and the observer. *Element size* is the angle from the road to the observer with respect to the roadway elevation. *Shielding* describes all acoustical shielding between the road and the observer and includes an adjustment for any barrier or divider on the road itself. *Observer relative height* describes the observer's vertical position with respect to the roadway. All of the above factors must be known for each section of road under study to predict a noise level for a specific observer location.

The HUSH computer model uses this and other information to estimate noise levels in terms of L_{50} and L_{10} for automobiles and trucks separately as well as a combined figure. The total noise impact at one observer location from more than one roadway is calculated by the computer model. The computer model removes much of the tedium and develops much more information in a much shorter time. However, only experts would be able to use it.

Conclusions. The three methodologies presented in this section vary in sophistication and purpose. The HUD method was developed so that people without technical training would be able to assess the exposure of a housing site to present and future road noise conditions. The EPA method was developed to determine the precise noise impact and the population impacted by noise. Most of the details of arriving at the known or predicted noise levels such as sampling procedure, adjustment for weather conditions, and variability in traffic flows was left to the designers of these methods. The final method is the most sophisticated and serves the purpose of a design guide for highway engineers.

In conclusion, if yours is a wealthy community, hire a consulting firm with the computer equipment to do an impact assessment. If your community is not wealthy, a noise meter and calibrator and a bit of practice can produce a meaningful picture of the ambient environment and of potential impacts. The HUD methodology is a fallback. If you cannot purchase a meter or borrow one from the U.S. EPA use the HUD methodology. If you have a meter, use the HUD methodology to check the results from the composite methodology.

Aircraft

Jet aircraft dominate the airways. There are two basic types in the current fleet. The first is the four-engine turbofan aircraft. These are used primarily on medium- and long-range flights and are powered by first generation turbofan engines. The second basic type is powered by two or three quieter and more advanced turbofan engines. They are used on short- and medium-range flights. Newer types such as the four-engine 747 jets, used for transcontinental and intercontinental flights, have within the last five years become a significant part of the commercial fleet.

The noise associated with jet aircraft is generated almost without exception by the jet engines. Noise production is at its highest level when an aircraft takes off and at a somewhat lesser level when the aircraft lands. This is because aircraft use full power during takeoff. Interior noise levels while cruising range typically from 79 to 88 dB(A). During takeoffs and landings, the noise levels are as many as 12 dB higher for periods of up to one minute.[29]

The Federal Aviation Administration (FAA) has developed a methodology to produce noise exposure forecasts to assist land use planners in defining the areas around an airport that are exposed to the highest cumulative noise from aircraft operations. This methodology begins with the noise exposure from a single aircraft flyover and combines it with frequency of occurrence, time of day, and aircraft track and flight profiles.[30]

The following simplified techniques have been developed for determining and rating the site exposure to aircraft noise. The runway is geographically located and contours are drawn around the runway as in the following diagram.

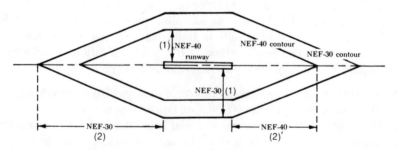

The size of the contours is determined by the amount and type of air traffic. First, the effective number of operations for the airport must be determined by multiplying the number of nighttime jet operations by 17. Then add the number of daytime jet operations to obtain the effective total. Any supersonic jet operation places the airport in the largest category of Exhibit 22. On a map of the area which shows the site and nearby airports, mark the locations of the site and of the center of the area covered by the principal runways.

EXHIBIT 22

NOISE EXPOSURE FORECAST DATA FOR AIRCRAFT

Effective Number of Operations	Distances to NEF-30 Contour		Distances to NEF-40 Contour	
	(1)	(2)	(1)	(2)
0-50	1000 feet	1 mile	0	0
51-500	½ mile	3 miles	1,000 feet	1 mile
501-1,300	1½ miles	6 miles	2,000 feet	2½ miles
More than 1,300 or any supersonic jet operations	2 miles	10 miles	3,000 feet	4 miles

SOURCE: T.J. Schultz and N.M. McMahon, *Noise Assessment Guidelines* (Washington, D.C.: HUD, 1971).

Then using figures from Exhibit 22 approximate the noise exposure forecast (NEF-30 and NEF-40) contours for the major runways and flight paths most likely to affect the site. Finally, use Exhibit 23 to evaluate the acceptability of the site.

EXHIBIT 23

EVALUATION OF SITE EXPOSURE TO AIRCRAFT NOISE

Distance from the Site to the Center of the Area Covered by the Principal Runways	Acceptability Category
Outside the NEF-30 contour, at a distance greater than or equal to the distance between the NEF-30 and NEF-40 contours	Clearly Acceptable
Outside the NEF-30 contour, at a distance less than the distance between the NEF-30 and NEF-40 contours	Normally Acceptable
Between the NEF-30 and NEF-40 contours	Normally Unacceptable
Within the NEF-40 contour	Clearly Unacceptable

SOURCE: T.J. Schultz and N.M. McMahon, *Noise Assessment Guidelines* (Washington, D.C.: HUD, 1971), pp. 2-5.

In addition to the NEF contour rating, the composite noise contour rating (CNR) is sometimes used. CNR is a measure of community response which was first used for industrial noise analysis and then applied to aircraft noise assessment by the FAA. The NEF-30 contour corresponds to the CNR-100 contour and the NEF-40 to the CNR-115 contour.

Summarizing, the 1976 and 1977 perspectives in the United States are focused on the Concordes. Detailed sampling and statistical analyses are being conducted to determine the impact on people and their property.[31] At the same time, additional work is needed to determine community noise exposure resulting from normal aircraft operations.[32]

RAILWAYS

Railways may be divided into two general groups: railroads and rapid transit systems. Railroads include locomotive drawn freight, long-distance passenger and commuter trains, and high speed intercity trains. Rapid transit systems include elevated trains and trolley lines.[33]

Railroad noise comes from two major sources, the locomotive and the individual cars pulled by the locomotives.[34] Locomotive noise is primarily caused by the engine in diesel types and by the cooling blowers and wheel-rail interaction in electric types.[35] The noise produced by the train vehicles is due primarily to the interaction between the wheels and the rails.[36] The major noise sources associated with rapid transit systems are wheel-rail interaction, the propulsion system, and auxiliary equipment.[37]

The noise levels experienced by people on the train or by persons waiting at the train station are in the range 60 to 75 dB(A) for long-distance and intercity passenger trains and 72 to 93 dB(A) on rapid transit systems.[38] Noise abatement programs have been initiated only in the last few years. Noise control standards for railways are practically nonexistent. However, they are being studied in other countries, for example England, where high speed railway operations are important.[39]

Evaluation of Site Exposure Due to Railway Noise.[40] In considering a site's exposure to railway noise, all above ground rapid transit lines and railroads within 3,000 feet of the site should be taken into account (Exhibit 24). The shortest distance from the site to the railway right-of-way should be recorded. The presence of a barrier that effectively shields the site from the railway should also be recorded. The number of nighttime railway operations should be recorded for each railway. The following table is based on the assumption that there are 10 or more nighttime railway operations. The table should be used directly if this is the case. If this is not the case, the distance from the site to the railway should be multiplied by the appropriate adjustment factor before proceeding to the table.

EXHIBIT 24

NOISE EXPOSURE DATA FOR RAILWAYS

Number of Nighttime Railway Operations	Adjustment Factor
1-2	3.3
3-5	1.7
6-9	1.2
10 or more	1.0

Distance from Site to Right-of-Way		Acceptability Category
Nonshielded Exposure	Shielded Exposure	
More than 3,000 feet	More than 500 feet	Clearly Acceptable
601-3,000 feet	101-500 feet	Normally Acceptable
101-600 feet	51-100 feet	Normally Unacceptable
Less than 100 feet	Less than 50 feet	Clearly Unacceptable

SOURCE: T.J. Schultz and N.M. McMahon, *Noise Assessment Guidelines* (Washington, D.C.: HUD, 1971).

CONSTRUCTION [41]

Once the baseline study for an industrial site has been completed and the ambient environment has been accurately characterized, the contribution to the noise environment that would arise from construction, operation, and maintenance of the development is analyzed. This section reviews the most recent and accurate methodology used to determine the impact of construction noise.

Construction projects, both industrial and residential, have increased in both scale and complexity. The result has been longer construction periods and more sophisticated construction equipment. Residents living in close proximity to a construction site usually can resign themselves at the very least to one or two years of construction impacts.

The analyst is faced by a seemingly infinite number of construction equipment combinations and phases, each with an individual noise spectrum. The best possible characterizations are based on representative situations. Certain similarities among construction noises justify the average situation analysis. The diesel engine, together with associated noises, such as exhaust and cooling, are invariably the characteristic noise factors in construction. Additional noises frequently cited are hydraulics and transmission noises in the diesel equipment. Another major noise source is impact equipment such as pile drivers, riveters, and jack hammers. Noise from all this equipment has been recorded to be in excess of 90 dB(A).

The construction process is one that can be categorized by equipment type and construction phase. Five construction phases can be found in differing degrees at all projects.[42]

1. a) Clearing
   b) Demolition
   c) Site preparation
2. Excavation
3. Placing of foundations
4. a) Frame erection
   b) Floors and roof
   c) Skin and windows
5. a) Finishing
   b) Cleanup

Road work as part of the development will undergo the following phases:

1. Clearing
2. Removing old roadbed
3. Reconditioning old roadbed
4. Laying new subbase, paving
5. Finishing and cleanup

Public works, which usually means the laying of utility pipes (water, sewer, electricity, gas) to the structure being constructed will contain the following phases:

1. Clearing
2. Excavation
3. Compacting trench floor
4. Pipe installation, filling trench
5. Finishing and cleanup

Classifying each phase and assigning it an individual noise level allows one to account for the variation in site noise output over the life of the project.

Although the use of construction equipment can be quite variant, there is high conformity among the major noise sources and patterns of operation. All equipment may therefore be categorized in a small number of groups. These groups and the associated noises are indicated in Exhibit 25.

EXHIBIT 25
CONSTRUCTION EQUIPMENT NOISE RANGES

			Noise Level (dBA) at 50 ft.					
			60	70	80	90	100	110
Equipment Powered by Internal Combustion Engines	Earth Moving	Compacters (Rollers)		⊢				
		Front Loaders		⊢——⊣				
		Backhoes		⊢———⊣				
		Tractors			⊢———⊣			
		Scrapers, Graders			⊢—⊣			
		Paver			⊢			
		Trucks			⊢—⊣			
	Materials Handling	Concrete Mixers		⊢—⊣				
		Concrete Pumps			⊢			
		Cranes (Movable)		⊢——⊣				
		Cranes (Derrick)			⊢			
	Stationary	Pumps	⊢					
		Generators		⊢—⊣				
		Compressors		⊢——⊣				
Impact Equipment		Pneumatic Wrenches			⊢—⊣			
		Jack Hammers & Rock Drills			⊢———⊣			
		Pile Drivers (Peaks)					⊢—⊣	
Other		Vibrator	⊢——⊣					
		Saws		⊢—⊣				

SOURCE: U.S.EPA, *Noise from Construction Equipment,* (Washington, D.C.: EPA, 1971), Figure 1, p. 11.
Note: Based on limited available data samples.

The principal noise source in construction activity is the prime mover, usually the diesel engine, used to provide operating power. There are three categories of diesel construction equipment, based on mobility (see Exhibit 25).

1. Earthmoving equipment (highly mobile)—excavating machinery, major noise source: engine and exhaust noise levels range from 73 to 96 dBA.
2. Materials handling equipment (mobility not part of work cycle)—cranes, concrete mixers, and pumps; noise source: engine noise levels range from 75 to 90 dBA.
3. Stationary equipment—air compressors and power generators; noise source: engine noise levels range from 70 to 80 dBA, usually have constant speed and load.

Impact noise comprises the second major construction noise source. The primary tools are the pile driver, jack hammer, and rock drill. Most impact equipment is pneumatically powered, necessitating air compression equipment. The dominant noises are the impact sounds and the high-pressure exhaust of the tool. The noise levels typically range from 80 to 97 dBA. Pile drivers reach over 100 dBA. All these equipment noise levels are measured at *50 feet,* a distance which is characteristic of a worst case urban environment situation.

To characterize the annoyance potential of a construction site, the EPA has developed a noise pollution level (NPL) criterion to describe each construction phase. The NPL is defined as the sum of the A-weighted sound pressure levels (dBA characteristics for each piece of equipment (energy averaged) added together utilizing the Leq equation) plus 2.56 times the standard deviation of the sound pressure level to account for the annoyance due to fluctuations. The major problem with using the NPL instead of the Leq criterion is explained by the EPA:

> Although a thorough study relating NPL to subjective descriptors of annoyance (e.g., acceptable) has not been accomplished, a provisional interpretation of NPL in such terms can be suggested. On the basis of an evaluation of domestic and foreign social surveys and psycho-acoustical studies, HUD has adopted a set of guideline criteria. . . (See Exhibit 26).

Based on the *Noise from Construction Equipment* study (1971), EPA has suggested the representative noise levels at construction site boundaries shown in Exhibit 27.

Once the potential noise characteristics of the site have been established, the next step is to determine noise propagation about the construction site. The degree of exposure to construction noise depends mainly on the distance from the construction site and the nature of the immediate environment (indoor-outdoor, open-closed windows, or immediate reflecting surfaces). The following formula is used to determine the attenuation caused by distance. It assumes two conditions: an open air propagation rule-of-thumb of a 6-decibel reduction in sound pressure level

EXHIBIT 26
PROVISIONAL CRITERIA RELATING NPL TO COMMUNITY NOISE LEVEL ACCEPTABILITY

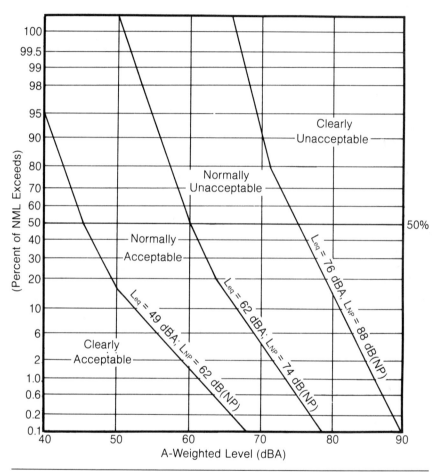

SOURCE: U.S. EPA, *Noise from Construction Equipment*, (Washington, D.C.: EPA, 1971), p. 17.

occurring as the distance from the source doubles, and that the receptor is indoors with closed windows.

$$A = 20 \log R/R_0 + 20 \; dB$$

where A is the attenuation achieved by distance and by being indoors, R is the distance from source to observer, R_0 is the reference distance from which the site noise was measured (usually 50 feet; 200 feet to be conser-

EXHIBIT 27
Typical Average Noise Level, dBA,
at Construction Site Boundaries

Phases of Construction	Domestic Housing	Office Building, Hotel, Hospital, School, Public Works	Industrial, Recreation, Store, Service Station	Highways, Roads, Sewers, Trenches
Ground clearing	83	84	84	84
Excavation	88	89	89	88
Foundation	81	78	77	88
Erections	81	87	84	79
Finishing	88	89	89	84

Source: U.S.EPA, *Information on Levels of Environmental Noise Requisite to Protect Public Health and Welfare with an Adequate Margin of Safety* (Washington, D.C., Doc. 550/9-74-004, March, 1974), p. 4-4.

vative), and 20 dB is the indoor noise reduction allowance. To determine the noise level at some distance from the site, find A for that distance and subtract A from the site noise level. For example, an industrial site in the excavation phase with all equipment present might generate a noise level of 89 dB. At 200 feet the indoor noise level would be 89 dB minus 32 dB (attenuation), or 57 dB, a significantly high level.

$$A = 20 \log R/R_0 + 20\ dB = 20 \log 200/50 + 20\ dB =$$

$$20 \log 4 + 20\ dB = 20\ (0.6021) + 20 = 32\ dB$$

It should be realized that this equation can provide only an estimate, and each attenuation situation is site specific. A later section of the chapter will treat the question of noise attenuation in greater detail.

By drawing radians about a construction site (based on attenuation contours) it is possible to determine the number of people exposed to differing noise levels in the vicinity of the site. This gives the planner an idea of the number of people impacted by the construction noise.

Once the exposure levels for the surrounding population have been determined, impact assessments can be projected. Usually the most conspicuous impact of construction noise is speech interference. When the noise level of the ambient environment exceeds 60 dBA, the ability to communicate by speech deteriorates rapidly. The immediate environment around a construction site (within 500 feet) is usually characterized in all phases by noise levels in excess of 80 dBA. Even taking into account the effects of attenuation through distance and transmission loss (walls), the interior noise level exceeds the criteria. It should be noted that peak levels of construction noise can prevent speech communication entirely.

Often stress is created when increased vocal effort is consistently required to overcome a high noise environment.

A second impact from construction noise is sleep interference, harming those individuals who must sleep during construction hours. This includes pre-school children, the sick, and those working night hours. Also in urban areas there are frequently instances of emergency public works repair activity. Construction noise levels of over 70 dBA, even for short peak levels, can awaken or change the sleep stage of approximately half of those exposed.

A third impact from construction noise is the risk of hearing damage which is not significant for those individuals who do not work directly on the construction site. While construction noise does not pose a severe threat to the general hearing public, it is potentially significant to those working on the site.

Another major impact from construction noise is annoyance. Both the surrounding population and passers-by are annoyed by their exposure to construction noise. People who must endure noises during the entire life of the construction project may become habituated. Task performance interference is prevalent around high-density urban construction areas. Business districts are especially vulnerable to this impact. Libraries, colleges, and hospitals share this high level of potential impact. By comparing the ambient construction noise levels to the impact criteria in all categories it is possible to identify the population that is likely to suffer from the various impacts. It is essential to realize, however, that the numbers generated are not precise quantities, nor do they necessarily possess legal clout.

We will now illustrate a simple construction impact assessment. We assume that construction will be representative of the noise generated during construction of a large industrial park. EPA research previously reported provides construction noise estimates for industrial facilities as shown in Exhibit 28.

The first potential residential impact area is an inn (site 5). The building is approximately 4,000 feet from the closest predicted construction site boundary. We will assume in this case that the boundary is 200 feet from the noise emitting sources. EPA estimates vary from 50 to 200 feet depending on project size, urban or suburban location, and site layout. To be conservative we will assume a reference distance of 200 feet. Using the previously reviewed distance attenuation formula, we calculate a dBA attenuation of approximately 26 for 4,000 feet.

$$A = 20 \ \log \ R/R_0$$

where A is the attenuation, R is the distance from source to observer, and R_0 is the reference distance (200 feet).

EXHIBIT 28
Typical Average Noise Level, dBA,
at Construction Site Boundary of an
Industrial Facility

Phase	Average Leq at Site Boundary
Ground clearing	84
Excavation	89
Foundation	77
Erection	84
Finishing	89

Source: U.S. EPA, Doc. 500/9-74-004, 1974, p. 4-4.

$$A = 20 \log 4{,}000/200 = 20 \log 20 = 26 \text{ dB}$$

As noise travels through the atmosphere its attenuation depends not only on distance but also on the frequency (Hz). Exhibit 29 specifies these effects. The curves within the graph represent a specific frequency range. If a spectral analysis specifying frequency content of the offending noise is available, then one can locate on the chart the curve which best represents the attenuation of that noise.

EXHIBIT 29
Noise Attenuation Distance and Frequency

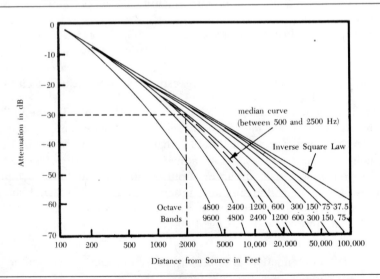

Source: U.S. EPA, *About Sound,* (Washington, D.C.: EPA, 1976), p. 8.

If a spectral analysis is not available for the noise emission (and they tend to be expensive, hence rare), then the next best course of action is to estimate the approximate frequencies of the noise source. Human speech tends to be in the range of 600–4,800 Hz, and this range is utilized in determining speech interference effects. Bulldozers emanate noise that has highest decibel levels of less than 1,000 Hz. Air compressors generate highest decibel levels in the 500–2,500 Hz range. The typical steam or diesel pile driver has the highest decibel levels at less than 250 Hz, but also significant levels between 500–2,500 Hz.

However one manages to characterize the noise sources by dominant frequencies, these frequencies can be matched to an appropriate attenuation curve in Exhibit 29. For example, air compressors are attenuated by approximately 30 dB over 2,000 feet and about 40 dB over 4,000 feet through the action of distance and atmosphere. To find the 30 dB attenuation, first locate the 600–1,200 and 1,200–2,400 Hz curves on Exhibit 29. Second, approximate a median curve between these two existing curves. Third, find 2,000 feet on the X axis. Fourth, trace a line up to the intersection of this line with the median curve previously determined. Finally, from this intersection trace a horizontal line to the left (Y axis) to see the attenuation which should occur. A similar analysis may be done for every piece of equipment. It may not, however, be feasible or necessary. Regional EPA officials should be able to advise you regarding this question.

Returning to the general 26 dBA attenuation estimated by the formula, an attenuation of approximately 26 dBA yields the following noise levels at the exterior of the inn.

Noise Levels Expected at Inn Exterior
(from Construction Activity)

		(average Leq facing the site)	
Phase	Average Leq Site Boundary	Air Attentuation Loss	Expected at Inn Exterior
Ground clearing	84	− 26	58
Excavation	89	− 26	63
Foundation	77	− 26	51
Erection	84	− 26	58
Finishing	89	− 26	63

The outdoor noise level proximate to the inn would violate the recommended EPA 55 dBA criterion. However, many temporary places of residence like this inn have little outdoor activity; therefore the fact that the outdoor levels are above 55 dBA is not very important. This particular inn has a parking lot surrounding the building, which is definitely not conducive to outdoor activities.

The inn is air conditioned, and the windows are shut. The transmission loss for this type of exterior is about 30 dB.[43] Thus the interior noise levels, by phase, will be approximately:

Noise Levels Expected at Inn Interiors
(from Construction Activity)

Phase	Expected Inn Exterior	(average Leq facing the site) Transmission Loss	Expected inside Inn
Ground clearing	58	− 30	28
Excavation	63	− 30	33
Foundation	51	− 30	21
Erection	58	− 30	28
Finishing	63	− 30	33

These levels easily fall within the EPA recommended indoor criterion (45 dBA). Most activities at the inn are indoor and would be adequately shielded from the construction noise. Our conclusion regarding the impact to this particular building is that it will experience a slight but unimportant impact from the construction noise.

The only other residential area with a potential of being impacted by the construction noise is the residential development across from site 4. The attenuation resulting from distance and air will be approximately 30 dB for a distance of about 6,000 feet. The ambient impact noise level at site 4 already exceeds 70 dBA. Accordingly, there will be no impact from the construction site.

The third, and last, potential impact area from construction activity includes the offices along the parkway leading to the site. This impact area is only about 2,000 feet from the construction site boundary. The distance attenuation is about 20 dB. This means that the construction noise levels, by phase, at the office area will be:

Noise Levels at Office Area
(from Construction Activity)

Phase	Average Leq of Site Boundary	(Average Leq Facing the Site)		
		Air Attenuation Loss	Expected Outdoor	Expected Indoor
Ground clearing	84	− 20	64	34
Excavation	89	− 20	69	39
Foundation	77	− 20	57	27
Erection	84	− 20	64	34
Finishing	89	− 20	69	39

A survey of the offices revealed little outdoor activity. Therefore, the exterior noise levels are not especially significant. These fairly high exterior noise levels mean, however, that if any of the offices have open windows, instead of air conditioning with sealed windows, there will be a definite and severe impact on regular office activities from the construction. A visual survey of most of these buildings indicated that they have air conditioning and sealed windows. Therefore, we would expect little impact on office activities from construction noises.

In conclusion, from the construction noise impact perspective, the location of the site both within the industrial park and within the development structure of the surrounding communities meets noise standards. There is almost no noise impact on the surrounding community. One standard cautionary note. If the site is developed for industrial and warehouse activities, its roads will have to be improved. Road construction noise could have an impact, although a short-lived one.

INDUSTRIAL OPERATIONS [44]

Noise from industrial plant operations and maintenance creates less noise impact on the residential population as a whole than surface-air transportation and construction noise because industry is more concentrated. However, if programs to reduce construction and transportation noise emissions are successful, industrial noise will quickly rise in relative importance. Furthermore, while not the focus of this volume, worker exposure is an extremely serious problem. More than four million American workers (primarily in the metals, printing, and textiles industries) are exposed to continuous sound levels exceeding 85 dB.

The most important determination in any industrial noise impact study is to locate and characterize plant noise sources. Once the major offending noise emissions are located, it is necessary to do a characterization, which consists of source noise levels, frequency characteristics in 1/3 octaves, and causes. Industrial noise sources can generally be categorized into the following types:

1. Impact noise sources, e.g., punch presses, stamping machines, and hammers
2. Mechanical noise sources, e.g., unbalanced machinery, resonant structures, gears and bearings
3. Fluid flow noise sources, e.g., fans, blowers, compressors, turbines, and control valves
4. Combustion noise sources, e.g., furnaces and flare stacks
5. Electromagnetic noise sources, e.g., motors, generators, and transformers

An urban plant usually has a greater number of neighbors than a suburban plant, but it also has a greater ambient noise level which masks the industrial noise. Based on a conservative estimate that the average impact community near an industrial plant is approximately 500 persons per plant and the conservative assumption that each of the 311,000 industrial plants in the U.S. is the principal noise source for the community, then about 16 million persons are affected, or 7.6 percent of the 1975 population. This is not a high percentage, but does roughly indicate the magnitude of potential noise emission effects from industrial sources.

The U.S. EPA *Noise from Industrial Plants* tried to identify as many sources of noise as possible in five typical industrial plants. The study considered in-plant source noise levels, ambient environmental noise in adjacent communities, and noise abatement technology. The 311,000 industrial plants in the United States were categorized into five groups for the study:

1. Molding, e.g., glass manufacturing
2. Process, e.g., oil refinery
3. Power, e.g., power plant
4. Assembly, e.g., automobile assembly plant
5. Metal fabrication, e.g., can manufacturing

In three out of the five typical industrial plants that were examined, transportation and construction activity noise predominated. In-plant industrial noise sources were less significant. Industrial noise sources can usually be controlled if anticipated during plant development. Noise reduction technology is aimed at reducing noise along its transmission path. High plant noise levels measured in the five-plant EPA study could have been reduced if plant design and construction had been more sensitive to reducing noise along transmission paths. To do so, one has to first recognize that noise sources may be connected to structural parts of the building through solid, air, or magnetic paths. These paths go through metals, concrete, wood, water, air, etc., which in turn vibrate sympathetically and reradiate the sound. The most common transfer of sound energy in industrial machinery is through solids or air.

The major transmission path noise sources in industrial operations are mechanical or structural connections between either different pieces of machinery or industrial machinery. Mechanical equipment coupling can be reduced by using shock absorbing connectors among the various equipment, such as the use of flexible hose in fluid pumping systems. Vibration coupling between machinery and the structure can be dampened by isolating the vibration source from the reradiating structure using shock absorbing mounts with low vibration transmissibility.

The second major transmission path in industrial operations is through air. Ambient airborn noise may be attenuated using different types of enclosures. The enclosure must be isolated from the vibration source (usually machinery) it is enclosing, and it also should be baffled on the inside to absorb some airborn vibrations. When the vibration source (machinery) is situated in a highly reverberant area, such as a corrugated steel structure with high ceilings, ambient reflected noise may be attenuated by covering the reflecting surfaces with a sound absorbent material. The typical example of this is the use of sound absorbent ceiling tiles in many home recreation areas. Noise reduction achieved by this technique is usually limited to about 7 to 10 dBA.[45] This technique is useful primarily when the exposed person is in the ambient reflecting area, or when the structure itself vibrates from the reflected sound. Finally, magnetic transmission paths can be reduced by replacing magnetic materials with nonmagnetic materials such as aluminum.

Even though noise is recognized as an important environmental factor by the EPA, most municipalities assign a low budget and interest priority in enforcing any noise regulations. Most municipalities presently utilize the nuisance code (a civil offense) to deal with noise complaints. This is a somewhat antiquated approach and is very slowly being replaced by municipal noise control ordinances (violations of which are a criminal offense) which are far more effective and impartial in dealing with noise complaints.

An EPA study notes that "little interest was expressed by any officials contacted regarding federal activity in the area of noise control legislation."[46] One of the reasons for this apathy is the division of powers to regulate noise. While EPA in essence is responsible for noise outside plant boundaries, employee protection from noise is governed by OSHA (Occupational Safety and Health Act) rules.[47] To help generate more interest, EPA has prepared a model noise ordinance for communities; we strongly recommend it.[48]   Overall, the slow rate of adoption of these municipal noise ordinances in the past reflects the low interest level regarding noise control.

The low level of interest in industrial operations noise generation led to an extreme paucity of information on industrial emissions. The EPA 1971 study covered only 1.5 percent of the total different types of industry in the U.S. Fortunately, in late 1975, the agency released a larger study of noise levels created by the construction industry and manufacturing industries grouped at the two-digit standard industrial code level.[49]   This study covers 236 machines of the 357 identified and provides overall dBA levels measured at a standard distance of 2–5 feet from the machine. An example of the EPA data is reproduced as Exhibit 30.

Since the literature on industrial noise impacts is not large, we present an illustrative case of a resource recovery park. A resource recovery park brings in solid waste and converts it to energy and other products such as steel, tin, newsprint, corrugated paperboard, and glass. The recovery park described here is a hypothetical design based on the raw material needs of secondary industries in the park and upon marketable materials from park operations.

EXHIBIT 30

INDUSTRY-MACHINE-NOISE LEVEL DISTRIBUTION (SIC CODE 33)

Industry	Machine	Level dBA
Primary Metal In-	Grinders	90*
dustries 38	Pneumatic Chippers	117*
machines, mean	Furnaces (Ingot Heating)	93*
dBA at 2–5 feet	Furnaces (Oil Heating)	93*
is 98	Wood Planers	107*
	Friction Saws	107*
	Shake Outs	103*
	Pneumatic Rams	84*
	Tumblers	99*
	Push Up Machines	99*
	Core Blowers	116*
	Core Draw Vibrators	108*
	Air Hoists	108*
	Electric Furnaces	96*
	Sand Slingers	96*
	Jolt Squeeze Machines	97*
	Crucible Heaters	81*
	Roughing Mills	102*

EXHIBIT 30 (Continued)
INDUSTRY-MACHINE-NOISE LEVEL DISTRIBUTION (SIC CODE 33)

Levelers	90*
Decoilers	116*
Anealing Furnaces	93*
Lectromelt Furnaces	95*
Open Hearth Furnaces	80*
Scarfing Equipment	86*
Bloomer Mills	90*
Strip Mills	97*
Conveyors	98*
Forging Hammers	109*
Coke Ovens	93**
Sinter Plants	100**
Blast Furnaces	93**
Basic Oxygen Furnaces	95**
Soaking Pits	98**
Rolling Mills	95**
Continuous Picklers	95**
Pipe Mills	96**
Wire Drawing	95**
Nail Mills	98**

NOTES: *SPL measured 0.61–1.52 meters (2–5 feet) from machine.
**SPL measurement distance not identified.
SOURCE: U.S.EPA, *Federal Machinery Noise Research, Development, and Demonstration Programs: FY73-75*, Doc. 600 2-75-008 (Washington, D.C.: EPA, 1975), pp. 101-02.

The resource recovery project is a prototype. There are no existing architectural plans that specify building design and materials, nor is there anything that indicates building interrelationships and road placement. The absence of a definitive site plan makes the task of accurately predicting noise levels more difficult than the usual industrial park. Hopefully, your case will be simpler.

We have assumed that the central source of emanation of all noise will be a single location approximately in the middle of all of the industrial plants and the front-end operation. Theoretically, this should be the loudest spot since it is the one most vulnerable to simultaneous operation of all activities. Noise theory indicates that there is a standard increment of about 2–3 dB for every noise source within 6–10 dB of each other, for up to about five noise sources.[50] A counterweight to the increasing impact of multiple noise sources is the attenuating effect of the actual building structures. Beranek considers the attenuating effect of intervening buildings to be somewhere in the range of 10–20 dB.[51]   This effect will be considered later in the impact assessment. Overall, in order to estimate the noise level at the centerpoint, each industry's manufacturing process will be considered independently, and then a general level will be estimated.

The first major noise producing activity is the front-end operation which contains several distinct steps. Indeed, this operation is the noisiest source. The receiving room is the first step in the process. The refuse trucks dump their contents into a pit. The trucks do not utilize a tilt-bed, but rather hydraulically shake and squeeze the refuse into the pit. While this activity lasts only about a minute per truck, the required size of the industrial park will necessitate almost continuous dumping during operating hours. An average level for these activities would be about 100 dBA.[52]

The next step of the front-end operation is to load the solid waste onto conveyor belts. Loading is mechanical and is not especially noisy. The conveyor belt passes by several stations, each of which recovers one specific material from the solid waste stream. The first station will consist of men handpicking bundles of newsprint. The second station is likely to be magnetic metal separation, which removes the metals from the conveyor belt and sends them through a chute to a hammermill and a metal nuggetizer, which shreds the metals and prepares them for detinning. This process is the noisiest activity in the entire front-end operation, producing levels of about 101 dBA at 50 feet.[53]

The next station, glass recovery, will initially not be needed. However, the glass recovery station should be designed into the front-end recovery activities, due to the potential addition of this operation. There are two general processes potentially available for glass recovery: one involving blower separation, the other electric eye separation. Electric eye separation is preferable due to its ability to sort different color glass. However, it is much more expensive and not perfected yet. This station will generate noise levels of about 90 dBA, primarily due to the recovered glass being fed into a chute.[54]

The last station along the conveyor belt is a pulverizer with a vibratory feeder. This activity pulverizes and grinds the remaining refuse (mostly organic wastes, plastics, and unrecoverable paper) for feeding into energy production processes. Noise levels of about 90 dBA are produced mainly due to the presence of unrecovered metals and glass and other dense materials that either escaped recovery or are not valuable.[55]   Lastly, the conveyor belt operation itself generates noise levels of about 90 dBA, primarily due to the noise of the drivers and the rollers.[56]

The overall noise level for the front-end operations is about 90–95 dB(A). How much of this noise escapes into the exterior environment depends on a number of variables including the type of structure made to enclose the operations, the number of openings in the structure, and the composition of the exterior walls. These variables will be considered in detail later in this section.

We will now turn to the secondary industries. The electric arc, continuous casting mini-steel mill is quite new in the industry. Studies are not yet available detailing the noise emissions from the operations. The process tends to be fairly quiet because electricity is used in the smelting process. Fortunately, a mini-steel mill exists in Sayreville, New Jersey. We measured the noise output on several occasions during April, 1976. The noise level at 50 feet from the structure was 70–75 dBA. At no time could we detect noise levels in excess of 75 dBA. In fact, the noise readings we obtained were influenced by other neighborhood conditions. The main source of noise was a tractor moving reinforcing bars next to the plant. While the actual steel smelting process is fairly quiet, the cutting of the bars formed in the process represents the major source of noise. The level of the cutting process is approximately 80 dB(A), which is attenuated by the building enclosure.

A detinning plant is another secondary operation. Normally, a detinning operation is not included in a recycling park. The shredding of the steel cans is usually done as part of the detinning operation. This leads people to attribute high noise levels to detinning, whereas the actual detinning process is basically a relatively quiet chemical reaction. We assume that the steel has been shredded in the front-end operation and only needs to be fed into the chemicals that remove the tin from the steel can shreds. The proposed detinning facility will emit noise only to the extent of the handling of the steel scrap and the turning of the steel scrap in the tank where it is mixed with chemicals. These activities should not exceed 75 dBA at 50 feet.

The third secondary industry is a newsprint mill. The front-end of the proposed project will separate bundles of newspaper by hand and then send them to the newsprint mill. The bundles of recovered newspaper are dumped off trucks onto the floor of the shredder room. Shredding is the first step in recovering newspaper. The shredder room is usually not sealed off from the exterior environment. A large amount of noise from this shredder will leak to the outside environment. A conveyor belt will reduce the noise. However, the opening in the wall to accommodate the conveyor belt will still leak a large percentage of the interior noise to the outside.

Baled newspapers are shredded into small strips which are chemically deinked and broken down into the basic components of paper manufacture. The noisiest part of this operation is the shredding of the newspapers which can generate levels as high as 80–90 dBA at 35 feet.[57]   The room which contains the shredder will have an ambient noise level of about 85–90 dBA when the shredder is in operation.

The fourth industry, the paperboard plant, is very similar in operation to the newsprint industry. Paperboard boxes, recovered by hand at the front-end, are collected and shredded before being chemically dissolved. The shredder operation for the paperboard is identical to that used in the newsprint plant, and the shredder noise levels are about 90 dBA. The shredding of the paperboard may be louder than the shredding of newsprint due to the more rigid and dense material being shredded.

Another component of the project is an energy recovery facility. Dry fuel is one energy recovery alternative. The solid waste must be dried and compressed, after being ground down into fairly small particles and mixed. The grinding, mixing, and compressing activities will be the major sources of noise. The loudest noises will come from the grinding of the refuse and should be approximately 85 dBA.

Pyrolysis, an anaerobic burning process, is the second energy producing facility we considered. The noise levels produced by pyrolysis itself should be low. The refuse will have to be ground up before being fed into the pyrolysis chamber in order to insure even burning. This grinding can take place at the finish of the front-end operation, thereby confining the noisy grinding to the building that is least likely to be impacted by it since it already contains many noisy processes. The major sources of noise associated with pyrolysis are the feeding operation (loading the ground refuse into the pyrolysis unit) and the removal and hauling away of the clean landfill material, which is one product of the pyrolysis process. The noise from these activities, being referenced to standard feeding and removal activities in utility stations should be no greater than 80 dBA at 50 feet.[58]

Overall, the interior average noise levels for the various potential industrial-recycling park tenants are:

Front-end operation	90–95 dBA	(interior level at 25′)
Mini-steel mill	70–75 dBA	(exterior level at 50′)
Detinning operation	70–75 dBA	(interior level at 50′)
Newsprint plant	80–85 dBA	(interior level at 25′)
Paperboard plant	80–85 dBA	(interior level at 25′)
Refuse dry fuel	80–85 dBA	(interior level at 25′)
Pyrolysis	75–80 dBA	(interior level at 25′)

After characterizing the noise sources, the next step in the noise assessment process is to gauge the effect of the building on noise emissions. We estimated the attenuating effect of an inexpensive plant enclosure, a moderately costly plant enclosure, and a relatively effective, but expensive, noise insulating enclosure.

An average, inexpensive building exterior used in most new warehouses and storage structures, is almost entirely composed of fluted steel (or some alloy) joined to 2-by-4 wooden supports. This material is light, easy to build with, relatively inexpensive (especially due to reduced construction time), but not very effective in dampening noise. Even when the joints between the sheets of fluted steel are caulked, there are many noise leaks in the exterior surface. The average sound transmission loss induced by this exterior is approximately 25–30 dB.[59]

Cinderblocks cemented together and painted are a moderately costly plant enclosure. These blocks are usually hollow, which makes them lighter to lay. A survey of industrial buildings in the study area suggests that most buildings are constructed of the 6″ or 8″ painted, hollow cinder blocks. The average sound transmission loss induced by these blocks is 45–50 dB.[60]

The most effective, but expensive, sound dampening materials are dense. Solid lead, which has a mass of 700 lb./ft.[3] is extraordinarily effective at dampening sound, a characteristic which makes it useful for specialized scientific applications. For a normal industrial building, poured concrete, which is very expensive, is the most effective noise insulating enclosure. The sound transmission loss through poured 4″ to 8″ thick reinforced concrete is approximately 55–65 dB.[61]

So far we have estimated the sound transmission loss for the three different structures as follows:

Cost of Enclosure	Material	Sound Transmission Loss
Low	Fluted Steel	25–30 dB
Average	Cinder Block (hollow)	45–50 dB
High	Poured, Reinforced Concrete	55–65 dB

These sound transmission loss factors are applicable only when there are no holes, such as doorways, windows, or openings for conveyor belts. The sound insulating quality of the wall is only as strong as its weakest link. Thus if a standard 2′ x 3′ window with 1/8″ glass is installed in a poured concrete wall, and the window is closed, the sound transmission loss for that window, and therefore the wall, will be about 30 dB.[62] Open windows virtually eliminate any sound insulating ability of an exterior wall. They are not recommended in industrial plants. The sound transmission loss of a steel door (well sealed) is about 40-45 dB.[63] Any opening in a wall to accommodate a conveyor belt allows a large proportion of the noise to escape.

The least-cost enclosure utilized fluted steel as the construction material, which is attached to 2-by-4 wooden posts and caulked. There will be few windows in this design, and most ventilation will be provided by ceiling fans, or perhaps air conditioning, although the insulating abilities of fluted steel are questionable. Ceiling fans require ducts and openings in the exterior walls near the roofline to admit fresh air for the ventilating equipment. Exhaust openings will also be necessary. These openings will reduce the insulating ability to 10–15 dB.

The transmission loss associated with fluted steel in our region is about 10–15 dB. The predicted noise level at 50 feet from each of the component operations in the project attenuation for a fluted steel enclosure will be the following:

Activity	After Structure Attenuation Noise Level, dB, Leq Average at 50 ft.	Baseline Average Levels dBA
Front-end operation	80	90–95 (interior at 25')
Mini-steel mill	70	70–75 (exterior at 50')
Detinning operation	60	70–75 (interior at 50')
Newsprint plant	70	80–85 (interior at 25')
Paperboard plant	70	80–85 (interior at 25')
Refuse dry fuel	70	80–85 (interior at 25')
Pyrolysis	65	75–80 (interior at 25')

The center point average noise level which we assume would represent the overall site noise level will be about 75 dB (not including any transportation noise) with fluted steel building enclosures.

In addition to dampening due to the industrial building structure, noise impacts will be further dampened by three factors. First, any buildings between the noise source and the impacted area will introduce a dampening of about 10–20 dB. The number of buildings is less important than the size of the intervening buildings.[64] Second, distance and atmosphere introduce an attenuation of about 20 dB to the office area and about 26 dB to the inn. Third, the attenuating abilities of the buildings containing activities potentially impacted (office and residential) will be about 30 to 40 dB if they are sealed from the outside environment. We previously noted that most offices and the inn are sealed.

Overall, of the 75 dB of noise generated by the industrial activities, less than 30 dB will reach the interior of the offices along the road and less than 25 dB will reach the interior of the inn rooms facing the project site. These levels are lower than ordinary activity noise levels generated indoors and considerably below the U.S.EPA 45 dB indoor threshold. Even with the least-cost structures there will not be any impact areas. Determining the noise levels in the impact areas for the two higher cost enclosures is unnecessary.

While it appears that from a noise protection perspective the site is an excellent one for a resource recovery facility, it should be recognized that noises from the industrial operations, and especially the transportation of the refuse into the park, will clearly mark the site as an unattractive site for outdoor activities. It could be argued that the proposed recovery project commits the entire area to industrial oriented land uses.

Summary and Additional Resources

This chapter has reviewed the processes of noise generation and impact assessment. Special attention has been given to the noises that accompany industrial facilities. Since readily available literature on this topic is sparse, a case study was drawn upon to illustrate the assessment procedures.

The chapter began by defining the basic concepts of sounds, frequency, amplitude, decibel, and loudness. Second, it reviewed measurements which are used to simulate people's reactions to sound including decibels, octave analysis, Leq and Ldn. The first section of the chapter concluded with a presentation on the following physical and psychological impacts of sound: hearing damage, speech interference, sleep interference, stress, startle, annoyance, and task interference. These reactions were associated with a range of decibel levels, and U.S.EPA criteria for taking these into account were presented.

The second part of the chapter presents methods for conducting ambient noise surveys. The goal of the section is to demonstrate to the readers that they can conduct a noise survey. Initially, the selection of monitoring stations is reviewed. Then, the British Standard is presented as an approach, which, while readily applicable, is probably not acceptable in the United States. New Jersey's procedure is briefly outlined to alert the reader to the fact that a critical step is to determine state and local requirements. The composite method is recommended as a monitoring procedure that the user, with a minimum of training, may employ. Equipment is discussed and the Leq and Ldn formulas are explained. Finally, the computer method is reviewed to inform the reader what a noise consultant can do.

The third part of the chapter focuses on measuring the impact of new noise sources. Three approaches of estimating the impact of automobiles and trucks are presented: HUD, the composite, and a computerized procedure. The HUD and composite methods are presented with an example because we believe that the reader should be able to use them. Next, relatively simple methods of measuring the impact of aircraft and railway operations are reviewed. Third, the impact of construction is considered. A case study is used to illustrate the process. Finally, methods of estimating the impact of industrial machinery are presented and illustrated with an example.

If this chapter has interested you enough to go further into noise pollution, we suggest that you next read the recently published books: *Industrial Noise Control Handbook* by Paul and Peter Cheremisinoff and *The Technical Feasibility of Noise Control in Industry* by Bolt, Beranek and Newman, Inc.[65]   *The Journal of Noise Control Engineering* is recommended as a source of current literature on industrial noise issues.

Government sources include the National Technical Information Service (NTIS) *Environmental Pollution and Control Abstracts;*[66] the ten regional EPA offices (see appendix); and state, county, and local environmental offices. Legal data are available from EPA's *Legal Compilation* which consists of separate volumes not only on noise, but on air, water, solid waste, pesticide, and radiation.[67]   The legal compilation presents the statutes, their legislative histories, executive orders, regulating guidelines, and reports.

Private sources of information include consulting firms which sell equipment, such as the General Radio Corporation of Concord, Massachusetts.

NOTES

1. Walsh Healey Public Contracts Act, Rule 50-204.10, *Federal Register,* vol. 34, no. 96, May 20, 1969.

2. U.S.EPA, *Noise from Construction Equipment,* NTID 300.1 (Washington, D.C.: U.S.EPA, 1971), p. 64.

3. *Ibid.,* p. 65, and L.L. Beranek, *Noise and Vibration Control* (New York: McGraw-Hill, 1971), p. 579.

4. L.L. Beranek, *Noise Control,* p. 579; U.S.EPA, 300.1, p. 69.

5. U.S.EPA, 300.1, p. 70.

6. H.E. von Gierke, *Noise—How Much is Too Much* (Springfield, Va.: NTIS, 1975); M.A. Whitcomb, *Effects of Long Duration Noise Exposure on Hearing and Health* (Springfield, Va.: NTIS, 1975); and Center for the Study of Science Policy, Pennsylvania State University, *The Effects of Mobile-Source Air and Noise Pollution on Residential Property Values* (Springfield, Va.: NTIS, 1975).

7. The following information in the text is drawn from U.S.EPA, *Information on Levels of Noise Requisite to Protect Public Health and Wel-*

fare with an Adequate Margin of Safety, Document 550/9-74-004 (Washington, D.C.: U.S.EPA 1974).

8. This section draws mainly from the following: National Bureau of Standards, *The Economic Impact of Noise* (Washington, D.C.: U.S.EPA 1971); U.S.EPA, *A Proposed National Strategy for Noise Abatement and Control* (Washington, D.C.: U.S.EPA, 1976); U.S.EPA, *Toward a National Strategy for Noise Control* (Washington, D.C.: U.S.EPA, 1977); U.S.EPA, *Policy and Implementation Questions* (Washington, D.C.: U.S.EPA, 1977).

9. See C. Duerden, *Noise Abatement* (London: Butterworths, 1970) for a description of the method; T.J. Schultz, *Community Noise Ratings* (London: Applied Science Publishers, 1972), pp. 52-54 stresses the importance of the method.

10. We would like to thank Mr. Don Dieso, instructor, Department of Environmental Science, Cook College, for helping us with this section.

11. New Jersey Administrative Code, 07:29-1.2, Noise Control Regulations Industrial and Commercial Operations, p. 181.

12. According to Don Dieso, the 3 dB figure is an accepted convention. The American National Standards Institute gives approval to Type II sound level meters when their accuracy is ± 1 dBA based on the electrical circuitry alone. Depending upon the quality of the microphone, the final accuracy of the meter can be anywhere from ± 3 to ± 7 dB. The ± 3 dB is usually used.

13. Information on the Waco study was obtained from H. Watson, Jr., G.J. Putnicki, and C.S. Riddel, *An Environmental Noise Assessment of the Waco, Texas, Metropolitan Area with a Low Cost Methodology* (Dallas: Region 6, U.S.EPA, 1973).

14. "Regulation for Certification of Environmental Compatibility and Public Need for Major Steam Electric Generating Facilities," New York State Public Service Commission, Article 8—Part 75; see U.S.EPA, *Noise Regulations in State and Local Noise Ordinances* (Springfield, Va.: NTIS, 1975) which provides a summary of noise source regulations in states and local governments.

15. U.S. Department of Transportation, Office of the Secretary, *Transportation Noise and its Control* (Washington, D.C.: U.S.DOT, 1972), p.1.

16. Wyle Laboratories, *Transportation Noise and Noise from Equipment Powered by Internal Combustion Engines* (Washington, D.C.: U.S. EPA, 1971), pp. 133-134.

17. C.G. Gordon, W.J. Galloway, B. Kugler, and D. Nelson, *Highway Noise—A Design Guide for Highway Engineers,* National Cooperative Highway Research Program Report 117 (Los Angeles: Bolt, Beranek, and Newman, 1971), p. 2.

18. U.S. Environmental Protection Agency, *Background Document for Proposed Medium and Heavy Truck Noise Regulations* (Washington, D.C.: U.S.EPA, 1974), p. 1-1.

19. *Federal Register*, "Environmental Protection Agency— Transportation Equipment Noise Emission Controls, Proposed Standards for Medium and Heavy Duty Trucks" (Washington, D.C., October 30, 1974), p. 38343.

20. U.S.EPA, *Background Document*, pp. 4-7.

21. *Ibid.*, pp. 8-17.

22. *Ibid.*, pp. 3-11.

23. Wyle Laboratories, *Transportation Noise*, p. 100.

24. U.S.EPA, *Background Document*, p. 8-3.

25. Much of the information in this section was derived from T.J. Schultz and N.M. McMahon, *Noise Assessment Guidelines* (Washington, D.C: HUD, 1971).

26. Much of the information for this section was derived from U.S.EPA, *Background Document for Proposed Medium and Heavy Truck Noise Regulations* (Washington, D.C.: U.S.EPA, 1974).

27. Several discussions were held with Fred Mintz of the U.S.EPA during January 1976 about compactor noise.

28. Information for this section largely comes from C. Gordon et al., *Highway Noise.*

29. Wyle Laboratories, *Transportation Noise*, p. 19.

30. U.S. DOT, *Transportation Noise*, p. 7.

31. R.L. Hershey, R.J. Kevala, and S.L. Burns, Booz-Allen Applied Research, Inc., *Analysis of the Effect of Concorde Aircraft Noise on Historic Structures* (Springfield, Va.: NTIS, 1975).

32. D.E. Bishop and W.J. Galloway, *Community Noise Exposure Resulting from Aircraft Operations: Acquisition and Analysis of Aircraft Noise and Performance Data* (Springfield, Va.: NTIS, 1975).

33. Wyle Laboratories, *Transportation Noise*, p. 132.

34. *Ibid.*, p. 135.

35. *Ibid.*, pp. 135-36.

36. *Ibid.*, p. 137.

37. *Ibid.*, pp. 141-42.

38. *Ibid.*, p. 147.

39. J.G. Walker, *Noise from High Speed Railway Operations* (Springfield, Va.: NTIS, 1975).

40. This section is based on T.J. Schultz and N.M. McMahon, *Noise Assessment*, 1971.

41. The U.S.EPA document *Noise from Construction Equipment*, NTID 300.1 (Washington, D.C.: EPA, 1971) was our major source for this section.

42. *Ibid.*, pp. 9-10.

43. American Industrial Hygiene Association (AIHA), *Industrial Noise Manual*, 2nd ed. 1966, pp. 124-25.

44. The major sources for this section were U.S.EPA, *Noise from Industrial Plants*, NTID 300.2 (Washington, D.C.: U.S.EPA, 1971), and U.S.EPA, *Federal Machinery Noise Research Development and Demonstration Program: FY73-FY75*, Document 600/2-75-008 (Washington, D.C.: U.S.EPA 1975).

45. U.S.EPA, NTID 300.1, p. 271.

46. U.S.EPA, NTID 300.2, p. 225.

47. *Ibid.*, p. 204.

48. The municipal noise ordinances are modeled after the EPA, *Model Community Noise Control Ordinance*, (Washington, D.C.: U.S.EPA Document 550/9-76-003, 1975).

49. U.S.EPA, 600/2-75-008.

50. R.H. Warring, ed., *Handbook of Noise and Vibration Control* (Modern Trade and Technical Press, 1970), p. 217.

51. Beranek, *Noise and Vibration Control*, p. 181.

52. U.S.EPA, *St. Louis/Union Electric Refuse Firing Demonstration Air Pollution Test Report*, Document 650/2-74-073 (Washington, D.C.: U.S.EPA, 1974), pp. 69 and 72.

53. *Ibid.*, p. 72.

54. U.S.EPA, 600/2-75-008, table E-12, p. 100.

55. *Ibid.*, table E-13, p. 101.

56. *Ibid.*, table E-13, p. 102.

57. *Ibid.*, table E-7, p. 94.

58. Extrapolated from *Ibid.*, table E-18, p. 108.

59. AIHA, *Industrial Noise Manual*, p. 125.

60. *Ibid.*, p. 125.

61. *Ibid.*, p. 124.

62. *Ibid.*, p. 124.

63. *Ibid.*, p. 124.

64. Beranek, *Noise Control*, p. 341.

65. P.N. Cheremisinoff and P.P. Cheremisinoff, *Industrial Noise Control Handbook* (Ann Arbor, Michigan: Ann Arbor Science, 1977); Bolt, Beranek, and Newman, Inc., *The Technical Feasibility of Noise Control in Industry* (Springfield, Va.: NTIS, 1976).

66. *Environmental Pollution and Control Abstracts* (Springfield, Va.: NTIS, weekly).

67. U.S.EPA, *Legal Compilation* (Washington, D.C.: U.S. Government Printing Office, Published as original volumes and supplements).

Chapter 4
Water Resources

THIS CHAPTER IS CONCERNED with the related questions of water quantity and quality. Unlike noise pollution, water resources management has received a good deal of public and private attention. Personnel principally trained in sanitary engineering and more recently in economics and law have developed a massive literature which includes many procedures for estimating the impact of industry on water resources. These procedures can be dichotomized: (1) industrial and related residential and commercial demand for water and (2) the impact of industrial discharges on water quality.

Water Quantity

Industrial development causes an increase in industrial, commercial, and residential water demand. This section will focus on methods for estimating water demand by industries. In addition, procedures for estimating public potable water demand will be reviewed because industries are important consumers of public potable water and because the direct, indirect, and induced employment impacts of many industries in sparsely developed regions may be substantial. This section ignores industries' demand for water of a particular quality for three reasons. First, the literature on industrial water quality requirements is extremely weak. Second, whereas it is rarely possible to anticipate special quality demands, industries which have such a demand will identify their specific needs to the responsible government or water agency before they are committed to a move. Third, long-term planning for a clean water supply is reviewed in the water quantity section.

INDUSTRIAL SELF-SUPPLIED WATER DEMAND

Water use in the United States has increased abut ten times since 1900. In 1900, daily water use was about 40 billion gallons (bg); in 1970, withdrawal was estimated to be 370 bg.[1] Electric utilities withdraw more than one-third of the total, much of it for cooling. Industry's total withdrawal is about 50 bgd; its use is more than double withdrawal. According to the latest United States Census of Manufacturing about 80 percent of this industrial use is fresh water, and about 8 percent is consumed by the processes or evaporated.[2]

For purposes of distinguishing among industrial water use estimating procedures, three impact circumstances may be specified.
1. Short-term impacts of a few plants
2. Regional planning for many industrial facilities in the near future
3. Regional planning for long-term economic development

Short-term Impacts of a Few Plants. The first impact situation assumes that specific industries are planning to locate in the region. They have presented a plan with information on water demand which you wish to check. Three sources of information are suggested. First, you should find a recently constructed facility in the same industry. National trade associations will provide the names of new plants. A call to a new plant can result in an excellent set of data. Second, federal and state environmental protection personnel are frequently familiar with the water requirements of new plants. The nearest regional office of the U.S.EPA is the best place to start. The engineers who specialize in specific industries can provide information from water pollution control and *Federal Register* documents and from their experiences.

The previously referred to federal census of manufacturing is the third source of industrial water use data. These volumes provide data on average water use by industries using more than 20 million gallons (mg) per year. The census tabulations include such important information as total water intake, water intake by purpose, source of water, fresh water intake, brackish water intake, public water use, gross water used, total water discharged, amount of water treated prior to discharge, and other variables. The tabulations are by two, three, and four-digit SIC codes. The four-digit code is the most appropriate for the case of a specific industry. Tabulations are provided for the entire United States, regions, and individual states. The state tabulations, however, are only at the two-digit level of aggregation, inappropriate for anything but a rough check against other sources of data.

Water intake coefficients are prepared by dividing the water information by employment and/or value added data provided in the census. Exhibit 1 provides a set of three- and four-digit level water intake coefficients which the reader may employ for a rough estimate of industrial needs. In general, for establishing water use for a few facilities, the census information should be used as a back-up.

Regional Planning for Many Industrial Facilities in the Near Future. When the goal of the impact analysis is short term planning for a large region, the census information becomes more important. Census based coefficients should be prepared from United States and regional tabulations. If the national and regional coefficients are not similar, then the coefficients will require further review. For example, assume the average national industry uses 100 gallons per employee and the average state industry uses 60 gallons per worker. Perhaps the state has progressed more rapidly than the nation in the introduction of water saving devices. A call to the nearest U.S. EPA office and/or state department of resources should produce explanations of the empirical results.

Regional Planning for Long-Term Economic Development. When the goal of the impact study is a long-range regional plan for economic development, the census tabulations and other published sources become the primary source of information. The major factors which will affect industrial water demand are amount of output and technological change. Projections of regional output are relatively rare. Employment projections at the two-digit SIC code level of aggregation are common and may be used as substitutes. Technological change is important insofar as it changes the per unit use of water. The degree of water recirculation is normally the clearest manifestation of technological changes which affect water use.

The long-range, regional plan procedure will be illustrated here. The URS/Madigan-Praeger and Conklin and Rossant study of industrial water

EXHIBIT 1
INDUSTRIAL WATER INTAKE, 1973

SIC Number	Industrial Category	Mean Annual Intake (Million Gallons per Employee)
201	Meat Products	0.59
202	Dairies	0.67
203	Canned, Frozen Foods	0.86
204	Grain Mills	2.18
205	Bakery Products	0.10
206	Sugar	3.49
207	Fats and Oils	2.04
208	Beverages	1.04
209	Miscellaneous Foods	2.85
2111	Cigarettes	0.09
2211	Weaving, Cotton	0.20
2221	Weaving, Synthetics	0.25
2231	Weaving, Wool	0.58
225	Knitting Mills	0.37
226	Textile Finishing	1.02
227	Floor Covering	0.54
228	Yarn, Thread Mills	0.27
229	Miscellaneous Textiles	0.34
242	Saw-Planing Mill	3.59
243	Millwork	0.68
249	Miscellaneous Wood	1.15
251	Household Furniture	0.15
2611	Pulp Mills	24.64
2621	Paper Mills	9.95
2631	Paperboard Mills	11.43
264	Paper Products	1.93
265	Paperboard Boxes	0.27
2661	Building Paper Mills	2.36
281	Basic Chemicals	11.04
282	Fibers, Plastics	4.05
283	Drugs	0.68
284	Soap, Toilet Goods	0.95
2851	Paint, Allied Products	0.43
286	Industrial Inorganic Chemicals	17.76

EXHIBIT 1 (Continued)
INDUSTRIAL WATER INTAKE, 1973

SIC Number	Industrial Category	Mean Annual Intake (Million Gallons per Employee)
287	Agriculture Chemicals	12.18
289	Miscellaneous Chemicals	5.12
2911	Petroleum Refining	3.45
295	Paving, Roofing	0.57
3011	Tires, Tubes	0.39
3069	Fabricated Rubber Products, N.E.C.	0.59
3079	Miscellaneous Plastic Products	1.09
3111	Leather Tanning	0.69
3211	Flat Glass	1.71
322	Pressed or Blown Glassware	0.25
3231	Products of Purchased Glass	0.40
3241	Cement, Hydraulic	3.39
325	Structural Clay	0.18
326	Pottery Products	0.15
327	Concrete, Plaster, Gypsum	1.32
3281	Cut Stone Products	0.78
329	Miscellaneous Nonmetallic Mineral	1.10
331	Blast Furnace, Basic Steel	8.52
332	Iron, Steel Foundries	0.49
333	Primary Nonferrous	10.17
334	Secondary Nonferrous	0.84
335	Nonferrous Rolling	0.71
336	Nonferrous Foundries	0.33
339	Miscellaneous Primary Metal	0.76
341	Metal Cans	0.18
342	Cutlery, Hardware	0.23
343	Plumbing, Heating	0.19
344	Fabric Structure, Metal	0.18
345	Screw Machine	0.22
346	Metal Forgings and Stamping	0.19
347	Metal Service, N.E.C.	0.95
348	Ordnance, Accessories, N.E.C.	0.17
349	Miscellaneous Fabricated Metal	0.36
351	Engines, Turbines	0.62

EXHIBIT 1 (Continued)
INDUSTRIAL WATER INTAKE, 1973

SIC Number	Industrial Category	Mean Annual Intake (Million Gallons per Employee)
352	Farm, Garden Machinery	0.37
353	Construction Equipment	0.17
354	Metalwork, Machinery	0.11
355	Special Industry Machinery	0.12
356	General Industrial Machinery	0.16
357	Office, Computing Machines	0.18
358	Service, Refrigeration Industrial Machine	0.20
359	Miscellaneous Machines	0.13
361	Electric Distribution Products	0.11
362	Electric Industrial Apparatus	0.18
363	Home Appliances	0.15
364	Light-wiring Fixtures	0.15
365	Radio-TV Receiving	0.06
366	Communication Equipment	0.06
367	Electronic Components	0.15
369	Miscellaneous Electric Products	0.17
371	Motor Vehicles	0.19
372	Aircraft and Parts	0.26
3731	Ship and Boat Building	0.23
3743	Railroad Equipment	0.10
376	Guided Missiles, Space Vehicles	0.05
3811	Eng., Scientific Instruments	0.09
382	Measuring, Controlling Devices	0.07
384	Medical Instruments	0.16
3851	Ophthalmic Goods	0.79
3861	Photographic Equipment	0.30
3873	Watches, Clocks	0.05
391	Jewelry, Silver	0.11
394	Toys, Sport Goods	0.18
396	Costume Jewelry	0.25
399	Miscellaneous Manufacturing	0.26

SOURCE: U.S. Bureau of the Census, *Census of Manufacturers, 1972 Special Report Series: Water Use in Manufacturing*, MC72(SRI-4) (Washington, D.C.: U.S.G.P.O., 1975), Table 2A. Calculated by author.

use for the Tocks Island Dam study is illustrative of the projection process.[3] The goal of the Tocks Island impact study was to determine if the projected water demands warranted the construction of a massive dam in the Delaware River.

The self-supplied water use estimating procedure is divided into six steps:

1. Estimate water intake per unit of output or value added or employment.
2. Estimate output or value added or employment.
3. Estimate output per employee.
4. Estimate recirculation and technological change to modify step 1 calculations.
5. Multiply data from steps 1, 2, and 3 to produce a baseline set of projections; multiply data from steps 1, 2, 3, and 4 to produce different water use projection.
6. Estimate consumptive water use.

The *first step* is to determine water intake per unit of output. Projected regional outputs were not available; consequently, employment was used. Exhibit 2 presents the water intake coefficients. The coefficients were prepared by dividing the water intake in gallons per day per employee for establishments using more than 20 million gallons per year by employment in those industries. The coefficients in Exhibit 2 are based on 1967 data. The latest water use census contains 1972 data (Exhibit 1). Previous censuses include 1964, 1959, and 1954. These may be used to determine if a trend exists.

The tabulations are for the four states which use Delaware River water and for the Delaware River Basin as a whole. The six standard industrial codes which are responsible for over 90 percent of the nation's industrial water intake are included. Three-digit SIC and perhaps four-digit SIC tabulations and estimates for other industries are appropriate for regions which are likely to attract a more specialized set of industries than those expected by the Delaware River study group.

At the two-digit level of aggregation, quite a bit of variation in water use by industry is manifested in Exhibit 2. The Tocks Island Dam research team used the New York and New Jersey estimates for their respective parts of the study region. The Delaware River Basin coefficients were selected to be representative of how much each industrial group was projected to be located in each state.

Employment projections, the *second step*, may be made by standard techniques or borrowed from published sources. The Tocks Island Dam research team used high, medium, and low employment projections. Exhibit 3 reproduces the high, medium, and low estimates for the primary metals and chemicals industries for the Delaware River Basin.

EXHIBIT 2

WATER INTAKE PER EMPLOYEE IN GALLONS PER DAY (1967)
FOR ESTABLISHMENTS USING MORE THAN
20 MILLION GALLONS PER YEAR

SIC	Industry	Delaware	Pennsyl-vania	New Jersey	New York	Delaware River Basin
20	Food	1,100	2,800	2,000	2,700	2,400
22	Textile	NA	900	1,700	1,000	1,300
26	Paper	39,800	12,300	6,800	14,100	9,600
28	Chemicals	15,900	16,000	9,100	11,700	16,000
29	Petroleum	NA	32,500	64,300	64,300	32,500
33	Primary Metals	NA	16,000	6,400	9,500	16,000

SOURCE: URS/Madigan-Praeger, Inc., and Conklin and Rossant, *A Comprehensive Study of the Tocks Island Project and Alternatives* (New York, 1975), Table 3-8, p. III-20.

The chemical industry is projected to be a growth industry even under the low growth estimates. Indeed, along with the paper industry, the chemical industry is the only significant water-using industry in the Delaware River Basin which is expected to increase employment.

Three employment projections may be too elaborate for most studies. Single, two-digit SIC level projections are not difficult to make. National projections such as the OBERS series establish a federal base. Shift and share analysis may then be used to allocate the national projections to states, regions, and counties.[4]

The *third step* in the process of estimating industrial water use is to translate employment into output. Standard sources are available. The Tocks Island group used gross product originating per employee. The values were derived from the above mentioned federal OBERS, Series E national average figures.[5] They represent earnings per employee estimates multiplied by projected ratios of gross product originating over earnings. Employee earnings were derived by dividing industry earnings by employees. The values derived by the Tocks Island Dam team are presented in Exhibit 4.

The gross product data in Exhibit 4 imply a huge increase in industrial output. The chemical industry is expected to increase in employment and increase almost four times in worker output. The other industries also are projected to substantially increase in output.

The increase in output would lead to a substantial increase in industrial water use were it not for technological changes which have reduced the

EXHIBIT 3
EMPLOYMENT PROJECTIONS FOR THE CHEMICAL
AND PRIMARY METALS INDUSTRIES FOR
THE DELAWARE RIVER BASIN

SIC		Year	Estimates 1000's
28		1985	120.7
Chemical	High	2005	148.2
		2025	180.7
		1985	117.5
	Medium	2005	138.1
		2025	162.1
		1985	104.7
	Low	2005	110.1
		2025	112.6
33		1985	52.2
Primary	High	2005	46.1
Metal		2025	43.1
		1985	50.8
	Medium	2005	42.8
		2025	37.5
		1985	47.2
	Low	2005	36.2
		2025	25.0

SOURCE: URS/Madigan-Praeger, Inc., and Conklin and Rossant, *A Comprehensive Study of the Tocks Island Project and Alternatives* (New York, 1975), Tables 3p12a, 3-12b, 3-12c, pp. III-24,-III-28.

per unit use of water. These changes are input in the *fourth step*. Exhibit 5 lists recirculation rates as of the late 1960s and early 1970s. They represent gross water use divided by water intake. National rates have been higher than the rates in the Middle Atlantic Region because the older industrial base of that region was constructed on the basis of once through flows of water. In addition, the Mid-Atlantic States are humid and therefore have had less incentive to recirculate water than the more arid western regions.

Since the passage and implementation of the Federal Water Pollution Control Act Amendments of 1972 (to be reviewed in detail later in the chapter), industry has dramatically moved toward process and water

EXHIBIT 4

GROSS PRODUCT ORIGINATING PER EMPLOYEE

		Dollars			
SIC	Industry	1970	1985	2005	2025
20	Food	12.59	17.29	29.18	45.77
22	Textiles	9.42	13.97	25.29	42.13
26	Paper	13.72	18.79	30.75	46.84
28	Chemicals	24.42	35.69	59.91	90.34
29	Petroleum	24.55	35.81	65.96	106.03
33	Primary Metals	13.67	18.35	26.54	37.04

SOURCE: URS/Madigan Praeger, Inc., and Conklin and Rossant, Table 3-14, p. III-28.

EXHIBIT 5

INDUSTRIAL RECIRCULATION RATE

SIC	Industry	U.S. 1967	Middle Atlantic States 1970
20	Food	1.66	1.46
22	Textiles	2.13	1.01
26	Paper	2.90	2.34
28	Chemicals	2.10	1.57
29	Petroleum	5.08	2.20
33	Primary Metal	1.55	1.42
	TOTAL	2.31	1.61

SOURCE: URS/Madigan Praeger, Inc., and Conklin and Rossant, Table 3-14, p. III-28.

cooling systems which decrease discharges and thereby increase recirculation. For example, the 1973 recirculation rate was 3.13, up 35 percent from 2.31 in 1967. The last column of Exhibit 6 indicates the levels of recirculation that might occur with a high degree of implementation of demand reducing policies. Perhaps even the high degree estimates may be low.

An additional decrease in industrial water demand is also likely to result from technological changes. For the Mid-Atlantic Region the Tocks Island

EXHIBIT 6
PRESENT AND PROJECTED RECIRCULATION RATES

| | | | Middle Atlantic States | |
| | | | Conservative Increase in Recirculation | High Degree of Recirculation |
SIC	Industry	1970	2025	2025
20	Food	1.46	1.77	2.49
22	Textiles	1.01	2.77	4.47
26	Paper	2.34	3.22	4.64
28	Chemicals	1.57	2.40	8.40
29	Petroleum	2.20	6.73	15.24
33	Primary Metals	1.42	1.61	3.25

SOURCE: URS/Madigan-Praeger, Inc., and Conklin and Rossant, Table 3-15, p. III-30.

study puts this as between 20 and 40 percent of projected industrial demand by 2025.[6]

Next, the *fifth step* is to multiply the information from steps 1–4 to produce different sets of projections. These multiplications will be illustrated with a fictitious industry group X. The relevant data and calculations for industry group X follow.

Step 1.

1. Present number of employees		100,000
2. Total water intake per day		300 mg
3. Water intake per employee (2/1)		3,000 gpd

Step 2:

4. Employment projections		110,000

Step 3:

5. Gross product originating per employee		
	present	$20.
	projection	$45.
	projection/present	2.25

Step 4:

6. Recirculation rates	present	2.00
	projection	3.00
	present/projection	0.667
7. Other technological change for water use reduction		0.80

Step 5:

8. Present water use
   (3,000 gallons per employee) x (100,000 employees)   = 300 mg
9. Projected baseline water use
   (3,000) x (110,000) x (2.25, gross product
   originating per employee ratio)   = 742.5 mg
10. Projected water use assuming projected
    recirculation rates and technological change
    for water use reduction
    (3,000) x (110,000) x (2.25) x (0.667, recirculation
    rate multiplier) x (0.8, technological change
    multiplier)   = 396.2 mg

Step 6:

The final step in the process is to estimate consumptive water use. Consumptive use represents the proportion of water intake (not water use, which includes recirculation) that is not put back into the water body because of evaporation, transpiration, or incorporation into the product. Consumptive use coefficients range from less than 1 percent for utility and industrial cooling to over 20 percent for some parts of the food industry.[7] The national average is about 5 percent. Average numbers are about 1 percent for industrial cooling and 10 percent for noncooling uses by industry. If we assume that 90 percent of the water use by industry group X is cooling, then consumptive use may be estimated.

11. Consumptive water use for cooling for baseline
    projection, 742.5 mg
    (0.9, proportion cooling) x (0.01) x (742.5)   = 6.68 mg
12. Consumptive water use for noncooling for baseline
    projection, 742.5 mg
    (0.1, proportion noncooling) x (0.10) x 742.5   = 7.43 mg
13. Total consumptive water use
    6.68 mg cooling
    7.43 mg noncooling

14. 14 mgd

PUBLIC POTABLE WATER DEMAND

Public water agencies have been responsible for a minor share of the water use in the United States, ranging from 7.5 percent in 1900 to 6.2 percent in 1955.[8] Water distribution by public agencies is generally divided into four sectors: domestic, commercial, public and other, and industrial. The following tabulation is the relative share of each of the sectors in per capita water distribution by public water agencies in the United States:

Sector	gpcd	Percent
Domestic	73	46
Commercial	28	18
Public and Other	20	13
Industrial	36	23
Total	157	100

Residential Demands for Public Potable Water. In the absence of better information, an average demand of 100 gpcd and 4 persons per residential unit is advised.[9] This combination of demand and family size results in an average residential dwelling unit demand of 400 gpd per unit. A maximum peak daily demand of 800 gpd per unit (200 percent) and a maximum peak hourly demand of 2000 gpd per dwelling unit (500 percent) are suggested. If extensive lawn sprinkling is common, the Federal Housing Administration recommends 2,800 gpd per dwelling unit. While the above numbers are a useful first-cut estimate, they ignore differences in residential water demand caused by the following: metered vs. nonmetered units; single-family vs. multiunit residences; septic systems vs. sewered homes; and east vs. west. Costly over- or underdesign of water systems may result if these four factors are not considered.

Exhibit 7 summarizes the relevant survey data developed by Linaweaver and Associates.

Price, public education, the saturation impact of water-using devices such as washing machines, and water-saving devices are factors, in addition to the factors distinguished in Exhibit 7, which are assumed to influence water demand. Regression equations developed by Hittman Associates, probability models developed by Whitford, and other mathematical techniques have been used to factor these variables into water demand projections.[10] An example is the URS/Madigan-Praeger, Inc., and Conklin and Rossant study of Tocks Island.[11] These studies suggest that, in the urban east, sprinkling demand could be substantially reduced and in-house use slightly reduced. Overall, under the best of circumstances, water use could be reduced about one-third below the average data found in Exhibit 7.

Water use, however, could increase. If the record of increase at the national level from about 90 gpcd in 1920 to over 150 gpcd in 1975 would continue, the estimates in Exhibit 7 would have to be increased. It is recommended that the numbers presented in Exhibit 7 be used as first estimates.

Commercial/Institutional Water Use for Public Potable Water. If the industrial project is of sufficient size, local service industries will grow.

EXHIBIT 7
RESIDENTIAL WATER USE
(gallons per day per dwelling unit)

		Avg. Annual	Avg. Summer	Max. Day	Max. Hour	Annual gpcd
Metered Public Water & Public Sewers: Western U.S.	High	679	1,108	1,534	3,643	166
	Low	316	398	554	1,651	90
	Avg.	458	658	979	2,481	123
Metered Public Water & Public Sewers: Eastern U.S.	High	421	582	1,172	3,135	113
	Low	212	273	503	1,695	59
	Avg.	310	438	786	1,833	76
Metered Public Water & Septic Tanks	High	309	395	728	1,745	63
	Low	189	209	381	1,173	54
	Avg.	245	328	726	1,835	61
Flat Rate Public Water & Public Sewers	High	1,487	3,024	5,014	9,366	437
	Low	504	1,069	1,862	5,300	107
	Avg.	692	1,284	2,354	5,170	193

SOURCE: Linaweaver, Geyer, and Wolff, *A Study of Residential Water Use*, (Washington, D.C.: U.S.G.P.O., 1967), Appendix A, pp. A2-A7.

Commercial and institutional water uses include water used in commercial and service establishments—schools, colleges, institutions, hotels, and others. Commonly found numbers for commercial/institutional water use are 20-35 gpcd. A reasonable average for an urban-suburban region is 25 gpcd. Researchers at Johns Hopkins University found a high correlation between water use and assorted measures of activity such as employment, number of square feet, etc. Coefficients were developed for twenty-eight of these commercial/institutional establishments (Exhibit 8).

Public/Unaccounted Water Requirements for Public Potable Water. This sector includes such activities as fire fighting, public buildings, parks, street cleaning, and unaccounted for water (leakage, meter malfunctions). The literature estimates a range from 10 to 15 percent of total public supply or about 20 gpcd.[12]

Industrial Water Requirements for Public Potable Water. Industrial water requirements for public potable water vary greatly. In the mid-1960s to early 1970s, public water systems supplied about 12 percent of the fresh water used by industries. With respect to the magnitude of their use of water from public agencies, industries can be divided into major and minor users. Minor users, such as apparel and printing and publishing, tend to duplicate the water use patterns of commercial establishments and homes. Conversely, six major users require substantial amounts of public potable water in their products or in their processing methods: food, paper, chemicals, petroleum refining, primary metals, and transportation equipment. In the mid-1960s to the early 1970s, these industries purchased almost four-fifths of the water sold to industries by public agencies.

Classification of industries according to broad requirement groups has not been difficult. However, measurement of industrial use for simulation and projection purposes has proven formidable. Though constrained by the lack of accurate data, several research groups have attempted to place industrial water use and discharge in an input-output framework.[13] Their purposes were to determine projected water needs, resultant pollution, and the effect of industries in one region on the water requirements in other regions. Significantly, both groups cite the lack of water use data as the major handicap in making their models operational.

Four factors account for the difficulty of obtaining a reliable set of industrial water use coefficients for both total water use and public potable use: (1) different processes in old as opposed to newer plants; (2) different water management practices, including the question of recirculation of water; (3) different climates; and (4) the availability of alternative sources

EXHIBIT 8
Commercial/Institutional
Public Potable Water Use

Category	Parameter	Expected Usage Coefficients (gallons/day/unit of parameter)		
		Mean Annual	Max. Day	Peak Hour
Barber Shop	Barber Chair	54.6	80.3	389.0
Beauty Shop	Station	269.0	328.0	1070.0
Bus-Rail Depot	Sq. Ft.	3.33	6.5	25.0
Car Wash	Inside Sq.Ft.	4.78	10.3	31.5
Church	Member	0.138	0.862	4.7
Golf-Swim Club	Member	22.2	22.2	22.2
Bowling Alley	Alley	133.0	133.0	133.0
College Resid.	Student	106.0	114.0	250.0
Hospital	Bed	346.0	551.0	912.0
Hotel	Sq.Ft.	0.256	0.294	0.433
Laundromat	Sq.Ft.	2.17	2.90	15.4
Laundry	Sq.Ft.	0.253	0.461	1.57
Medical Office	Sq.Ft.	0.618	1.66	4.97
Motel	Sq.Ft.	0.224	0.461	1.55
Drive-in Movie	Car Stall	5.3	5.33	5.33
Nursing Home	Bed	133.0	146.0	424.0
New Office Bldg.	Sq.Ft.	0.093	0.173	0.521
Old Office Bldg.	Sq.Ft.	0.142	0.264	0.797
Jail and Prison	Person	133.0	133.0	133.0
Restaurant	Seat	24.2	83.4	167.0
Drive-in Rest.	Car Stall	100.0	144.0	547.0
Night Club	Person Served	1.33	1.33	1.33
Retail Space	Sale Sq.Ft.	0.106	0.154	0.271
School, Elem.	Student	3.83	6.39	37.4
School, High	Student	8.02	17.7	79.9
YMCA-YWCA	Person	33.3	33.3	33.3
Service Station	Inside Sq.Ft.	0.251	0.590	4.89
Theater	Seat	3.33	3.33	3.33

of supply. Despite these drawbacks, Exhibit 9 is presented as a first-cut method of estimating public potable water demand by industry.

Summarizing, industrial and related residential and commercial demand for water can be estimated by two general approaches. One approach is interviewing, most appropriate for short-term forecasting of a few industries. The second approach is statistical analysis of published water use data and is most appropriate for long-range, regional planning studies.

WATER SUPPLY

An industrial water supply must be satisfactory in both quantity and quality. Local streams, lakes, and bays usually provide plenty of water. Frequently, however, nearby untreated surface water supplies are not of suitable quality. Accordingly, many industries turn to underground water supplies and, if necessary and possible, to more expensive public agencies.

While an adequate amount of water may not be conveniently available at a plant site, water is continuously recirculated between the continents and the oceans. The hydrologic (or water) cycle is the never ending circulation of water and water vapor over the entire earth.[14] This circulation penetrates the three parts of the total earth system: the atmosphere, the hydrosphere (the water covering the surface of the earth), and the lithosphere (the solid rock beneath the hydrosphere). The energy for the circulation is provided by the sun and gravity.

The hydrologic cycle is continuous and indivisible. Water is evaporated from the oceans and the land, with the largest amounts coming by far from the oceans. The evaporated water is carried into the atmosphere, usually drifting up to hundreds of miles before being returned to the earth as rain, snow, hail, or sleet. This precipitated water may be intercepted, may run over the ground surface and wind up in stream channels, or may filtrate into the ground. A considerable part of the intercepted and transpired water and the surface runoff returns to the air by evaporation. The infiltrated water may seep down to deeper zones of the earth, forming ground water storage pools which may later flow out to streams as base flow. The runoff from the streams will empty into the ocean, where water will evaporate into the atmosphere to complete the hydrologic cycle. Thus the hydrologic cycle involves the processes of evaporation, precipitation, interception, transpiration, infiltration, seepage, storage, and runoff.

The quantity of water going through the hydrologic cycle during a given period for an area can be evaluated by the hydrologic equation (or continuity equation):

$$I - 0 = \Delta S$$

where I is the total inflow of surface runoff, ground water, and precipita-

EXHIBIT 9
INDUSTRIAL PUBLIC POTABLE WATER DEMAND

S.I.C. Number	Industrial Category	Mean Annual Usage Coefficient (gal/day/employee)
201	Meat Products	903.
202	Dairies	791.
203	Canned, Frozen Foods	784.
204	Grain Mills	488.
205	Bakery Products	220.
206	Sugar	1,433.
207	Candy	244.
208	Beverages	1,144.
209	Miscellaneous Foods	1,077.
211	Cigarettes	193.
221	Weaving, Cotton	171.
222	Weaving, Synthetics	344.
223	Weaving, Wool	464.
225	Knitting Mills	273.
226	Textile Finishing	810.
227	Floor Covering	297.
228	Yarn, Thread Mills	63.
229	Miscellaneous Textiles	346.
230	Whole Apparel Industry	20.
242	Saw-Planning Mill	223.
243	Millwork	316.
244	Wood Containers	238.
249	Miscellaneous Wood	144.
251	Home Furniture	122.
259	Furniture Fixture	122.
261	Pulp Mills	13,494.
262	Paper Mills	2,433.
263	Paperboard Mills	2,464.
264	Paper Products	435.
265	Paperboard Boxes	154.
266	Building Paper Mills	583.
270	Whole Print Industry	15.
281	Basic Chemicals	2,744.
282	Fibers, Plastics	864.
283	Drugs	457.
284	Soap, Toilet Goods	672.

EXHIBIT 9 (Continued)
INDUSTRIAL PUBLIC POTABLE WATER DEMAND

S.I.C. Number	Industrial Category	Mean Annual Usage Coefficient (gal/day/employee)
285	Paint, Allied Products	845.
286	Gum-Wood Chemicals	332.
287	Agriculture Chemicals	449.
289	Miscellaneous Chemicals	984.
291	Petroleum Refining	3,141.
295	Paving, Roofing	829.
301	Tires, Tubes	375.
302	Rubber Footwear	82.
303	Reclaimed Rubber	1,031.
306	Rubber Products	371.
307	Plastic Products	527.
311	Leather Tanning	899.
321	Flat Glass	590.
322	Pressed, Blown Glassware	340.
323	Products of Purchased Glass	872.
324	Cement, Hydraulic	279.
325	Structural Clay	698.
326	Pottery Products	326.
327	Cement, Plaster	353.
328	Cut Stone Products	534.
329	Nonmetallic Mineral	439.
331	Steel-Rolling	494.
332	Iron, Steel Foundries	411.
333	Prime Nonferrous	716.
334	Secondary Nonferrous	1,016.
335	Nonferrous Rolling	675.
336	Nonferrous Foundries	969.
339	Prime Metal Industries	498.
341	Metal Cans	162.
342	Cutlery, Hardware	459.
343	Plumbing, Heating	411.
344	Structure, Metal	319.
345	Screw Machine	433.
346	Metal Stamping	463.
347	Metal Service	1,806.
348	Fabricated Wire	343.

EXHIBIT 9 (Continued)
INDUSTRIAL PUBLIC POTABLE WATER DEMAND

S.I.C. Number	Industrial Category	Mean Annual Usage Coefficient (gal/day/employee)
349	Fabricated Metal	271.
351	Engines, Turbines	197.
352	Farm Machinery	320.
353	Construction Equipment	218.
354	Metalwork, Machinery	196.
355	Special Industry Machinery	290.
356	General Industrial Machinery	246.
357	Office Machines	138.
358	Service Industrial Machine	334.
359	Miscellaneous Machines	238.
361	Electric Distribution Products	272.
362	Electric Industrial Apparatus	336.
363	Home Appliances	411.
364	Light-Wiring Fixtures	369.
365	Radio-TV Receiving	235.
366	Communication Equipment	86.
367	Electronic Components	203.
369	Electric Products	393.
371	Motor Vehicles	318.
372	Aircraft and Parts	154.
373	Ship and Boat Building	166.
374	Railroad Equipment	238.
375	Motorcycle, Bike	414.
381	Scientific Instruments	181.
382	Mechanical Measure	237.
384	Medical Instruments	506.
386	Photographic Equipment	120.
387	Watches, Clocks	164.
391	Jewelry, Silver	306.
394	Toys, Sport Goods	213.
396	Costume Jewelry	423.
398	Miscellaneous Manufacturing	258.
399	Miscellaneous Manufacturing	258.

SOURCE: Hittman Associates, Inc., *Forecasting Municipal Water Requirements* (Columbia, Maryland: 1969), pp. vi-3-vi-5.

tion; O is the total outflow which includes evapotranspiration (the combined processes of evaporation and transpiration), and subsurface and surface runoff from the area; and ΔS is the change in storage in the various forms of retention and interception.

Precipitation is the sole source of the surface and ground water supplies of the earth. Evapotranspiration, or water loss, can be considered the reverse of precipitation, as it represents the total transport of water from the earth back to the atmosphere. Transpiration is the process whereby water is brought up through the plant structure, and finally returned (transpired) to the atmosphere as water vapor. Evaporation and transpiration are generally grouped together in one term since they are difficult to measure separately.

A distinction must be made between the actual amount of evapotranspiration (AE) and the potential evapotranspiration (PE). AE depends mainly on the availability of water whereas PE is the maximum amount of water that could be evaporated from vegetation and land surfaces assuming an unlimited supply of water in the ground. There is very little difference between AE and PE when the soil is sufficiently moist.

The applications of the concept of PE are numerous. For example, the determination of evapotranspiration in the hydrologic cycle has been used to estimate soil moisture, water needs for lawn sprinkling, and surface and subsurface runoff.

There are several methods for calculating PE. One of the commonly used procedures is that of Thornthwaite.[15] The major parameters of Thornthwaite's empirically derived technique are temperature and precipitation. Thus, one advantage of the method is the use of two easily available meteorological elements rather than difficult to obtain solar radiation data employed in other methods.

It is estimated that two-thirds of the precipitation falling on the land areas of the world is returned to the atmosphere by evapotranspiration, leaving one-third going into the groundwater or into streams for transportation to the oceans. The proportions for New Jersey, as an example, are approximately half-and-half. Fifty percent of the average annual precipitation of 45 inches is evapotranspired, leaving a residual of 21 to 23 inches of runoff which is available to localities for storage.[16]

Surface runoff is an important part of the hydrologic cycle; however, it varies considerably. In New Jersey, for example, it ranges from 8 inches in a dry year to 35 inches in a wet year.[17] This range of 27 inches in year-to-year runoff variation poses problems for water resource planners. The fourteen major water supply reservoirs in New Jersey have a total capacity of 129 billion gallons. This storage capability is equivalent to approximately 1 inch of runoff from the 7,509 square miles of land area in the state. Thus, only a small portion of the residual runoff in New Jersey can be stored for use in drought periods. One factor which hinders the storage of runoff in urban regions is the absence of reservoir sites. Also, in urban areas, runoff is often seriously polluted which results in a quality problem.

Since precipitation varies seasonally and annually, stream discharge also varies from month to month and from year to year. During certain times of the year a stream may carry minimal amounts of water, while the same stream following heavy rains may become a raging torrent. Given this variability in discharge, reservoirs are constructed in order to store excess water from periods of high flow for use during periods of drought. Regardless of the size of the storage reservoir or the ultimate use of the water, the major function of a reservoir is to stabilize flow over time.

Estimating Water Quantity

One of the most important aspects of reservoir design is the study of the relationship between yield and capacity. Yield is defined as the amount of water which can be obtained from a reservoir during a specified period of time. This time period can vary from a day to several years depending upon the size of the reservoir. Since yield depends upon inflow, it will vary from year to year.

Safe yield is defined as the maximum amount of water which will be available from a reservoir during a critical dry period. Often the time of the lowest natural flow on record for the stream is selected as the critical period. Since the historical record represents only a small portion of the total period of the streamflow, there is a definite probability that drier periods may occur with yields less than the safe yield. Thus, yield must always be considered in probabilistic terms.

The maximum possible yield of a basin equals the average inflow minus evaporation and seepage losses. If the flow of a river were absolutely constant, it would not be necessary to build a reservoir. However, as streamflow variability increases, the required reservoir capacity also increases. The question arises as to the degree of risk of inadequate water supply which the given water system will tolerate. For example, a reservoir which serves as a municipal water supply should have a low design yield in order to reduce the risk (to about 5 percent) of encountering a time in which the actual yield will be less than the design yield. In contrast, an irrigation system can tolerate a 20 percent risk of failing to meet the design yield, since the deficiency will have a much smaller impact on the public.[18]

Another useful term in this connection is *secondary yield*, which is defined as the amount of water which is in excess of safe yield and can be obtained from a watershed during high flow conditions. *Spill* refers to the amount of water which cannot be stored in the reservoir when it is full and may therefore flow out of the watershed and be lost. During wet periods the amount of spill can be enormous. Barring additional new reservoir construction, the management of spill can be facilitated by the following procedures: (1) Optimize the operation of separately owned reservoirs so as to draw down the reservoir which is spilling and conserve water in those reservoirs which are not at capacity. (2) Institute conjunctive management of surface and ground water resources, such as using New York City's reservoir spill to supply Nassau County on Long Island during the winter, thereby allowing Nassau's ground water levels to build up, and then reverse the procedure in the summer when New York City's reservoirs are characteristically low.[19]

Standardized techniques exist for the development of reservoir storage-yield relationships. As far back as 1883, W. Rippl suggested a method using mass curves which are a cumulative plot of reservoir inflow on the ordinate against time on the abscissa for obtaining a graphical evaluation of the yield.[20] A number of modifications and improvements have been made to the Rippl method since that time, including the use of statistical techniques to generate synthetic streamflow records many times longer than the historical record. The "synthetic hydrology" technique may yield critical low flow periods which do not appear in shorter historical records.[21]

Even though procedures for estimating the safe yield of surface water systems are supposed to have been standardized, one encounters a number of problems with the resulting values. One set of problems has to do with the selection of the critical dry period, another with yield interpretation, and still another with estimation variability.

For many systems in the Northeast, the 1929-32 drought was one of the worst on record and was accordingly chosen as the critical dry period. The 1961-66 drought, with subnormal precipitation lasting as many as 60 consecutive months in some places, markedly exceeded in severity the earlier 1929-32 drought. Reservoirs fell to record lows, and the governor of New Jersey declared a water emergency. Plans were even being discussed for bringing potable water to Newark by rail car and tank ship.

The 1961-66 drought prompted the recalculation of safe yields for the water systems in the region—many had to be reduced. For example, the safe yield of the New York City system was radically revised downward from 1,800 to 1,330 mgd, a reduction of 29 percent.[22]

The 1960s drought has an estimated recurrence interval of 200 years. This means that the probability of the drought occurring in any particular year is only 0.5 percent, and the probability of its occurring in consecutive years is even less. Nonetheless, the issue of selecting a recurrence interval remains, and there is some conflict over the selection. Generally, the agency managers prefer the conservative approach, which means the selection of the more critical drought period, and consequent yield reduction.

The second set of problems pertaining to yield estimation relates not only to the selection of the critical dry period but also includes interpretation of reserve storage assumptions. For example, the safe yield of the Wanaque system of the North Jersey District Water Supply Commission (NJDWSC) is either 69, 79, or 85 mgd. The 69 mgd value is based on the 1960s drought; the 79 mgd estimate is based on the 1930s drought and assumes a reserve storage of 25 percent; and the 85 mgd value assumes complete depletion of available reservoir storage based on the 1930s drought.[23] Adding to the confusion is the Wanaque reservoir's 10 mgd release requirement. The requirement is on the books, but it was relaxed during the drought. Therefore, is it a realistic requirement?

Since the Wanaque reservoir is oversized for its drainage area, full utilization of its capacity requires interbasin transfers of water. Consequently, NJDWSC applied to the state of New Jersey in 1950 for permission to divert 25 mgd from the Ramapo River and pump the water up into Wanaque. Permission was granted and the yield of the system is now estimated at either 94, 104, or 110 mgd. The NJDWSC prefers to use the 104 mgd estimate based on the 1930s drought, while the state prefers the more conservative 94 mgd value.[24] Overshadowing the two estimates of 94 and 104 mgd is the average annual diversion which in 1972 reached 111.6 mgd and is clearly in excess of both yields.

The third set of problems with safe yield determination is simply estimating variability. For example, even though identical methodologies were employed by two teams of experienced engineers on the same watershed, different safe yield estimates were obtained. Using the drought of the 1960s as the critical period, the Department of Water Resources of New York City estimated the yield of the Delaware system to be 482 mgd, while a team of consultants came up with an estimate of 510 mgd, a difference of 28 mgd or 5.8 percent. The estimates for the total New York City reservoir system were 1,297 and 1,332 mgd, or a difference of 35 mgd (2.7 percent). An even larger difference developed when the outside consulting firm included all useable storage space in its calculation of total yield. Mindful that New York City estimates its yields with 25 percent of useable storage held in reserve, the difference in estimates

(1,297 and 1,422 mgd) amounted to 125 mgd or only 9.6 percent. Note that both estimates were less than the 1971 average consumption in New York City of 1,512 mgd.[25]

Clearly, the estimation of safe yield for surface water systems is imperfect, but given the variation inherent in natural hydrologic systems, this observation is not surprising. Safe yield estimates for readers' purposes should be obtained from water purveyors and/or the relevant county and state agencies. In cases of discrepancy, and there are many, the lower or more conservative estimate should be used, unless the lower estimate is obviously unreasonable.

Estimating ground water resources is fraught with even greater uncertainty than estimating surface water safe yields, because the ground water portion of the hydrologic cycle is more complex, less well understood, and not visible to the observer. The term *safe yield* of an underground reservoir was first introduced in 1932 by O.E. Meinzer who defined it as "the practicable rate of withdrawing water from it [the aquifer] perennially for human use."[26] Todd defined safe yield as "the amount of water which can be withdrawn from [the ground water basin] annually without producing an undesired result."[27]

For a particular basin, the amount of discharge must be balanced by a comparable amount of recharge over a period of time, less any change in storage. In short, calculating this balance safe yield involves the collection of data on:

1. Surface inflow and outflow
2. Water imports and exports
3. Precipitation
4. Consumptive use (processes or evapotranspiration)
5. Changes in ground and surface water storage
6. Subsurface inflow and outflow

Several of these items are difficult to measure: subsurface inflow and outflow discharges cannot be directly gauged; and ground water storage changes require detailed information about the existence of ground water in the basin. Adequately measuring ground water storage would thus require the delineation of aquifers and an analysis of all well logs.

The concept of safe yield has come under criticism, partly because it is often misinterpreted by laymen as implying a fixed underground water supply. Kazmann considers safe yield to be a pseudo-hydrologic term, inasmuch as it may depend more on the particular well location rather than on general aquifer characteristics.[28] A similar criticism is noted in the 1972 edition of the *Glossary of Geology*, wherein usage of the term is discouraged because feasible withdrawal rates depend on the relationship between aquifer boundaries and well locations.[29]   Indeed, the U.S. Geological Survey (U.S.G.S.) does not even include the term *safe yield* in its 1972 list of revised definitions of ground water terms.[30]

Subject to the foregoing criticisms, it would still be helpful to have some estimate of the magnitude of the ground water resource. In the absence of detailed and specific well log and aquifer data, one approximation of the long-term yield of an area can be obtained by a consideration of the underlying geology. Clearly, different physiographic regions would have varying amounts of ground water as a consequence of their differing geohydrologic properties. For example, the Bergen County, New Jersey, Water Study Committee in 1957 estimated that the yield from the fractured sandstone and shale deposits in the county would be 0.4-0.5 mgd per square mile.[31]   A more conservative estimate of 0.2-0.3 mgd per square mile was made by the U.S. Geological Survey.[32]   Both of these estimates presume maximum development of the aquifer and a large number of widely dispersed wells.

For the purposes of readers' studies, yield estimates of the ground water resources should be obtained from the water purveyors or the state and county agencies, or from published records. Consequently, the estimates will vary in reliability and age. Quite often the estimate represents installed well pump capacity rather than aquifer yield.

Note that the terms *permissive yield, long-term yield, cumulative yield,* and *dependable yield* are sometimes used in lieu of safe yield. Whatever the term used, however, the resulting value remains an uncertain estimate at best.

Overall, data for estimating the current and future availability of water vary considerably. The U.S.G.S. has available published stream flow and sometimes groundwater records. State water resource divisions, county planning units, and geology and health agencies may have the U.S.G.S. data and additional information. Public potable water supply agencies normally have excellent records and can advise on the reliability of other data. If potable water is required, the feasibility of transfers will have to be reviewed. In many regions the U.S. Army Corps of Engineers has been involved in projects which have produced massive reports which discuss not only the current status of water supply but also possible new projects and alternative approaches such as re-use. Local universities and even consulting firms are sometimes sources of free suggestions and data.

Next, appropriate water laws and standards must be carefully reviewed with state and local officials. In some regions the riparian doctrine is appropriate—its essence is that water adjacent to or underneath land is owned by the landowner. The owner may use the water as long as the quantity is not depleted or· the quality is not degraded. Riparian doctrines, however, are frequently unclear as to what constitutes degraded quality.

In other regions, usually arid, the appropriation doctrine is law. This doctrine holds that the first water user is entitled to the same quantity and quality of water as long as he or she wants it. Later users are restricted to what is left over. This first-come-first-served doctrine, however, has been severely challenged in western court cases where urban regions needed water which had been used by ranchers and farmers.

Having obtained the data, you will want to match demand and supply. The calculations performed below cover typical situations for surface and ground water supplies. For surface water supplies the options are purchasing water from another utility, diverting water from a reservoir and from a river.

Purchasing water is dependent on the ability of one utility to transfer water to another. The quantity available may be predetermineed by pipe and pumping capacities. Cost is usually the crucial consideration.

Water diversion from a reservoir is dependent upon the constructed yield of the reservoir and minimum release requirements. For illustrative purposes, let us make the following assumptions about a basin:

size of basin	20.0 square miles
minimum stream flow necessary	
to protect aquatic ecosystems	0.150 mgd/square mile
reservoir yield	15.0 mgd

The minimum release requirement is 3.0 mgd [0.150(20.0)]. The available water for further development is therefore 12.0 mgd (15.0-3.0).

If further development is dependent upon a stream that is not impounded, then the low flow of the stream must be taken into account. In the illustrative case, we will continue to require a minimum stream flow of 0.15 mgd per square mile. In addition, it will be assumed that the low flow of the river which will be exceeded 95 percent of the time is 0.55 mgd per square mile. The difference between the low flow (0.55 mgd) and minimum requirement (0.15 mgd) is available for development.

$$(0.55 - 0.15 \text{ per sq./mile}) (20 \text{ square miles}) = 8 \text{ mgd}$$

In the illustrative case, the reservoir provides 4 mgd more than the stream for possible industrial and associated use.

If ground water is a possible source, the following data and calculations are necessary. The analyst must determine the estimated water yield from the geological formations and the proportion of the region composed of these formations. For illustrative purposes, let us make the following assumptions about the 20 square mile basin:

geologic formations	yield mgd/square mile in dry year	proportion of region
shale	0.4	60
sandstone	0.3	40

The calculations are

shale: 20 sq. mi. (.60) = 12(.4) = 4.8 mgd
sandstone: 20 sq. mi. (.40) = 8(.3) = 2.4 mgd

Total yield   7.2 mgd

The 7.2 mgd cannot all be used because of allowances for base-flow and loss of ground water due to existing development. If all the available ground water was taken, the rivers would eventually dry-up. Assuming the 0.15 mgd per square mile minimum stream flow requirement is necessary to protect the river's ecosystems, the available ground water supply is reduced to 4.2 mgd.

ground water yield	7.2 mgd
stream flow requirement (0.15 × 20)	3.0 mgd
	4.2 mgd

The above calculations are based on the assumption that the region is not developed. As development increases, land is paved over and precipitation rapidly flows into rivers instead of becoming ground water. Reliable estimates of yield reduction are rare. It would not, however, be unusual to find yield decreased between 15 and 35 percent by moderate single-family residential development of a basin. As the reader can see, the combination of losses due to development and minimum stream flow requirements can quickly eliminate ground water as a source.

If the planner chooses to ignore the conservative principles of yield estimation or rely on ground water as a supplementary supply, far more water will be available.

Many cases will require additional refinement. For example, if homes use septic tanks, 60-75 percent of the residential use will be returned to the streams and count as part of the stream flow requirement. Spray irrigation also recharges ground water supplies. Suffice it to say, knowledge of local conditions will be necessary in order to make the best estimates.

Summarizing, the first section of this chapter has focused on two major questions. How much water will industry and related activities require? How can you determine if enough water is available? The demand question was approached from the perspective of the person responsible for estimating demand. Three types of studies were reviewed: short-term impacts of a few plants; regional planning for many industrial facilities in the near future; and regional planning for long-term economic development. Public potable water demand was also considered because industry directly uses public water supplies and indirectly increases public potable water demands through increasing regional job opportunities.

The water supply section defined basic hydrologic concepts, focusing on the difficulty of relating such terms as *safe yield* and *dependable yield* to the amount of water that can be delivered to customers. Finally, sources of water supply data were presented.

Water Quality

A polluted water body has physical, chemical, or biological properties which interfere with water uses. These physical, chemical, and biological characteristics are normally present in all water bodies in acceptable concentrations; but they become pollution when the concentrations are no longer acceptable. This section will review procedures for estimating the impact of industrial activity on water quality in three parts: (1) establishing the ambient environment through biological and chemical analyses and aquatic and terrestrial surveys; (2) estimating industrial discharges; and (3) estimating the impact of effluent discharges on water quality, fauna, and flora.

ESTABLISHING THE AMBIENT ENVIRONMENT

This section provides an introduction to water quality, overviews the role of industry in degrading water quality, and reviews sources of water quality data.

An Introduction to Water Quality. The most important characteristics of water quality insofar as they influence use are turbidity, temperature, and the presence of dissolved gases and solids.[33]

Turbidity (opaqueness), color, and odor are physical indicators. A dirty looking and smelly water body containing floating solids is unappealing to potential users, even if it is perfectly safe. Highly colored and odorous water bodies typically receive drainage from industrial sites, urbanized watersheds, and swamps which are overloaded with plants. A highly turbid water body may suffer from reduced light penetration and deposition of silts and mud. In turn, bottom organisms and flora as well as fauna which are dependent on bottom plants and organisms for food will die.

With respect to lakes, completely pure water absorbs all light and appears black. Suspended solids scatter light and cause a blue color. A highly productive lake usually appears grey-blue and sometimes yellow because it possesses a large mass of organic matter which scatters incoming light. Less productive lakes tend to shade toward blue and green.

Streams do not vary in color as much as lakes, especially during non-flood periods. Upper reaches contain little organic matter and are clear. As one moves downstream, increased organic matter leads to brown colors.

Streams sometimes turn black from an accumulation of leaves. Algae will impart a greenish tint to the surfaces of streams. During floods, suspended solids will scatter nearly all the incoming light and impart a brown color characteristic of the area's soil.

Overall, solids in suspension and marked turbidity are characteristics of rivers, while lakes are marked by deposition of solids and clear colors. Streams vary little in color, except during flood stages, while lakes vary considerably depending upon their size, shape, biological characteristics, and water sources.

Temperature affects the ability of plants to produce oxygen and the activity of biological organisms. High temperatures reduce the ability of fluids to contain oxygen and other dissolved gases. In the absence of man-made discharges, the sun's rays control the water temperature of streams. On clear, summer days the stream will be warm; during cloudy days and evenings the water body will be cold. Relatively little stratification occurs in streams. Smaller streams experience greater temperature variations than larger, deeper streams. Downstream areas contain more suspended sediments which absorb heat and therefore fluctuate less than upstream stretches.

The thermal characteristics of lakes are much more complicated than those of streams and estuaries. Lakes have a pronounced thermal stratification which changes drastically between winter and summer. During the winter, water temperature in moderately deep water is warmer than water at the surface. Shading from floating snow and ice reduces light penetration which leads to the depletion of dissolved oxygen and decreased biological activity at lower lake levels. When spring arrives, the ice and snow melt and runoff increases. The upper part of the lake becomes dense. Mixing of lake waters occurs, driven by density differences and winds.

During summer, the lower layers are colder than the upper layers. Dissolved gases may be depleted at all depths. The process starts a new cycle in autumn. The above description is the relatively simple case of a lake which undergoes two temperature circulations each year.

Estuaries are water bodies that lie at the interface of the fresh continental water and salty ocean waters. Estuaries have a much higher salt content than streams and lakes; they are deeper than streams and shallower than most lakes. Sea water heats up faster in response to the sun's rays than large streams and lakes. The thermal properties of estuaries are also related to the characteristics of waters flowing down from streams and back from oceans.

Dissolved Gases and Solids. The hydrogen bonding of water molecules is weak. Therefore, water contains dissolved gases and organic and inorganic solids, and biological organisms. The most important dissolved gases are oxygen, carbon dioxide, methane, and hydrogen sulfide.

Dissolved oxygen (DO) is the most important dissolved gas in water. It regulates both the metabolism of fauna and the photosynthesis of flora. The value of dissolved oxygen in water varies with temperature, salinity, and atmospheric pressure. As the temperature increases, the amount of dissolved oxygen in water decreases. As a result, many water bodies have dissolved oxygen debts during the summer, especially at night when aquatic plants are no longer producing oxygen.

Salty waters (estuaries and oceans) contain less dissolved oxygen than streams and lakes. The higher the atmospheric pressure (altitude), the lower the amount of dissolved oxygen. In general, salty waters at high altitudes during the summer months are more likely to suffer natural oxygen depletion than are fresh water bodies at or near sea level.

A water body derives oxygen from two natural sources. First, oxygen is mixed from the atmosphere into water by winds, wave action, and other disturbances, such as water running over rock outcrops. Second, photosynthesis, the process by which plants produce carbohydrates, produces oxygen as a byproduct.

Dissolved oxygen is the most important indicator of the oxygen status of water. Biochemical oxygen demand (BOD), chemical oxygen demand (COD), and total organic carbon (TOC) are three other standard indicators of oxygen content. BOD is the rate at which dissolved oxygen is used by bacteria and other micro-organisms to decompose organic matter. A high BOD reading suggests that a good deal of organic matter is present to be decomposed. A low BOD reading means either that the water is clean or that the organisms have been killed, usually by toxic pollutants.

COD is a test of oxygen demand in which the organic matter is chemically oxidized instead of being biologically oxidized. COD values are higher than BOD values because the chemical test oxidizes all of the organics, while the biological test is selective.

TOC tests for organic matter by combusting a sample and measuring the amount of resultant carbon dioxide (CO_2). TOC is a better test than BOD or COD, but it requires relatively expensive equipment.

The second important dissolved gas is CO_2, which acts as a buffer against rapid shifts in the acid-base balance of water, and along with dissolved oxygen helps regulate biological processes in aquatic communities. Carbon dioxide is highest when dissolved oxygen is lowest. Sources of CO_2 include respiration by plants and animals, contact of water with rocks containing carbonates (e.g., limestone), contact between the air and water, and bacterial decomposition of organic matter.

The acid-base balance exists because water molecules disassociate (ionize). In neutral waters an equal concentration of H+ (hydrogen ions) and OH− (hydroxide ions) are present. An overabundance of H+ makes a water body acidic, while too few hydrogen ions makes the water body basic. Basic waters have too many hydroxide ions.

Aquatic species are extremely sensitive to the acid-base balance. CO_2 is an indicator of the balance. However, pH is a clearer indicator. The pH value is the negative power to which the number 10 must be raised to equal the hydrogen ion concentration.

$$pH = log \frac{1}{H+} \quad or \quad H+ = 10^{-pH}$$

The concentration of H+ and OH− ions is measured in molecular weights in grams per litre of water. The product $(H+) \times (OH-) = 10^{-14}$. If the H+ concentration is 10^{-8}, the OH− concentration is 10^{-6}, and the water is slightly basic. For a neutral solution, the pH value is 7 and H+ is 10^{-7}. If the hydrogen ion concentration is high (e.g., H+ = 10^{-2}; = 10^{-3}) the pH is low and the water is acidic. If the hydrogen ion concentration is low (e.g., H+ = 10^{-11}; = 10^{-12}), the pH is high and the water is basic.

The acid-base balance may differ considerably because of regional variations in geology. Water draining through limestone regions may have pH values of 9 or more. Lakes born from volcanic activity may be extremely acidic because of high sulfur levels which are converted to sulfuric acid in water. Water bodies which pass through bogs and swamps usually are acidic because the decay of organic matter produces humic and tannic acids.

Organic matter may be decomposed in two ways: using free oxygen (aerobically) or in the absence of free oxygen (anaerobically). When anaerobic decomposition takes place, methane (CH_4) and hydrogen sulfide (H_2S) result. Methane, also known as marsh gas, is produced by the breakdown of carbohydrates by anaerobic bacteria, especially during the summer when free oxygen is not available at the bottom of swamps, ponds, lakes, and other slow-moving water bodies. Hydrogen sulfide is a foul smelling gas produced during anaerobic decay. When methane and hydrogen sulfide are found in a water body, the water body will have very limited use.

There are many inorganic dissolved solids in water. Chief among these are carbonates, sulfates, calcium, iron, magnesium, nitrates, and phosphates. If the dissolved solids are found in low concentrations, the water body may be devoid of life. For example, nitrogen compounds are important in the synthesis and maintenance of protein, phosphorus compounds in the transfer of energy in the aquatic system, sulfates for protein metabolism, and iron in animal respiration. If the concentrations are too great, the water body may be choked with plants which will lead to oxygen depletion.

In general, natural differences among water bodies in solids content occur because of differences in the geology of drainage basins and rainfall quantities and frequencies.

Human activity contributes many of the most dangerous solids. Toxic inorganic solids such as arsenic and lead may be present in trace concentrations because of river basin geological formations. When the concentrations exceed a trace level, the change is usually drastic. Some chemicals react to produce a more harmful effect (synergism). Other reactions reduce the harmful impact (antagonism). For example, cadmium and zinc react synergistically to produce a toxic effect on fish much greater than either chemical produces by itself. Calcium and lead react antagonistically to reduce the impact of lead.[34] The literature on toxic pollutants is large, continuously growing, and extremely complicated. Basic references are contained in the chapter notes.[35]

Biological organisms that are potentially harmful to humans and other species are found in water bodies. Coliforms are plentiful and easily found microbes that are associated with warm-blooded animals. They have become a standard test for bacterial pollution. However, a coliform count need not be associated with water-borne diseases such as cholera and typhoid. Fecal coliform and fecal streptococci are better indicators of bacterial pollution, but are more expensive to obtain.

Finally, excessive solids deposited on the bottom of a water course can exert a deleterious effect long after deposition. When stirred by natural flushing or by man's activities (e.g., dredging) they can circulate oxygen demanding, toxic wastes.

To the swimmer, floating solids and odors may be the only signs of an unacceptable water body. To fish, plants, and other aquatic species the signs of a water pollution problem are quickly apparent and complex. Organisms require resources such as phosphates, nitrates, potassium, calcium, magnesium, dissolved oxygen, and CO_2 for metabolism. And they possess limited physical adaptations to such characteristics as temperature, salinity, and the strength of currents. Organisms occupy a portion of a water body as long as one limiting factor is not reached. A single physical, biological, or chemical change may suddenly eliminate them or force them to migrate. Fauna and flora exhibit great variations in their tolerances of discharges. Some organisms possess wide tolerances for organic wastes, solids, and temperature variations. Others possess little tolerance; most possess little or no tolerance for toxic discharges.

Given the above introduction to water quality, we can review leads for establishing the ambient water environment. While the ambient noise environment usually has to be established by the analyst with a meter, the water environment may be monitored in three ways:

1. By biological and chemical analyses of the water.
2. Bioassay in which organisms are placed in water samples and their reaction compared with controls. At present this approach is receiving a good deal of attention for monitoring toxic discharges.
3. By the use of plants and animals which experience has shown to be reactive to types and degrees of pollution. The absence of organisms known to be highly intolerant of pollution also serves as an indication of pollution, and the presence and expansion of pollution tolerant organisms is a related index of pollution.

Biological and Chemical Analyses of Water

In general, the ambient water environment is established by biological and chemical testing. If possible, you should rely on available monitoring records. If such records do not exist or important parameters have not been tested, then a kit may be used to fill gaps.[36]

Public and private agencies have accumulated a good deal of water quality data. Ward has distinguished six major duties involving monitoring, surveillance, and dissemination for branches of government: (1) planning, (2) research and development, (3) aid programs, (4) regulation of water quality, (5) technical assistance, and (6) legal enforcement.[37] The first three require primarily a long-term record for the identification of long-term trends and for the isolation of problem areas. The last three require data which have a reasonably high probability of detecting stream standard and legal permit violations and of withstanding legal challenges. The following agencies, following U.S.EPA technical regulations, collect water quality data to meet these six objectives: the U.S.EPA; state health, water resources, and environmental agencies; regional water quality and supply commissions; the United States Geological Survey; and water purveyors. Many of these data have been stored in a centralized storage and retrieval system called STORET, a system which we will shortly discuss.[38]

Monitoring has three dimensions—parameters, frequencies, and locations. EPA's STORET system contains fields for more than 900 parameters of water quality. The literature on what parameters should be sampled range from classical articles extolling the virtues of a limited number of parameters—usually DO, BOD, temperature, and pH[39]—to books which describe suggested inventories for streams and estuaries,[40] and to literature which implies that a single index of water quality may be derived.[41]

An effective means of examining the adequacy of the ambient parameter selection in the study area is to compare the existing data set with parameters mentioned in the federal rules, with the region's water quality standards, and with standards promulgated by other regions. The federal rules require monitoring in the streams and in sediments of the following parameters and others depending upon water quality standards: DO, temperature, specific conductance, pH, total phosphorous, total Kjeldahl nitrogen, pesticides, dissolved nitrite plus nitrate, COD, TOC, heavy metals and other toxic materials, and oil and grease.[42] Most of these parameters have been sampled in urbanized areas. The record of sediment samples is much smaller than the ambient water records.

Schultz has classified more than fifty water quality parameters into four groups based on the frequency of their use in state water quality standards.[43] Nine parameters are classified as found in all the state standards: DO, pH, coliform, temperature, floating solids (oil-grease), settleable solids, turbidity-color, taste-odor, and toxic substances. Three groups of parameters are categorized as found in 50 to 99 percent of the state standards. These "frequently" sampled parameter groups (radioactivity, total dissolved solids, and U.S. Public Health Service Drinking Water Standards parameters) have been sampled less frequently in most regions than the first nine. Next, Schultz identifies sixteen parameters which are found in 20 to 49 percent of the state water quality standards. Eleven of these parameters are heavy metals and other toxic substances. Finally, Schultz identifies eighteen parameters which appear in less than 20 percent of the state standards.

Sampling frequencies vary from systematic to special and from daily to annually. In studies of the Delaware River estuary and the New York metropolitan region, the senior author found that the most reliable data were daily and weekly readings by public potable water companies; state data were the least frequent and least useful.[44]

Sampling locations usually emphasize one or more of the following: major dischargers, potable water supplies, important commercial or recreation fishing areas, political boundaries, and locations where tributaries join larger water bodies. With respect to the number of sampling locations in 1950, Velz made the following argument which is relevant to most water bodies more than twenty-five years later.

> Ordinarily, too many stations are established, with an insufficient number of samples collected at any one. A few locations with a sufficient number of samples to define results in terms of statistical significance are much more reliable than many stations with only a few samples at each. If valid conclusions are to be drawn from the data, enough samples must be taken to define the variability by statistical treatment and determine the degrees of confidence in any mean condition.[45]

Hopefully, you will have a nearby station with a weekly or at least monthly record of readings dating back for at least three or four years. Such a data set will enable you to calculate measures of central tendency and dispersion, as well as look for historical trends.

The EPA STORET data appear to be the ideal source of water quality records.[46] All the agency data are available and central tendencies and dispersions are calculated. This set has three major problems. Readings are lumped together so that data from the 1950s, 1960s, and 1970s are averaged. Second, in transcribing the data between the collecting agency and the STORET system some agencies neglected to check their data. The result is data errors which lead to erroneous central tendencies. Third, much of the STORET data are of such short duration that they will not be of use. Overall, if STORET can be of use to you, we recommend that you request the original input data of a limited number of reliable collection agencies. The nearest U.S.EPA office will have an individual who is responsible for interacting between users and the computer.

If you are lucky, a friendly public potable purveyor will be monitoring the stream. If you are not so lucky, then U.S.EPA, state, and U.S.G.S. data will be your major sources.

Aquatic and Terrestrial Surveys [47]

Surveys range from reviews of existing literature, to one-shot baseline field studies, to long-range monitoring programs. The purpose of the survey is to learn enough about the existing aquatic and related terrestrial environments to indicate the potential impact of a proposed project. In order to understand why particular organisms are studied, we will briefly review biological systems.

Biological Systems. The basic building block of the biological system is the *individual* who belongs to a particular *species* based on shared inheritance. Groups of similar species occupying the same space compose a *population* for that space. Populations of different species occupying the same place are called *communities*. Finally, a group of interacting communities constitutes an *ecosystem*.

Waterbodies such as ponds, lakes, estuaries, and rivers may be viewed as ecosystems. Each of these ecosystems contains different individuals, species, populations, and communities which occupy their own niche in the system. They interact with each other in many ways, including through the control of the food chain, birth and death rates, and the provision of suitable living spaces.

The food chain will be briefly reviewed as an illustration of these interactions. Species maintain a supply of food for one another by assuming a specific role in the transfer of energy through the system. Some species are capable of producing living organic material through the utilization of inorganic materials and solar radiation. These *producers* include green plants, phytoplankton, and some bacteria. The producers are fed upon by *consumers* who are not capable of directly producing organic matter. Consumers may be dichotomized into *herbivores*, which feed directly upon the producers, and *carnivores*, which consume herbivores or other carnivores. The interactions between producers and consumers result in dead organic materials which are decomposed and converted back into elemental nutrients. The *decomposers* are principally bacteria and fungi.

In order for the food chain to continue, for some species not to overpopulate the living spaces, and for the living areas to remain viable, physical, chemical, and biological characteristics of the ecosystem must be maintained within tolerance limits. For example, water temperature, salinity, and the strength of the current are usually important characteristics of a water body which control the maintenance and spread of different populations. Among the previously mentioned critical resources are dissolved gases such as oxygen and CO_2 and inorganic nutrients such as magnesium and nitrates.

All species do not react in the same way to changes in their environment. Some species have wide tolerances (prefix eury,) others have very narrow tolerances (prefix steno). For example, fresh-water species are stenohaline because they require water with little salt content. Since they require high levels of salt in the water, ocean species are also stenohaline. Estuarine species are euryhaline because they can tolerate relatively wide fluctuations in the salinity of their water environment. Adaptation to changes in salinity is related to temperature, the presence of nutrients, and other biological, physical, and chemical factors.

As is apparent from this brief description, the ecosystem is a complex chain of interactions among individuals and the environment. The purpose of the aquatic and related terrestrial surveys is to determine if and how industrial development might disrupt the ecosystem. Probable impacts of industrial development on an ecosystem can be estimated by establishing the composition of the present ecosystem and by knowing how industrial activities, especially effluents, might affect the nutrient base, temperature and other tolerances, and living spaces of each community.

Aquatic Field Survey. An aquatic field survey begins with a literature search, the goal of which is to learn as much as possible about any of the following: species in the area, population density and diversity, and aggregate biomass. Identification of species is important because, in general, the presence or absence of particular species is usually directly indicative of the hospitality of the environment. For example, the presence of trout is one indicator of a moderate to high dissolved oxygen. Furthermore, species identification is vital because the presence of *rare or endangered species* and/or a *unique ecosystem* can immediately preclude or delay development. Federal and state officials can supply lists of rare or endangered species.

Population density is the number of individuals per unit volume or area. Generally, the greater the density the more productive the area. Numerous species and individual diversity are indicators of biological stability. Finally, total biomass is the amount of living material in an area. It may be measured in a variety of ways including total dry weight of green materials per unit area, net yield of green materials per unit of area and time (equivalent to the concept of safe yield of water), and rate of production of biomass per unit of time and space.

Aquatic surveys focus on key producers, consumers, and decomposers. In water bodies without a swift current, plankton is found and collected as an indicator of biomass and sensitivity of the biological community to the changed environmental conditions. The collection is done with a variety of instruments, including nets. Gravity and/or a centrifuge is used to concentrate the plankton. If a particular chemical is to be discharged from the proposed industry, laboratory tests of the impact of the effluent on the plankton can be made.

Benthos organisms are species such as worms, insects, and mollusks which lie along the floor of the water body. Benthic species consume organic material which drops from the upper layers of the water body and, in turn, are consumed by higher carnivores such as fish. Benthos are good indicators of water quality because they are relatively immobile. Fish are generally the highest level of carnivores in a water body. Accordingly, their presence or absence is a good indicator of water quality. Finally, bacteria are collected in water quality sampling bottles as an indicator of decomposition.

Most industrial impact assessments include a literature review of aquatic species; fewer include a baseline survey and impact assessment; and still fewer include the baseline assessment and a monitoring program designed to trace the impacts during the construction and operation of the facility. The monitoring program is, in essence, the same as the baseline study, though the level of detail may not be as fine.

When the proposed site is marshland, other wetland, or near a bay and estuary, one can expect that a terrestrial survey will be necessary to support the aquatic survey. Depending upon available budgets, a terrestrial baseline study will involve analyses of the following: soils, vegetation, insects, birds, mammals, amphibians, and reptiles.

Soils are analyzed for four major reasons: (1) to estimate the value of the land from the agricultural perspective, (2) to calculate the loss to the region should the land be developed for nonagricultural purposes, (3) to estimate the quality and quantity of runoff from the site during construction and during the operation of the facility, and (4) to develop appropriate land management practices during the life of the facility.

Vegetation is studied to determine the dominant plant species in each area. Actual plant counts are taken in sample areas and mapped to provide a perspective on the spatial distribution of species. Studies of mammals and birds, when combined with vegetation studies, help analysts estimate areas which may be damaged by industrial development. The survey techniques range from counting the number and types of species along a route to trapping, tagging, and following species.

Insects are an important part of the aquatic and terrestrial ecosystem because they are the food for many higher order species. Finally, reptiles and amphibians such as toads, snakes, frogs, turtles, and alligators provide a direct link between the land and water environments.

Summarizing, one of the three key steps toward determining whether industrial development will be acceptable from the water quality perspective is establishing the quality of the ambient environment. Physical, chemical, and biological surveys are all relevant methods toward this end. The second step is to estimate the quantity and quality of the industrial discharge. It is this step to which we now turn.

ESTIMATING INDUSTRIAL DISCHARGES

Public law 92-500, the Federal Water Pollution Control Act Amendments (FWPCAA) became law on October 18, 1972.[48] The law represents the most comprehensive federal effort to abate and control water pollution. Its stated goal is to "restore and maintain the chemical, physical and biological integrity of the nation's waters." All dischargers were to have been brought up to at least secondary treatment by July, 1977 (now 1978). By July, 1983 (now 1984), if possible, waters are to be suitable for contact recreation and for the propagation and protection of fish. The 1972 act establishes a 1985 goal (which is probably unrealistic for most industries) of no discharges.

The FWPCAA goals are to be achieved by providing federal funds, legal, and technical assistance. This section will overview the FWPCAA and present a detailed review of those provisions that are most relevant to industrial water pollution.

An Overview of the Federal Water Pollution Control Act Amendments of 1972 and 1977 Amendments. With respect to industrial water discharges, the effluent limitation provisions are the most critical parts of the legislation. The effluent limitations set average and maximum discharge for mid-1977 and mid-1983. In the 1977 amendments, the 1977 and 1983 deadlines were set back to 1978 and 1984. The average and maximum numbers differ for existing and new facilities. The effluent limitations are uniform throughout the United States. Effluent limitations will be reviewed in much greater detail later in the chapter.

The 1965 Water Quality Act required the states to establish water quality standards for coastal and interstate waters. The standards were based on water uses, typically contact recreation, potable water supply, propagation of fish, and agriculture. The water quality standards were approved by public hearings, and include plans for implementing and enforcing the standards. State responses differed greatly. For example, Illinois designated all its waters for use as a general supply or for a public and food processing water supply. Missouri designated seventeen categories including irrigation, livestock watering, and others.[49] Horowitz studied the water quality standards of California, Maryland, Ohio, and Oregon and concluded that none of the four states

> even vaguely approximates [an] integrated application of water quality standards. What's usually behind the words is a simple insistence that primary treatment be upgraded to secondary, or secondary to tertiary. Water quality standards are neither the most logical nor the most compact mediums for making simple statements of that kind. We have not seen a straight-forward case of water quality standards being translated into cleaner water through sharp inspections, competent and honest predictions of assimilative capacity, sound local allocations and enforced compliance.[50]

The 1972 amendments continue to require water quality standards, but two important changes were made. First, intrastate waters are included in the program. Second, in essence, the water quality standard is relegated to the role of a tool for judging the success of effluent standards. The states are required to tailor effluent discharge programs to the water quality goals. Each segment of a water body has to be monitored at specified intervals and the impact of each discharger evaluated.

On the basis of the evaluations, each segment of a water body is put into one of two groups: effluent limited or water quality limited. Effluent limited water bodies are bodies in which the standards are being met or will be met if the nationwide effluent limitations are implemented. Water quality limited bodies will not meet the water quality standards even with the application of the nationwide effluent limitations. Accordingly, more stringent effluent limitations are required.

Clearly, the management of a water quality limited body of water is considerably more complex than its effluent limited counterpart. Effluent requirements have to be tailor-made for every discharger along the water quality limited body of water.

Application of the effluent and water quality limited standards requires long-term and short-term planning and funding programs. The short-term program consists of determining the extent of present discharges and abating these discharges back to levels required to meet the effluent limitations and, if necessary, water quality standards. This program is called the national pollutant discharge elimination system (NPDES). All dischargers must file a standardized report which indicates the quality and quantity of their discharges with the U.S.EPA and their state agency.

The state and/or the U.S.EPA reacts to the report with a set of effluent limitations, an abatement schedule to meet the effluent limitations, and a monitoring schedule. Upon agreement by the discharger, interested citizens, and the state and federal EPA groups (open public meetings may be required) a permit is then issued. The permit specifies a set of legally enforceable steps which the discharger must take to meet effluent limitations. More than 45,000 permits have been issued to public and private dischargers.

In order to secure a local permit you may go to your state EPA or the nearest regional office of the U.S.EPA. The full set of documents is available to the public. Most of the permits were prepared by the federal EPA based on promulgated effluent limitations, on engineering approximations of what the effluent standards would be, and on the economic impact of the limitation on the discharger. The long-term responsibility for enforcing and modifying existing permits and issuing new permits lies with both the state and federal governments. The U.S.EPA is responsible for issuing the technical documents establishing the nationwide effluent limitations.

Other than this federal responsibility, the federal and state governments can interact in two ways. The regional U.S.EPA office can maintain the permit program with state certification. Or the U.S.EPA can certify the state as the designated body to maintain the permit program. The U.S.EPA regional office monitors the state program and has to approve each permit.

If the project you are interested in falls in a state certified program, then the state staff is probably a strong one which can assist in determining the relevant effluent limitations and environmental impact of the proposed industrial facility. If the state does not administer the permit program, then the regional U.S.EPA office will probably be your major source of help. The engineers tend to specialize along industry lines, and therefore you will have to find out which engineer or set of engineers is concerned with your project.

Data collected by the permit program are extremely useful because they can demonstrate the initial and permitted effluent discharges of existing facilities in the standard industrial group of the proposed project. The states and/or the U.S.EPA must regularly monitor effluent quality. Different combinations of monitoring have been promulgated, including regular inspections four times a year and spot checks by the government. Major dischargers are required to monitor on a daily basis. These data are sent to the permitting agencies. A major discharger is defined as a discharger of toxic substances and/or more than 50,000 gallons per day. The effluent monitoring reports are extremely helpful in determining the spatial distribution of effluent discharges.

Frequently, relatively small dischargers located in urban regions will release their effluents into a municipal system. The industrial discharger is not required to determine the quality and quantity of industrial inputs into a municipal system. Usually, a consulting firm is hired to make the determination for the public treatment facility and has filed a report which is appended to the documents required for the issuance of a municipal permit.

While the federal agency is establishing the technological bases for permit limitations and the federal and state agencies are issuing and enforcing the permits of existing dischargers and new dischargers, long-term planning processes have been established by the FWPCAA of 1972 to plan basin water resources activities in the foreseeable future. The long-term planning processes of the 1972 amendments may be briefly reviewed under three headings: (1) municipal facilities, (2) areawide planning, and (3) state and other agency long-term planning. At the municipal scale, short-term plans are required to determine the most useful public treatment facilities in the immediate future. Municipal facilities planning is irrelevant with respect to industrial development with two major exceptions. The first exception is the case of the industry which might tie into an already planned public system. The second case is the possible need of the local government to provide a treatment facility to handle the urban development which will result from siting the industry.

The second planning mechanism is areawide planning in urban-industrial regions. (Section 208 of the act). The areawide planning agency has the general goal of establishing a comprehensive approach to improve, or at least control, water quality in areas which are already seriously degraded or are likely to be degraded in the near future. Its more specific goal is to develop a plan to secure federal and other monies for upgrading existing facilities and constructing new facilities over the next twenty years.

The areawide planning regions are quite variable in size and jurisdiction. They are designated by the state governors. Sometimes they are political entities such as counties; other times they are basins; and still other times they cross state boundaries.

The areawide planning process interacts with potential industrial water dischargers in two important ways. First, the plan is supposed to include specifications for twenty years for all treatment works and collection systems necessary to handle all wastes, including industrial. Second, the areawide planning agency must identify industrial dischargers using public treatment facilities and insure that industrial pretreatment standards are being met. Perhaps the most important planning impact with respect to industrial location is that the areawide agency has the authority to refuse to allow new sources to tie into the public system if the effluent from the new source will lead to the violation of an effluent and/or water quality standard.

The third planning process requires the states to plan a long-range solution to water quality problems and to coordinate these plans with other interested agencies. Included in the state mandate is the classification of water bodies as water quality limited or effluent limited, a means for running the permit program, and priorities for allocating resources among alternative treatment and collection projects.

The FWPCAA has strong legal and financial bases. With respect to industry, the U.S.EPA may bring legal action for a permit violation including an effluent standard, monitoring inspection, pretreatment requirement, and any other permit condition. The states play the major investigative role in the legal process. Finally, citizen suits are limited to those "adversely affected." A citizen has to establish individual special damages in order to bring suit.

Economic factors are explicitly woven into the FWPCAA of 1972 in two places. First, the act requires the U.S.EPA to determine the economic cost of water pollution control. This economic consideration is most apparent in the definitions of "best practicable" and "best available treatment" technologies applied to existing dischargers. The U.S.EPA has sponsored studies of the economic impact on specific industries of meeting the 1977, 1983, and 1985 goals. These studies are extremely worthwhile. They review the processes, the costs of different control technologies, and the likely economic impact of requiring alternative technologies. If your industry/industries have been studied, then we strongly recommend that you secure a copy of the report/reports from the U.S.EPA or from the National Technical Information Service which publishes all of the reports.[51]

The second economic consideration in the FWPCAA is the increased federal funding role. The federal government will pay 75 percent of the cost of municipal treatment facilities. In return for this federal share, the U.S.EPA must be assured that the state has an ongoing planning process and that the facility meets relevant technological specifications.

Effluent Limitations. With respect to industrial development, it is vital to understand the effluent limitations, especially the new source standards. Three levels of effluent limitations were promulgated: (1) best practicable technology, (2) best available technology, and (3) new source technology. Best practicable technology was the July 1, 1977, goal (now 1978). EPA technical documents, permits, and conversations with EPA engineers lead us to conclude that this first level of technology is largely a stop-gap. U.S.EPA engineers study each industry's permit application. They compare the treatment achieved by the permit applicant with existing plants characterized by a low effluent level. If the plant has already achieved an acceptable treatment level, EPA will usually allow a continuation of the existing discharge and move toward setting best available technology goals for the facility.

More often than not, existing industries do not approach a good treatment performance. EPA engineers examine the existing equipment, the production processes, and engineering and economic considerations in applying different technologies to the facility. Sometimes, a higher level of performance can be obtained by minor process changes, by switching raw materials, and by controlling leaks. At other times treatment facilities have to be upgraded, and still other times the industry is asked to pretreat and then send the bulk of the effluent to a municipal facility.

The best available technology limitations have been developed to meet the 1983 goals of the FWPCAA. They represent the best technologies that can be economically applied by July 1, 1983 (now 1984). Most of these technologies have already been promulgated by EPA and are being applied in the permit process.

New source standards will be applied to any industrial facility constructed after January, 1974, and perhaps to existing sources which are modified. A new source is expected to use all available treatment and process changes to achieve a high level of treatment. Once a new source has been given standards, these standards cannot be changed for the period of equipment depreciation or for a decade, whichever is shorter.

An important, though not completely resolved, part of the FWPCAA is toxic pollutants. EPA was required to promulgate a standard which recognizes an "ample margin of safety" for any pollutant which will "cause death, disease, behavioral abnormalities, cancer, genetic mutations, physiological malfunctions . . ." in an organism or its offspring. Lists of hazardous and toxic pollutants and an enormous literature on toxics is available.[52] Hazardous waste management is one of the most complicated scientific, social, and economic issues in urban-industrial society and will require years of study before the vast majority of people will be convinced that appropriate restrictions have been promulgated.

The 1972 act amendments required that standards be achieved within one year of their promulgation. Economic and technological factors were not to be weighed as important factors. The 1977 amendments postpone the deadlines and explicitly require the consideration of cost and technical feasibility. The amendments require twenty-one industries to use the best available control technology for effluents of 129 specific "toxic" pollutants by 1984 and for other potential toxics by 1987. The toxicity of another set of "nonconventional" pollutants including some heavy metals and pesticides is to be determined before action is to be taken.

The 1972 FWPCAA also addressed overflows and accidental spills o toxic substances. Discharges of such substances were prohibited, and the discharger was to be held liable for cleanup costs. Finally, the discharge of hazardous water emissions could be regulated under the 197𝔢 FWPCAA water quality standards.

Whereas toxic provisions were written into the 1972 act, these prov sions have been little used. Only four proposed standards have been formally reviewed. The problems have been the difficulty of defining "hazardous quantities" and "removable," the prohibition against considering economic and technological factors, and the 1972 act's strict timetables.

EPA proposed rules designating hazardous substances and defining "hazardous quantities" in late 1975. EPA is also working on effluent, new-source, and pretreatment standards. Specifically, the settlement of a suit by environmental groups requires EPA to issue new-source, effluent, and pretreatment standards for sixty-five pollutants discharged by twenty-one industries by mid-1983. These proposed standards are being issued in 1978. EPA is to weigh economic and technological as well as health and environmental factors in the standards.

Municipal effluent limitations are less complex than industrial limitations. By July 1, 1977, all municipal plants were required to meet a secondary treatment level. This level of treatment implies the following technologies: mechanical removal of solids by screening and settling; removal of additional organic wastes and solids by treating the waste with air or oxygen and by allowing bacteria to consume organic materials; and chlorination.[53] The 1977 Amendments allow a waiver of secondary treatment in the case of facilities meeting specific pretreatment standards and preconditions. The senior author interprets the waiver to be only for west coast plants discharging into the ocean and islands. Whether this interpretation is correct will probably be tested in the courts. A secondary treatment facility is usually able to remove between 75 and 95 percent of the organics and solids in the waste stream. Much of this material becomes sludge which has been dumped into the oceans. Ocean dumping is reviewed in the solid waste chapter. Land application and reuse alternatives are now receiving a good deal of attention.

Estimating Effluent Discharges. Once they are agreed upon, the federal effluent limitations are relatively easy to apply. The permit application filed by an industry must indicate the quality and quantity of more than seventy physical, chemical, and biological indicators of the effluent quality. The discharger must indicate if the discharge contains any of the pollutants in Exhibit 10A and others which will be added as the toxic regulations are passed. The discharges must be described in detail later in the permit application. The companion list of parameters (Exhibit 10A) is the list of specific industries for which specific effluent limitations have been proposed and in some cases promulgated. In the event that readers wish to examine some of these regulations, the list is in the order of the date the limitations were proposed in the *Federal Register*.

By July 1, 1983, the goal was to introduce new approaches such as re-use of waste water and to upgrade municipal plants to handle wastes from urban runoff and from industries. Secondary treatment is not effective in treating many industrial wastes. Indeed, the introduction of industrial wastes into a municipal plant may kill the bacteria which decompose organic wastes. Accordingly, pretreatment standards for industrial wastes are important if the proposed industry would like to use a public plant. In essence, the goal of pretreatment requirements is to prevent new industries from getting around new source standards by going through a public plant.

As indicated above, EPA has been slow in responding to the hazardous waste provisions of the FWPCAA of 1972. About half of the nation's major

EXHIBIT 10A
Effluent Identification Check List
for Industrial Dischargers

Parameter Name	Code	Parameter Name	Code
Color	00080		
Turbidity	00070	Chromium	01034
Radioactivity	04050	Copper	01042
Hardness	00900	Iron	01045
Solids	00500	Lead	01051
Ammonia	00610	Magnesium	00927
Organic Nitrogen	00605	Manganese	01055
		Mercury	71900
Nitrate	00620	Molybdenum	01062
Nitrite	00615	Nickel	01067
Phosphorus	00665	Selenium	01147
Sulfate	00945	Silver	01077
Sulfide	00745	Potassium	00937
Sulfite	00740	Sodium	00929
Bromide	71870	Titanium	01152
Chloride	00940	Tin	01102
Cyanide	00720	Zinc	01092
Fluoride	00951	Algicides	74051
Aluminum	01105	Oil and Grease	00550
Antimony	01097	Phenols	32730
Arsenic	01002	Surfactants	38260
Barium	01007	Chlorinated Hydrocarbons	74052
Beryllium	01012		
Boron	01022	Pesticides	74053
Cadmium	01027	Fecal Strepto-cocci Bacteria	74054
Calcium	00916		
Cobalt	01037	Coliform Bacteria	74056

Source: U.S.EPA, Engineering Form 4345-1, page 2, May, 1971.

municipal dischargers (those serving 10,000 or more people) did not meet the July 1, 1977, compliance date. According to an EPA source, the typical reason was the absence of pretreatment standards. In comparison, only about 16 percent of industrial dischargers were not in compliance with their 1977 requirements.

In February, 1977, the EPA proposed rules for the development of pretreatment standards and requested feedback on alternative regulatory

EXHIBIT 10B
INDUSTRIES WITH EFFLUENT GUIDELINES
PROPOSED OR PROMULGATED

Industry	First Proposed Date in *Federal Register*
Insulation, fiberglass	1/22/74
Beet sugar	1/31/74
Feedlots	2/14/74
Glass	2/14/74
Cement	2/20/74
Phosphate	2/20/74
Rubber	2/21/74
Ferroalloys	2/22/74
Asbestos	2/26/74
Meat products	2/28/74
Inorganic chemicals	3/12/74
Cane sugar refining	3/20/74
Grain mills	3/20/74
Fruits and vegetables	3/21/74
Electroplating	3/28/74
Plastics and synthetics	4/5/74
Nonferrous metals	4/8/74
Fertilizer	4/8/74
Leather tanning	4/9/74
Soap and detergent	4/12/74
Timber products	4/18/74

strategies. In addition, the pretreatment mandate has been modified in 1977 and again in 1978 by requiring pretreatment of the previously discussed 65 pollutants produced by 21 industries.

Effluent limitations are set for each pollutant. The nature and discharge frequency of the pollutant will dictate the manner in which the effluent limitation will be expressed. Most of the pollutants are measured as concentrations which can be converted into pounds or kilograms. Some parameters are measured uniquely, for example, temperature, pH, coliform, turbidity, and color.

Continuous discharges are usually limited by assigning a daily average and a maximum load in pounds of pollutant per pound of manufactured product. Discontinuous processes necessitate more complex limitations. The following limitations illustrate the discontinuous discharge limitation: (1) average concentration is not to exceed 30 ppm of total suspended solids and maximum concentration not to exceed 60 ppm; (2) no discharge is

EXHIBIT 10B (Continued)
INDUSTRIES WITH EFFLUENT GUIDELINES
PROPOSED OR PROMULGATED

Industry	First Proposed Date in *Federal Register*
Organic chemicals	4/25/74
Petroleum refining	5/9/74
Builders paper	5/9/74
Dairy	5/28/74
Pulp and paper	5/29/74
Seafood	6/26/74
Iron and steel	6/28/74, 8/21/75
Textiles	7/5/74
Steam electric stations	10/8/74
Wood furniture	11/14/74
Paving and roofing	1/10/75
Paint and ink	2/26/75
Poultry products	4/24/75
Oil and gas extraction	8/15/75
Mineral mining	10/16/75
Coal mining	10/17/75
Ore mining	11/6/75

permitted to exceed 100 pounds of BOD more than once a week; and (3) no continuous discharge of a concentration exceeding 100 ppm of total solids is to occur over a twelve-hour period.

Now, it is appropriate to illustrate the impact of the effluent limitations on existing and new sources. One comparison is between pre-permit discharges and permit limited discharges. A dramatic comparison may be made using state of New Jersey data. New Jersey has the dubious distinction of ranking first in two indicators of economic development: population density and value added by chemical manufacturing. Indeed, the production of chemicals in the 7,521 square miles of New Jersey greatly exceeds the output of chemicals in the more than 1.8 million square miles comprising the eighteen New England, Mountain, and Pacific states taken together.

Thirty-three of the more than one thousand petroleum and chemical plants in New Jersey are major water effluent dischargers. In 1974, the discharges of BOD and suspended solid wastes from these thirty-three plants was the equivalent of the treated discharges from a city of about four million people. In addition, these plants discharged numerous toxic

EXHIBIT 11
DISCHARGES BY THIRTY-THREE MAJOR CHEMICAL
AND PETROLEUM PLANTS IN NEW JERSEY

Parameter (all in lbs./day except flow)	(A) Present Discharge Net Fall, 1974	(B) Draft Permit Limitations July 1, 1977	(C) (B)/(A)
Discharge, mgd	764.4	N.A.	—
Biochemical Oxygen Demand (BOD)	357,227	34,520	0.10
Total Suspended Solids	204,832	30,672	0.15
Total Organic Carbon (TOC)	239,306	44,871	0.19
Ammonia	97,830	7,397	0.08
Oil & Grease	86,379	15,670	0.18
Phenols	15,046	165	0.01
Titanium	7,167	1,180	0.16
Chromium	3,130	316	0.10
Zinc	2,980	754	0.25
Lead	1,315	199	0.15
Copper	1,598	228	0.14
Arsenic	128	2.38	0.02

SOURCE: Permit applications and draft permits.

wastes, some of which are summarized in the accompanying table (Exhibit 11, column A).[54] By July 1, 1977, the discharges from these plants were to be reduced to between 25 and 1 percent of the present total (Exhibit 11, columns B and C). These drastic reductions have not yet been carried out by all the industries.

A second comparison is between initial discharges, permit limitations, and new source standards. One of the important industries in resource recovery is corrugated paperboard production. The permitted discharges of an existing plant and allowable initial discharges at a new plant are found in Exhibit 12. The existing plant discharges over 100,000 pounds of BOD_5 into the Mississippi River. The permit calls for a reduction to one-fifth of the initial discharge. A new plant would reduce the discharge to about 1/87 of the BOD_5 discharge from the existing plant. The total suspended solids difference is less, but still substantial.

The U.S.EPA has promulgated new source effluent standards for most of the important direct discharges as well as pretreatment standards for

EXHIBIT 12
Effluent Discharge by Existing and New Corrugated Medium Facility, SIC 2631

	Existing Plant		New Plant
	Existing Discharge	Initial Permit Discharge	Discharge
BOD₅, lbs/day			
30-day Daily Avg.	100,600	20,000	750
Daily Max.	126,000	40,000	1,500
BOD₅, lbs/ton of product			
30-day Daily Avg.	130	26	1.5*
Daily Max.	164	52	3.0
TSS, lbs/day			
30-day Daily Avg.	20,800	4,200	2,000
Daily Max.	31,200	8,400	4,000
TSS, lbs/ton of product			
30-day Daily Avg.	27	5	4.0*
Daily Max.	41	11	8.0

*Average of daily values for 30 consecutive days shall not be exceeded.
Source: Permits provided by Jack R. Newman, chief, Industrial Unit, Permit Branch, U.S.EPA Region V, and EPA rules and regulations for "Pulp, Paper, and Paperboard Point Source Category, Subpart E—Paperboard from Waste Paper Subcategory," *Federal Register*, vol. 39, no. 104, May 29, 1974, pp. 18751-18752.

new sources which hope to use public facilities. These are published in the *Federal Register* and the *Environment Regulations Handbook*[55] and are available along with expertise in the U.S.EPA regional offices and some state offices. The engineers will be able to assist you with industries for which no limitations exist and industries for which some of the effluents have not been assigned standards. While you are speaking with the engineers, you had better find out if any rules and regulations limit effluents from holding lagoons and other impoundments on the site. Currently runoff from industrial sites is a controversial question.

New source standards are available for specific processes. If your study is long range at the two- or three-digit SIC code levels of aggregation, you will have to aggregate four-digit groups. A reasonable approach is to allow each four-digit SIC group to represent its percent of projected share of

EXHIBIT 13
ILLUSTRATION OF ESTIMATING EFFLUENT LIMITATIONS
FOR 2 AND 3-DIGIT
SIC CODE AGGREGATIONS

Industry	Average Daily Production, Tons	30-day Daily Average BOD_5 Limitation per Ton	30-day Daily Average BOD_5 Permitted
4-digit subcategory X1	200	3.0	600
4-digit subcategory X2	300	1.5	450
4-digit subcategory X3	100	4.0	400
All other X4[a]	1,000	0.1[a]	100
Total	1,600	-	1,500

NOTE: [a]Represents estimate of all other 4-digit categories in SIC code X in which the waste stream is minimal.
The total 30-day daily average BOD_5 limitation estimate is 0.969 pounds per ton of production.

employment and/or output. Results produced by the averaging of shares are illustrated by a hypothetical example in Exhibit 13.

THE IMPACT OF DISCHARGES ON WATER QUALITY AND ORGANISMS

Using knowledge about the quality of the ambient environment and the quantity and quality of industry effluents, this section reviews the impact of industrial effluent discharges on water bodies. Before proceeding into a detailed presentation on water quality impacts, a few words should be said on land treatment and disposal of industrial wastewater. This technique is becoming an increasingly attractive disposal method for organic nontoxic wastes and sludge. If the 1985 "zero discharge" goal is not modified, land disposal could become an extremely important method. The recent book by Sanks and Asane is the most useful reference.[56]

We know that when effluent containing organic wastes, for example from a paper plant, is discharged into a water body, turbidity increases, sunlight penetration is reduced, and plants die. Organisms multiply to consume the oxygen demanding wastes. If the discharge is large enough and persists, all the dissolved oxygen will become depleted, and anaerobic decay and associated impacts will result. Anaerobic decomposition is slow. The water turns black, it smells, and fauna and flora die.

Depending upon stream configuration, organic and other solids particles will move along with the stream in suspension or drop to the bottom. As previously indicated the bottom deposits (benthal) may cover and smother bottom organisms and can exert a later oxygen demand if and when stirred by a strong current or man's activities.

If the discharge is not repeated, the organic wastes will be slowly decomposed by bacterial action and the stream will recover. Indeed, limited amounts of organic and solids pollution can contribute to the fertility of an infertile water body by providing a nutrient base for organisms. While a small amount of pollution may fertilize a barren water body, human and industrial organic wastes, if not properly treated, always pose the threat of bacterial pollution. Toxic organic and inorganic industrial wastes pose hazards which have caused them to be severely limited or completely banned by effluent limitation regulations.

The fate, and consequently the impact, of a discharge depends upon a host of factors including the configuration of the water body, the regional meteorology, and the uses of the water body. If the discharge is into a stream, the water will move steadily downstream with some horizontal diffusion. The movement of wastes in a stream is relatively simple and has been described by mathematical equations. If the effluent is discharged into an estuary, the effluent may move toward the ocean, then back upstream. The net movement is, however, downstream and modeling is therefore feasible. If the discharge is into a lake, effluent movements will be extremely difficult to predict. Most lakes are relatively sluggish and accordingly the waste may move in a random pattern about the discharge point. Whether by movement downstream or by dilution in the mass of the water body, water bodies can usually recover from the discharge of organic wastes.

Discharges into the ground are decomposed through a significantly different process. The quantity and variety of decomposers in the limited spaces of the ground are less than the biological organisms available in water bodies. The reduction of biological activity is more than compensated for by the soil and rocks which act as filters.

The Role of Industry in Degrading Water Quality. Industrial development directly affects water quality and organisms in three ways: (1) direct discharges of waste, some of which may be toxic; (2) construction, which results in increased erosion, leading to turbid waters and sedementation; and (3) increased municipal waste discharge through population growth.

While not specifically made for industrial pollutants, Reid developed the following classification of zones of pollution in a polluted water body:[57]

1. *Zone of Recent Pollution:* Much organic material present. Early stages of decomposition. Dissolved oxygen content usually high. Green plants present. Fish may be abundant.
2. *Zone of Active Decomposition — Septic Zone, Polysaprobic Zone:* Great amount of oxidation occurs here. Zone may be nearly depleted of dissolved oxygen. Much carbon dioxide and hydrogen sulfide. Bacteria abundant. Green plants mainly absent (blue-green algae may be present). Many kinds of protozoans live in this zone. The rat-tailed maggot, Tubifera (-eristalis), abounds. If a small amount of oxygen is present, tubificid worms may be found, often in great abundance. Through decomposition of organic matter, this zone grades into the
3. *Strongly Polluted Zone — Alpha-Mesosaprobic Zone:* Green algae present, although in reduced numbers. Dissolved oxygen content low, particularly at night. Fauna more varied and a greater number of species present than in the preceding zone.
4. *Mildly Polluted Zone — Beta-Mesosaprobic Zone:* Green algae and "higher" plants common in this zone. Dissolved oxygen usually above about 5 ppm. Diminishing oxidation of organic matter. Conditions within range of tolerance of many animals. Fishes such as eels, carp, and minnows may inhabit this zone.
5. *Zone of Cleaner Water — Oligosaprobic Zone:* This section is essentially free of pollution, although decomposition occurs. Dissolved oxygen content generally above 5 ppm, even at night. Green plants are abundant. Animal populations are generally those of typical "healthy" streams of the region.

There are unfortunately many polluted water bodies in the United States. The Water Information Center has published a water atlas of the United States.[58] Using U.S.EPA data, the center's maps graphically illustrate the degraded water quality of American river systems. Every state had at least one seriously polluted lake, stream, or estuary. Many states did not have a single major stream which had less than 10 percent of its length polluted. The water bodies of the densely developed northeastern and north central states and the intensively farmed midwestern and southeastern regions are predominantly or seriously polluted.

Industry is generally responsible for the quality of American water bodies insofar as it is part of a "use and discard" oriented society. If the general responsibility issue is side-stepped, we would still find that direct industrial discharges are a major contributor to water quality problems. Powers and his associates estimated that about 2,000 American industrial facilities discharged almost twice as much BOD and about 40 percent more suspended solids than the entire population of the United States.[59] In addition, the industrial discharges are more detrimental because they contain substantial amounts of toxic wastes and because major industrial dischargers tend to be concentrated in limited stretches. The result is serious and concentrated degradation.

The final part of this section discusses water quality models. The reader who does not have a mathematical background will find this part difficult. The mathematical segments may be skipped.

Mathematical Water Quality Models. Mathematical models have been designed to quantify the impact of effluents on water quality and biological communities. The simplest of these models relates to oxygen demanding wastes. In order to prevent anaerobic activity from taking place, depletion of a water body's dissolved oxygen (deoxygenation) by discharges, benthal deposits, and respiration must be less than rates of dissolved oxygen buildup by atmospheric mixing, plant photosynthesis, and turbulence. Oxygen deficit in a stream has been simulated by a mathematical equation called the Streeter-Phelps equation. The Streeter-Phelps equation is

$$dD/dt = k(La\text{-}y) - rD$$

where dD/dt is the net rate of change in the DO deficit; $k(La\text{-}y)$ is the oxygen utilization by BOD in the absence of reaeration; and $-rD$ is the rate of oxygen absorption by reaeration in the absence of BOD. Transforming the equation yields

$$D = \frac{La}{(f-1)} \, e^{-kt} \left\{ 1 - e^{-(f-1)kt} \left[1 - (f-1)\frac{Da}{La} \right] \right\}$$

where D is the DO deficit; f is the rate of self-purification; k is the rate of deoxygenation; La is the first-stage BOD: Da is the DO deficit at the point of reference where the effluent mixes with the water.

Given $f = 2.4$
$k = 0.23$ per day
$Da = 3.2$ ppm
$La = 20.0$ ppm
$t = 1$ day after the discharge

Find DO at point of reference one day later.

$$D = \frac{20}{1.4} \, e^{-0.23} \left[1 - e^{-1.4 \times 0.23} \left(1 - \frac{1.4 \times 3.2}{20} \right) \right]$$

$D = 5.0$ ppm at the end of one day. At 1.93 days the oxygen sag has reached a maximum of 5.3 ppm, whereupon the net balance of reoxygenation and deoxygenation begins to favor reoxygenation.[60]

The Streeter-Phelps equation was the jumping-off point for Thomann [61] and others who in the early 1960s began to produce water quality models which are capable of estimating the impact of discharges on receiving waters. Models currently exist for streams, estuaries, lakes and reservoirs, and groundwater bodies. Numerous stream and estuary models have been developed and applied.[62]   A recent study by Water Resources Engineers concluded that "many [of these models] are similar, most are quite useable and helpful for some purposes, all have some weaknesses, and none is perfect."[63]   The latest models can estimate the impact of more than twenty parameters, light, temperature, phytoplankton, fish, and benthic organisms.[64]

The earliest estuary modeling occurred in the mid-1960s. The Delaware estuary was initially modeled, and studies of the San Francisco Bay and Sacramento-San Joaquin Delta followed between 1967 and 1969. The 1967-69 period also included some limited lake and groundwater modeling.[65]   Next, the ability to model chemical constituents was developed and backfitted to the numerous existing models.

Since the passage of the FWPCAA of 1972, efforts have been focused on estimating the impact of urban runoff on receiving waters. Water Resource Engineers acknowledge the long strides that have been taken since 1962, but conclude that

> Throughout the roughly 15-year history of modelling of receiving waters, the capabilities of the developed models have lagged behind the importance of the problem being faced by urban water management decision makers.[66]

One, if not the, major problem has been the inability of the developers of water quality models to apply them to more than one case and to explain the working limitations of the models. Unless the reader has had calculus, statistics, and computer programming, the mathematics and computer language will be formidable barriers to overcome.

A DO Model for a River Basin. Some of the mathematical models are not very difficult. One such model, which was developed by the senior author and associates, has been used to simulate twice monthly values of DO in river systems.[67]   It has been customary in engineering practice to calculate the dissolved oxygen level of a body of water by developing a mass-balance relationship based upon reoxygenation and deoxygenation processes as set forth initially by Streeter and Phelps and subsequently developed through numerous studies.

Because equations which serve as the structure for this approach involve coefficients of deoxygenation and reoxygenation which are themselves exponential functions of water temperature, the calculations based upon these equations may be very cumbersome. For most engineering purposes, the DO behavior of a stream under the impact of organic pollution (measured in BOD) is sought over a short time period—24 or 48 hours, perhaps. To all intents and purposes, it may be assumed that water temperature does not fluctuate much in that period of time; thus the values of the coefficients remain constant. Under these conditions, the calculations of the Streeter-Phelps equations are simplified, since the equation parameters are invariant.

This assumption cannot be made about the simulation of DO over an entire year for a given stream station. An approach is required in which estimation calculations would be simple enough to computerize for several dozen stations on a river system simultaneously, preserving mass-balance effects wherever untreated or undegraded BOD from upstream is passed on downstream.

Furthermore, detailed data on the sewage introduced by various effluents into the stream at each station for each episode of water quality measurement are not available. Due to the inadequacy of effluent data it is typical for analysts to have at their disposal only monthly or twice monthly arithmetic means of effluent introduced by treatment facilities over two to three years.

For these reasons, an alternate to the Streeter and Phelps model is presented below. In an unpolluted stream, DO is inversely related to water temperature. But because of the astronomical motions of the earth, water temperature is a trigonometric function of time. DO may be predicted by means of a harmonic function with time as the independent variable. For the ith observation at the jth station:

$$DO_{ij} = DO_{\mu j} + A_j \cos\left(\omega t_i - \theta_j\right). \tag{1}$$

DO symbolizes dissolved oxygen, t is time ω is a scale factor which transforms times into radians, θ is a phase angle and A is the amplitude of the curve. DO_{uj} is the mean value of dissolved oxygen about which the curve oscillates at the jth station (Exhibit 14).

When pollution is introduced into the stream, the mean dissolved oxygen $(DO\mu)$ will be diminished. Thus, we say,

$$DO_{\mu j} = \Sigma_i \alpha_{ij} P_{ij} + \Sigma_k b_{kj} F_{kj} + \epsilon \tag{2}$$

For the jth station of a river system, the mean DO, $DO_{\mu j}$, is a function of the mean load of the i pollution variables, P_i and the value of k stream parameters F_k. The α_i and b_k are regression coefficients, and ϵ is a normal

EXHIBIT 14
GRAPHIC REPRESENTATION OF EQUATION (1)

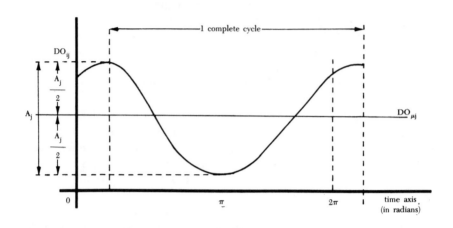

random variate. But the range over which DO_{ij} and $DO_{\mu j}$ may vary is not unlimited. Fresh water under standard conditions becomes saturated near 14.6 ppm of DO. And clearly, values of DO may not be negative. Thus the constraint:

$$O \le (DO_{ij} , (DO_{\mu j}) \le 14.6. \tag{3}$$

This produces an interesting relationship between the two parameters of equation (1), $DO_{\mu j}$ and A_j. In a polluted stream, where $DO_{\mu j}$ is depressed, the harmonic function will be constrained against the lower horizontal axis, at $DO_{ij} = 0$ (Exhibit 15).

Since the variance of DO_{ij} is a function of the amplitude in a harmonic curve,

$$\sigma_j^2 = \frac{A_j^2}{2}, \tag{4}$$

at the jth station, where σ_j^2 is the variance. Thus, we assert that when $DO_{\mu j}$ is low, σ_j will also be low. Moreover, when values of DO_{ij} are high, the curve will impinge upon the upper asymptote representing saturation (Exhibit 16).

EXHIBIT 15
Harmonic Function with Low DO_{1j}

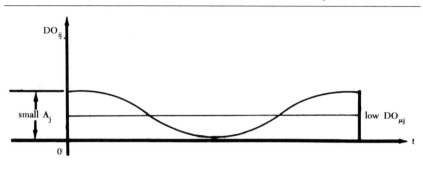

In intermediate ranges of $DO_{\mu j}$, the A_j will reach a maximum. This situation is well represented in the analysis of Wastler (Exhibit 17).[68]

Accordingly, one might entertain the idea of estimating the amplitude of DO_{ij} by means of a curvilinear regression against $DO_{\mu j}$. In fact, we did not

EXHIBIT 16
Harmonic Function with High DO_{1j}

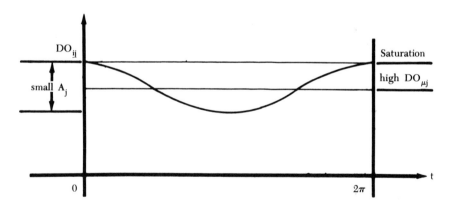

have the data to do this since our stations all demonstrated $DO_{\mu j}$ values which fell on the right-hand branch of the curve—only a very few were so polluted as to fall on the left-hand branch. We therefore adopted the following approximation, where $DO_{\mu j}$ is mean DO and D_j is a dummy variable applying to points to the left of 7.5 ppm on the DO_{uj} scale. This is

EXHIBIT 17
DO Variance as a Function of Mean DO, Potomac Estuary, August, 1959

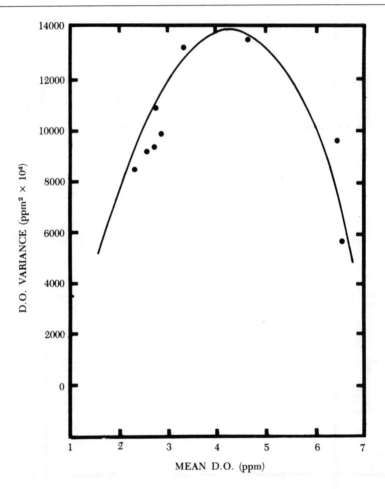

equivalent to estimating most of the points by means of a straight line approximation, and the left-hand branch points (which were closely clustered) as a group.

$$A_j = b_1 \, DO_{\mu j} + b_2 \, D_j + \epsilon \tag{5}$$

By virtue of the fact that rivers are flow systems, and the phase angle is a parameter which estimates the time when DO reaches a maximum, we hypothesized that for river systems relatively free of impoundments and impediments to flow, the θ at all stations should be similar. The values assumed by θ in Exhibit 18 verify this assumption.

EXHIBIT 18

PHASE ANGLE VALUES

Station	θ	Station	θ	Station	θ	Station	θ
0154	6.0	0175	5.9	0186	5.9	0170	5.7
0155	5.9	0176	5.9	0187	5.9	0171	5.7
0162	5.8	0177	5.9	0188	5.8	0182	5.8
0165	5.8	0178	5.8	0164	5.8	0183	5.8
0168	5.8	0179	6.0	0166	5.8	0185	5.9
0172	6.0	0180	6.1	0167	5.6	Mean	5.8
0174	5.9	0181	5.9	0169	5.6		

Regrouping, these equations form the basis for estimating DO on the river system.

$$DO_{ij} = DO_{\mu j} + A_j \cos (\omega t_i - \theta_j) \tag{1}$$

$$DO_{\mu j} = \Sigma_i \alpha_{ij} P_{ij} + \Sigma_k b_{kj} F_{kj} + \epsilon \tag{2}$$

$$0 \leq (DO_{ij}, DO_{\mu j}) \leq 14.6 \tag{3}$$

$$\sigma_{j^2} = \frac{A_j^2}{2} \tag{4}$$

$$A_j = b_1 DO_{\mu j} + b_2 D_j + \epsilon \tag{5}$$

Knowing the pollution variable and stream parameter inputs in (2) allows us to proceed to (5), under the boundary conditions set forth in (3) and (4). Having estimated the A_j from (5) and the $DO_{\mu j}$ from (2), the parameters of (1) are completely specified, since θ may be empirically estimated for the system and t is dependent on the frequency of observation of the data. We must now indicate how the P_{ij} and F_{kj}, which start the simulation, are specified.

The independent pollution and stream parameter variables relating to the effect of pollution load in the stream on DO include: (1) Organic loads from wastewater sources, (2) Reoxygenation from stream turbulence, (3) Factors of basin geometry related to flow and current, and (4) Runoff from land surfaces.

Percent of impervious surface was used as a surrogate for runoff. Reliable average annual BOD values or treatment capacities were obtainable from sewage treatment facilities, while more detailed data from those sources were useless. To address the questions of stream turbulence, and stream geometry related to oxygen sag and reoxygenation, the following parameters were utilized: stream slope, cross-sectional area, and the nature of the underlying geologic formations. A detailed discussion now follows.

  1. BOD. This variable enters a given stream segment in one of three ways: discharge of effluent, runoff, or downstream flow from the segment next upstream. In the model, all of the stream segments are centered on observation stations and arranged from upstream to downstream. The mean BOD entering into the segment through effluent discharge is stipulated, and the BOD accruing from upstream is added to it according to a table function related to velocity (using slope as a surrogate).
  2. Turbulence. The longitudinal profile of a stream tends to a logarithmic slope in which the steeper upstream reaches manifest greater turbulence than the more hydraulically efficient downstream reaches. Thus, the logarithm of slope was used as a surrogate for this variable.
  3. Geologic formations. Two structural regions form the basis for our Raritan area simulation. This was expressed by a dummy variable which assumed a value of 0 for the upland region, and 1 for the coastal plain region. On the Passaic, the contrasting regions were swamp versus upland.
  4. Runoff. Impervious surface, as estimated from population density was used as a surrogate for runoff plus unmonitored and bypassed effluents.

Then using regression we derive a relationship based on equation (5) above as follows:

$$DO_{\mu j} = 9.542 - 0.634B_j - 5.191I_j + .544 L_j - 1.55G_j + \epsilon. \quad (6)$$

B_j is the calculated BOD load at the jth station according to the method outlined above. I is impervious surface (a surrogate for BOD from bypass and runoff), L is slope (a surrogate for turbulence), and G is the geological dummy variable. The equation was calculated for 38 stations in the sample watershed by stepwise, least-squares multiple regression.

  Once the $DO_{\mu j}$ are calculated, the A_j and the DO_{ij} may be calculated as well. These DO_{ij} form a matrix whose rows represent 26 bi-weekly observation dates, and whose columns represent stations. This is reflected in Exhibit 19.

We also prepared a stream standard goal matrix which establishes minimum DO standards for each segment at each time of record. Representing this matrix by U, we find the difference matrix $\overline{\Delta}$.

$$\overline{\Delta} = \overline{U} - \overline{S} \quad (7)$$

Every entry of negative sign in $\overline{\Delta}$ indicates a failure of a segment at a given time to meet the policy goal. When such entries materialize, we go

EXHIBIT 19
SCHEMATIC REPRESENTATION OF THE
DISSOLVED OXYGEN SIMULATION OUTPUT

	Station 1	Station 2	Station 3	...	Station 38
Jan. 1					
Jan. 15					
Feb. 1					
Feb. 15					
		SIMULATED DATA			
Dec. 15					

back to the start, and adjust inputs by tightening up on effluent control and urbanization policy—which bears upon runoff—through operations on variables B and I in equation (6) until we produce a nonnegative $\overline{\Delta}$. The chart in Exhibit 20 summarizes the procedure.

EXHIBIT 20
FLOW CHART OF DISSOLVED OXYGEN SIMULATION

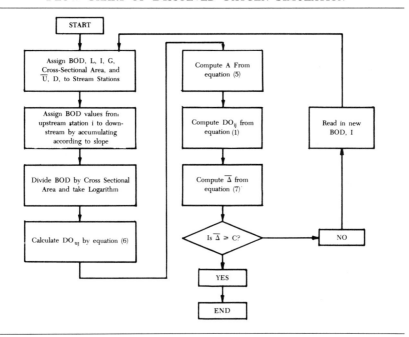

Calibration of the model on the Raritan system of New Jersey. Empirical validation was accomplished for 38 stations on the Raritan River basin by the procedure outlined above. Then we backfitted our *simulated data* to the *known data* from a past year of record (1969-1970) with results as shown in Exhibits 21 and 22.

EXHIBIT 21
Validation of Raritan Simulation Model:
Correlation Analysis

R^2	Number of Stations
greater than 0.90	9
.85 - .900	15
.80 - .849	8
.75 - .799	3
.70 - .749	2
.60 - .699	1
TOTAL	38

EXHIBIT 22
Validation of Raritan Simulation Model;
Standard Error of Estimate

Standard Error of Estimate, ppm	Number of Stations
0.50 - .749	5
0.75 - .999	14
1.00 - 1.249	13
1.25 - 1.499	4
1.50 - 1.999	2*
TOTAL	38

Note: *Stations 0156 and 0157 both had covariation and constant errors significantly higher than the remainder of the stations. These stations are near New Brunswick in the tidal stretch of the river system.

Thirty-two stations (84 percent of all stations) had a value of R^2 in excess of 0.80—corresponding to correlation coefficients in excess of 0.90. These results seem excellent considering the data deficiencies which we had to overcome. Moreover, of the remaining six stations, only one manifested an R^2 below 0.70, corresponding to a correlation coefficient between 0.82 and 0.78—usually considered quite respectable.

The data on standard error of estimate is even more encouraging. Only two stations revealed a standard error above 1.5 ppm, and even these fell within the 2.0 ppm range. Half of the stations had a standard error below 1 ppm.

Furthermore, by examining the data themselves, we can point out that our model tended to err—small though those errors were—on the side of conservatism. In other words the simulated DO readings tended to be slightly above the actual DO readings. Thus, if a stream segment fails to meet standards on the simulated data, we have grounds to suspect that the situation in respect to actual conditions is, if anything, slightly worse. In only two stations, 0156 and 0157, is the reverse true—but existing data show that these two are already known to be highly polluted.

Additional tests of this model were made. For example, the model uses many estimated parameters. The sensitivity of the results to parameter changes was tested. Overall, this DO model is one of the simpler water quality models. Its relative simplicity stems from the fact that it simulates twice monthly, not instantaneous, changes of water quality in fresh-water bodies. However, like the more complex mass-balance models, it requires data of high quality.

Assuming that the proposed project required modeling and that the modeling disclosed that the impact would be serious, three alternatives should be considered. First, the level of treatment could be raised; pre-treatment is a possibility if a limited number of pollutants will cause the problem. A second solution is to pretreat toxic wastes and send the remaining waste to a public facility which would be capable of handling the load. Pretreatment and pipeline facilities are, however, extremely expensive. Third, if the discharge problem is one which can be solved by dilution with a greater volume of water or by aerating the water, the low-flow augmentation and/or mechanical aeration can be tried.

Summarizing, qualitative assessments of the impact of effluent discharges are readily available from the literature. Mathematical models capable of quantifying the impact have been under development since the early 1960s. Stream models are not difficult to apply. The supply of estuarine models is limited, but growing. Lake and groundwater impact models are rare. Dissolved oxygen, BOD, and temperature are the usual parameters described by the models. The newer models simulate a much larger set of parameters.

Summary and Additional Resources

This chapter began by dichotomizing the massive water resources literature into water supply and water quality. The initial goal was to show the reader how to estimate the demand for water. Data and methods for three types of water demand studies were reviewed: short-term impacts of a few facilities; regional planning for many industrial facilities in the near future;

and regional planning for long-term economic development. Tables which the reader may use were presented, and a case study was used to illustrate the regional planning studies. The final part of the demand section presented estimates and tables for estimating industrial, residential, commercial-institutional, and public/unaccounted for public potable water requirements.

The water supply section defined the following important hydrologic concepts: hydrologic cycle, safe yield, maximum possible yield, secondary yield, and spill. The variability of surface and groundwater supplies was stressed. Finally, sources of water supply data were discussed.

The three-part water quality section began with an introduction to establishing ambient water quality. Differences between lakes, streams, and estuaries were overviewed. A variety of dissolved gases and solids, toxic substances, and biological organisms were treated in the introduction. Next, biological and chemical means of establishing the quality of the ambient environment were reviewed. Major issues include the choice of parameters, frequency of sampling, and siting monitoring stations. Sources of chemical and biological water quality data were identified. The third section of the ambient water environment section described the goals and methods of aquatic and terrestrial surveys.

The second major part of the water quality section explained how to estimate the quantity and quality of industrial effluents. Relevant provisions of the FWPCAA of 1972 and subsequent 1977 and 1978 revisions were presented. Use of effluent limitation provisions is the focus.

The third part of the water quality section began with a qualitative description of the impact of effluent on water quality. The final section presented an overview of mathematical water quality models. A relatively simple dissolved oxygen model was presented.

Numerous sources of additional information have already been presented in this chapter. While trying to keep repetition to a minimum, the following sources are especially valuable. Fair, Geyer, and Okun's text, *Elements of Water Supply and Waste Water Disposal*, is the most useful general volume.[69] James Patterson's *Waste Water Treatment Technology* presents an evaluation of more than twenty industrial pollutants and methods of treating them.[70] *Water Resources Research* and *Water Resources Bulletin* are two of the most useful journals. Finally, N.T.I.S. reports most of the valuable government sponsored research and the U.S. EPA and consulting firms will provide specific advice on a case-by-case basis.

NOTES

1. W.L. Picton, *Water Use in the United States, 1900-1980* (Washington, D.C.: U.S.G.P.O., 1960) and C.R. Murray and E.B.

Reeves, *Estimated Use of Water in the U.S. in 1970*, Geological Survey Circular 676 (Washington, D.C.: U.S. Geological Survey, 1972).

2. U.S. Bureau of the Census, *Census of Manufacturers, 1972, Subject Statistics: Water Use in Manufacturing* (Washington, D.C.: U.S.G.P.O., 1975), various tables.

3. URS/Madigan-Praeger, Inc., and Conklin and Rossant, *A Comprehensive Study of the Tocks Island Lake Project and Alternatives* (New York: The Firms, 1975).

4. U.S. Water Resources Council, *1972 OBERS Projection of Regional Economic Activity in the United States.* Series E Population, 1974. See M. Greenberg, D. Krueckeberg, and C. Michaelson, *Population and Employment Projections: A Manual and Computer Programs* (New Brunswick, N.J.: Center for Urban Policy Research, Rutgers University, 1977).

5. *Ibid.*

6. URS/Madigan-Praeger, *Study of Tocks Island*, Table 3-16, p. III-31.

7. U.S. Bureau of the Census, *Water Use in Manufacturing* (Washington, D.C.: The Bureau, 1972), developed from various tables.

8. Picton, *Water Use*, p. 2.

9. F.P. Linaweaver, Jr.; C. Geyer; and J.B. Wolff, *A Study of Residential Water Use* (Washington, D.C.: U.S.G.P.O., 1967), p. 3.

10. Hittman Associates, Inc., *Forecasting Municipal Water Requirements*, 2 vols., HIT-43 (Columbia, Maryland: Hittman, 1969); and P. Whitford, *Forecasting Demand for Urban Water Supply*, Rep. EEP-36 (Stanford, Calif.: Stanford University Press, 1970).

11. URS/Madigan-Praeger, *Study of Tocks Island*, pp. III-11-19; III-33; III-38-40.

12. Hittman, *Forecasting Requirements*, pp. VII-1-4.

13. W. Isard, E. Romanoff, with the assistance of G. Tschannerl, *Water Utilization: Input-Output Coefficients*, Technical paper no. 5 (Cambridge, Mass.: Regional Science Research Institute, 1967), p. 4; and E.M. Lofting and H. Craig Davis, "The Interindustry Factor-Content Matrix: An Application for the Analysis and Projection of Regional Water Requirements," paper presented at the American Water Resources Association Conference, 1968.

14. This section borrows from M. Greenberg and R. Hordon, *Water Supply Planning* (New Brunswick, New Jersey: Center for Urban Policy Research, Rutgers University, 1976), pp. 60-74. Professor Hordon prepared the material.

15. C.W. Thornwaite and J.R. Mather, *Instructions and Tables for Computing Potential Evapotranspiration and the Water Balance*, Publica-

tions in Climatology, vol. 10, no. 3 (Centerton, New Jersey: Drexel Institute of Technology, Laboratory of Climatology, 1958).

16. J.E. McCall, "New Jersey Water Resources," in *New Jersey Trends,* ed. T.P. Norman (New Brunswick, N.J.: Institute for Environmental Studies, Rutgers University, 1974), pp. 194-202.

17. *Ibid.,* p. 195.

18. See C.S. Russell, D.G. Arey, and R.W. Kates, *Drought and Water Supply* (Baltimore: Johns Hopkins Press, 1970) for an extended discussion of water supply and yield.

19. The literature on conjunctive management of surface and ground water sources is quite extensive, particularly in California. For example, see J.A. Dracup, "The Optimum Use of a Ground-Water and Surface-Water System: A Parametric Linear Programming Approach," Contribution no. 107 (Berkeley: University of California, 1966), 134 pages; R.L. Leonard, "Integrated Management of Ground and Surface Water in Relation to Water Importation: The Experience of Los Angeles County," Ph.D. dissertation, University of California at Berkeley, 1964, 157 pages; transfers between New York City and Long Island are discussed in Nebolsine, Toth, McPhee Associates, *Water Supply: Wastewater Management Aspects for Northern New Jersey, New York City, Western Connecticut Metropolitan Area,* Contract no. DACW 52-73-C-006 with North Atlantic Division, Corps of Engineers, New York, 1973.

20. The Rippl method is explained in R. Dorfman, "The Production Function: Hydrologic Aspects," eds. A. Maass *et al., Design of Water-Resource Systems* (Cambridge, Mass.: Harvard University Press, 1962), pp. 118-27.

21. For additional details on the use of synthetic (or operational) hydrology in the simulation of water-resource systems, see M.M. Hufschmidt and M.B. Fiering, *Simulation Techniques for Design of Water-Resource Systems* (Cambridge, Mass.: Harvard University Press, 1966). A manual of practice on operational hydrology involving minimal mathematical derivations but containing a large number of formulas and examples is provided in M.B. Fiering and B.B. Jackson, *Synthetic Streamflows,* Water Resources Monograph no. 1 (Washington, D.C.: American Geophysical Union, 1971).

22. A. Groopman, "Effects of the Northeastern Water Crisis on the New York City Supply System," *Journal of the American Water Works Association* 60, 1:37-48.

23. The estimates are based on a personal communication from Robert E. Cyphers, chief, Bureau of Water Resources Planning and Management, Department of Environmental Protection, Trenton, New Jersey, November 8, 1974; and a personal interview with Dean Noll, chief engineer, NJDWSC, July 11, 1974.

24. Dean Noll, chief engineer, NJDWSC, statement before the Water Policy and Supply Council, State of New Jersey, Trenton, New Jersey, November 8, 1974.

25. For a clear presentation of safe yield estimation for New York City, see Temporary State Commission on the Water Supply Needs of Southeastern New York, *Water Supply Needs* (Albany, New York: The Commission, 1972), pp. 75-95; and New York City Board of Water Supply, *Annual Report*, 1972.

26. O.E. Meinzer, *Outline of Methods for Estimating Groundwater Supplies*, U.S. Geological Survey Water-Supply Paper 638-C (Washington, D.C.: U.S.G.S., 1932), p. 119.

27. D.K. Todd, *Ground Water Hydrology* (New York: John Wiley and Sons, 1959), p. 200.

28. R.G. Kazmann, *Modern Hydrology*, 2nd ed. (New York: Harper and Row, 1972).

29. M. Gary, R. McAfee, and C.L. Wolf, eds., *Glossary of Geology* (Washington, D.C.: American Geological Institute, 1972).

30. S.W. Lohman, et al., *Definitions of Selected Ground Water Terms—Revisions and Conceptual Refinements*, U.S. Geological Survey Water-Supply Paper 1968 (Washington, D.C.: U.S.G.S., 1972).

31. Bergen County Water Study Committee, *Report on the Present and Future Water Supply of Bergen County, New Jersey* (Hackensack, New Jersey: The Committee, 1957).

32. J. Vecchioli and E.G. Miller, *Water Resources of the New Jersey Part of the Ramapo River Basin*, U.S. Geological Survey Water-Supply Paper 1974 (Washington, D.C.: U.S.G.S., 1973).

33. This section draws heavily on G.K. Reid, *Ecology of Inland Waters and Estuaries* (New York, N.Y.: Van Nostrand Reinhold, 1961); E. Odum, *Fundamentals of Ecology* (Philadelphia: W.B. Saunders, 1971); F. Ruttner, *Fundamentals of Limnology* (Toronto: Univ. of Toronto Press, 1963); and R. Wetzel, *Limnology* (Philadelphia: W. B. Saunders, 1975).

34. R.F. Schneider, *The Impact of Various Heavy Metals on the Aquatic Environment*, PB-214-562 (Springfield, Va.: NTIS, 1971), pp. 6-11.

35. R. Eisler, *Annotated Bibliography on Biological Effects of Metals in Aquatic Environments*, PB-228-211 (Springfield, Va.: NTIS, 1973); Battelle-Columbus, *Water Quality Criteria Data Book, Effect of Chemicals on Aquatic Life* PB-213-210 (Springfield, Va.: NTIS, 1971); R. Dorn, *Study of Lead, Copper, Zinc, and Cadmium Contamination of Food Chains of Man*, PB-223-018 (Springfield, Va.: NTIS, 1972); R.J. Straub *et al.*, *Effects of Industrial Effluents on Primary Phytoplankton Indicators*, PB-220-741 (Springfield, Va.: NTIS, 1973); J.B. Berkowitz, *et al.*, *Water Pollution Potential of Manufactured Products*, PB-222-249 (Springfield,

Va.: NTIS, 1973); D.K. Button, *et al.*, *Biological Effects of Copper and Arsenic Pollution*, PB-201-648 (Springfield, Va.: NTIS, 1971).

36. The Hach Chemical Company of Ames, Iowa, manufactures a number of inexpensive sampling kits.

37. R.C. Ward, *Data Acquisition Systems in Water Quality Management*, PB-222-622 (Springfield, Va.: NTIS, 1973).

38. This section draws heavily from M. Greenberg, "Monitoring and Surveillance Analysis," in Betz Environmental Engineers, *Regional Assessment Study of the Delaware River Basin for the National Commission on Water Quality*, PB-249-910 (Springfield, Va.: NTIS, 1975).

39. For an early example see C.J. Velz, "Sampling for Effective Evaluation of Stream Pollution," *Sewage and Industrial Wastes* (May 1950) 22, 5:666-84.

40. See, for example, T.A. Wastler and L.C. de Guerrero, *National Estuarine Inventory: Handbook of Descriptors* (Washington, D.C.: FWPCA, 1969).

41. See, for example, R.M. Brown, N. McClelland, and R. Tozer, "A Water Quality Index—Do We Dare?" *Water and Sewage Works* (October, 1970), pp. 339-43.

42. Environmental Protection Agency, "Water Quality and Pollutant Source Monitoring," notice of proposed rulemaking, *Federal Register* vol. 39, no. 168 (August 28, 1974), pp. 31500-31505.

43. S. Schultz, *Design of USAF Water Quality Monitoring Program* AD-756-504 (Springfield, Va.: NTIS, 1972), see table 4, p. 13.

44. M. Greenberg, see note 38, and G. Carey, L. Zobler, M. Greenberg, and R. Hordon, *Urbanization, Water Pollution, and Public Policy* (New Brunswick, New Jersey: Center for Urban Policy Research, Rutgers University, 1972).

45. Velz, "Sampling," p. 668; the trade-off of locations for frequencies has been suggested as a general working rule by R.C. Ward, *Data Acquisition Systems in Water Quality Management* (Springfield, Va.: NTIS, 1973); D. Vanderholm, *Planning Water Quality Surveillance* (Ann Arbor, Mich: University Microfilms, 1972); and F. Kittrell, *A Practical Gude to Water Quality Studies of Streams*, FWPCA Pub. CWR-5 (Washington, D.C.: U.S. Department of the Interior, 1969).

46. See U.S.EPA, Water Quality Office, *Storage and Retrieval of Water Quality Data Training Manual* (Springfield, Va.: NTIS, 1971) for a review of the STORET system. *Demonstration of a Water Quality Management Information System*, Publication no. 40 (Harrisburg, Pa.: Department of Environmental Resources, Bureau of Water Quality Management) describes the WAMIS system.

47. See E.P. Odum, *Fundamentals of Ecology* (Philadelphia: W.B.

Saunders, 1959); E.J. Kormondy, *Concepts of Ecology* (Englewood Cliffs, New Jersey: Prentice-Hall, 1969); and P. Dansereau, *Biogeography* (New York: Ronald Press, 1957).

48. Federal Water Pollution Control Act Amendments of 1972, Public Law 92-500, 92nd Congress, October 18, 1972, available from EPA. The following two reports indicate the intent of the Senate and House committees: *Senate Report, S-2770*, Report no. 92-414, Senate Public Works Committee, October 28, 1971; *House Report, H.R. 11895 and 11896*, Report no. 92-911, House Public Works Committee. The following paper is the best available brief summary of the Act: Isaak Walton League, *A Citizen's Guide to Clean Water* (Washington, D.C.: U.S.EPA, 1973).

49. R.P. Pikul, *Fixed vs. Variable Environmental Standards* (Washington, D.C.: Mitre Corp., 1973), p. 9.

50. J. Horowitz *et al.*, *Evaluation of Water Quality Standards in California, Massachusetts, Ohio, and Oregon: Case Studies 1965-1972*, PB-234-979 (Springfield, Va.: NTIS, 1974), pp. 5-6.

51. Three good examples are the following: A.D. Little, Inc., *Economic Analysis of Effluent Guidelines for the Inorganic Chemicals Industry*, PB-234-457 (Springfield, Va.: NTIS, 1974), A.T. Kearney, Inc., *Economic Analysis of Effluent Guidelines Ferroalloys Industry*, PB-234-045 (Springfield, Va.: NTIS, 1974); H.C. Bramer, *Economic Feasibility of Minimum Industrial Waste Load Discharge Requirements*, PB-221-490 (Springfield, Va.: NTIS, 1973).

52. The U.S.EPA has sponsored numerous studies: U.S.EPA, *Proposed Criteria for Water Quality*, 2 vols. (Washington, D.C.: U.S.EPA, 1973) suggests the large number of parameters involved. See A.D. Little, *Assessment Models in Support of the Hazard Assessment Handbook*, AD-776-617 (Springfield, Va.: NTIS, 1974). The most general document is U.S.EPA, *Report to Congress on the Disposal of Hazardous Wastes* (Washington, D.C.: U.S.G.P.O., 1974); and "Hazardous Substances—Spills," Sec. 311, Federal Water Pollution Control Act Amendments of 1972; *Federal Register 39* (164): 30466-30471, August 22, 1974.

53. See U.S.EPA, *A Primer on Waste Water Treatment* (Washington, D.C.: The Agency, 1971), for an introduction to the types of treatment.

54. This table was originally prepared by M. Greenberg, C. Koebel, D. Krueckeberg, and B. Krugman for "Public Participation in the Industrial Pollution Discharge Elimination Program: The Performance in New Jersey," Report to project petroleum industry in the Delaware River estuary, NSF and RANN, September 20, 1974.

55. Environmental Information Center, Inc., *Environmental Regulations Handbook* (New York: The Center, 1973) updated.

56. R. Sanks and T. Asane, *Land Treatment and Disposal of Municipal*

and *Industrial Wastewater* (Ann Arbor, Michigan: Ann Arbor Science, 1976).

57. G.K. Reid, *Ecology of Inland Waters*, p. 319.

58. *Water Atlas of the United States* (Port Washington, N.Y.: Water Information Center, 1975).

59. T.J. Powers, B.R. Sacks, and J.L. Holdaway, *National Industrial Waste Assessment* (Cincinnati, Ohio: FWPCA, 1967), compiled from various tables.

60. This example is taken from G.M. Fair and J.C. Geyer, *Elements of Water Supply and Waste Water Disposal* (New York: Wiley, 1961), pp. 516-19.

61. R.V. Thomann, *Systems Analysis and Water Quality Management* (New York: Environmental Sciences, Services Division, 1972).

62. See Thomann, *Systems Analysis*, for an overview; E.J. Lehmann, *Water Quality Modeling: A Bibliography with Abstracts*, COM-74-10938 (Springfield, Va.: NTIS, 1974); and G. Ward and W. Epsey, *Estuarine Modeling: An Assessment* (Washington, D.C., U.S.EPA, 1971).

63. Water Resources Engineers, Inc., *Future Direction of Urban Water Models*, PB-249-049 (Springfield, Va.: NTIS, 1976), p. 48.

64. C.W. Chen and G.T. Orlob, *Ecologic Simulation for Aquatic Environments* (Washington, D.C.: OWRR, 1972); L.A. Genet, D.J. Smith, and M.B. Sonnen, *Computer Program Documentation for the Dynamic Estuary Model* (Washington, D.C.: U.S.EPA, 1974).

65. C.W. Chen and G. T. Orlob, *Ecologic Study of Lake Koocanusa—Libby Dam* (Walnut Creek, Calif.: Department of the Army, Seattle District, Corps of Engineers, 1973); and D.J. Glanz and G.T. Orlob, *Lincoln Lake Ecologic Study* (Springfield, Va.: U.S. Army Corps of Engineers, Louisville District, Water Resources Engineers, 1973).

66. Water Resources Engineers, Inc., *Future Direction*, p. 13.

67. M. Greenberg, G. Carey, L. Zobler, R. Hordon, "A Statistical Dissolved Oxygen Model for a Free-Flowing River System," *Journal of the American Statistical Association 68, 342 (June 1973)*, pp. 279-83. George Carey has prepared a lengthier draft of the model which appears in G. Carey, L. Zobler, M. Greenberg, and R. Hordon, *Urbanization, Water Pollution, and Public Policy* (New Brunswick, N.J.: Center for Urban Policy Research, Rutgers University, 1972). Professor Carey's description of the model has been modified for presentation in this volume.

68. T.A. Wastler, *Spectral Analysis, Applications in Water Pollution Control* (Washington, D.C.: FWPCA, 1969).

69. G. Fair, J. Geyer, D.A. Okun, *Elements of Water Supply and Waste Water Disposal* (New York, N.Y.: Wiley, 1971).

70. J.W. Patterson, *Wastewater Treatment Technology* (Ann Arbor, Mich.: Ann Arbor Science, 1975).

Chapter 5
Air Resources

THE PURPOSE OF THIS chapter is to provide a basic understanding of air pollution and methods for measuring the impact of industrial development on air quality. The chapter is divided into five parts. The first three parts overview air pollution and the fourth and fifth sections present practical methods of assessing the impacts of emissions. Part one identifies the pollutants and discusses the health, materials, and economic impacts of air pollution. The second part overviews the properties and origins of man-made pollutants. The third presents legal and administrative machinery used to manage air resources. Part four considers the problem of acquiring and using emissions and ambient air quality data. The fifth part discusses the processes which govern the dispersal of emissions and some of the simplest models used to simulate the dispersal of emissions.

In dealing with the subject of air pollution within a brief chapter such as this, one must necessarily make decisions regarding scope and content. Accordingly, we have decided to omit the subject of nuclear radiation, since it represents a much more specialized type of air pollution problem.

The Impacts of Polluted Air

An air pollutant is a substance which, because of its physical, chemical, or biological properties, produces a measurable adverse effect on man, other life, and materials. Contaminants emitted into the air can affect the health of living organisms either directly, by interfering with their life processes, or indirectly, by interfering with the climate and food chain. In addition, air pollution damages material goods and can affect the economy through loss of value, costs of clean-up, costs of pollution control or costs of avoidance. Safety is another issue, since air pollution can create hazardous conditions for aircraft and motor vehicles.

Control of air pollution is important, not only because of health and other impacts, but also because contaminants which enter the environment are never really removed. Air emissions enter the water as acid rainfall; equipment which captures or cleans the emissions results in captured pollutants which must be disposed of via land dumping or water discharges. Water borne contaminants may enter the air through wind or wave action, and incinerated solid wastes produce gaseous and particulate contaminants.

The need to control air pollution is important at three geographical levels:

1. *Global view:* pollution of the atmosphere and its effects on the biosphere, especially climate.
2. *Urban view:* localized effects that do not necessarily alter global balances. These effects may be only transient, the result of insufficient mixing, but they are nonetheless serious.
3. *Enclosed space view:* mines, factories, laboratories, etc. Effects are generally characterized by a limited time of exposure defined by "toxic limits" or threshold limit values specified by industry or government groups.

The global, urban, and enclosed space perspectives are all important. This primer concentrates on the urban view, the perspective which is most relevant to the intended audience.

The past twenty years have produced legislation designed to control some of the major air pollutants at these three spatial levels (e.g., nuclear test ban treaty, Clean Air Act). There are other known and most likely some unknown contaminants which also are damaging but are not subject to control. One of the problems in abating air and water pollution lies in the difficulties of determining and proving cause-effect relationships which occur over a long period of time (e.g., twenty or more years to contract lung cancer after exposure to asbestos in the workplace) or which would result in consequences so serious that they should not be empirically demonstrated (e.g., changes in global temperatures or precipitation patterns). Few studies can graph the relationship between specific levels of pollution and specific levels of damage.

In the case of conflicting information or contrary conclusions, the economics and politics of allowing the suspect air emissions to continue unabated can be very seductive. Political decisionmakers are caught between the need for economic growth in the shortrun (e.g., electric power) and the need to preserve environmental resources in the long run. Sometimes, decisions can be rationalized by assuming that future technology will produce nonpolluting processes for industry, energy production, and transportation. Other, well meant decisions are undermined by the fact that current technologies cannot meet the legislative deadlines which have been set for emission reduction. Monetary quantification provides a convenient common denominator for comparing air pollutant effects; it can lead to inequities where, for example, public health may be compromised because elimination of pollutants is perceived as a poor short-term economic strategy.

Measurement units most commonly used to describe air contaminants are based on either weight or volume. The annual average emission of a pollutant is often expressed in terms of millions of tons. Volumetric measurement parameters include parts per million (ppm), parts per hundred million (pphm), and parts per billion (ppb). Parts per million means the number of parts of pollutant by volume in a million total parts. Other important measurement parameters include milligrams per liter (mg/1), pounds per day, micrograms per second (ug/sec), tons per day, and, as cited above, millions of tons per year. In many instances, data used will be available in either volumetric or gravimetric (by weight) form, but not both, and conversion from one form to the other will become necessary. Standard conditions for reporting are 25°C and 760 torrs of pressure. Use the following formula to convert:

$$ug/(m)^3 = \frac{(ppm)\,(M)\,(10^3)}{24.5}$$

or

$$ppm = \frac{(ug/(m)^3\,(24.5)}{(10^3)\,(M)}$$

---

where: M = molecular weight of gas of interest

Thus, 35 ppm of carbon monoxide (molecular weight = 28.0 amu) is equivalent to 40 mg/m³ of carbon monoxide.

Appendix A provides additional weight and measure information.

HEALTH AND SAFETY OF PEOPLE, PLANTS, AND ANIMALS

Air pollution causes adverse effects in man or his possessions. These effects range from a variety of inconveniences to total destruction.

Pollution reduces the aesthetic quality of an area by creating odors, reducing visibility, soiling or eroding works of art, and attacking the vegetation of planned and natural landscapes. Sky darkening and haziness caused by atmospheric pollutants reduce visibility. A reduction in visibility is the result of light attenuation due to the scattering and absorption of the light by fine particles. This scattering effect tends to reduce the brightness contrast of distant objects and under severe conditions reduces visual range to as little as several hundred yards. When humidity levels reach 70 percent, salt, sulfate, and other particles attract moisture to create fog droplets and sulfuric acid droplets (formed from SO_2) which can further diminish visibility. Bates points out a relationship between specific concentrations of particulate air contaminants and decreased visibility. At 50 micrograms per cubic meter (ug/m^3), visibility is considered to be 10 miles; at 200 ug/m^3, visibility is given as 2 miles; and at 600 ug/m^3, visibility is down to less than or equal to one mile.[1]

Though decreased visibility is an extremely hazardous air pollution problem, objectionable odors represent the most frequent complaint aired about air pollution episodes. An insult to the senses can stir up a great deal of community opposition to a variety of odor producing activities.

Many of the adverse consequences of air pollution may be directly or indirectly measured in dollars. These losses include damage to vegetation or livestock, deterioration to all kinds of exposed materials, soiling, and above all, damage to human health. These losses generally run into the billions of dollars per year, and represent a major incentive toward regulation and reduction of air pollution.

Damage to vegetation is often the easiest to detect, but also it is often the most difficult form of air pollution damage to assess. Plants are ubiquitous in their distribution on the surface of both land and water and provide a source of food for almost every form of life on earth. The number of plant species found on the earth is enormous. In general, in assessing the effects of air pollution on plants, one must keep in mind that each plant species is affected by a specific air pollutant in a specific way because of its differing structure (morphology) and function (physiology).

Leaves, because of their direct exposure to the atmosphere, their large surface area relative to the remainder of the exposed parts of the plant, their high metabolic network, and gas exchange through their surfaces, are usually the most obvious and important site of air pollution damage. The nature of injuries to plants by various air pollutants can be conveniently divided into visible effects and the suppression of growth. Both types of damage are difficult to assess, particularly under natural conditions, given the complex nature of the environment. Visible effects are difficult to pinpoint because certain types of air pollution damage are difficult to distinguish from effects produced by diseases and by natural changes in the environment. Suppression of growth is also difficult to pinpoint because of the large number of variables affecting plant growth in the natural environment.

Estimating economic losses in the form of vegetation damage due to air pollution is difficult for the reasons stated above. Relating vegetation damage to a particular cause is an even more complex problem, particularly in metropolitan areas where each of numerous industrial sources emits a unique composite of gases and/or particulates into an atmosphere already containing air pollutants.

Methods to reduce the adverse effects of air pollution on plants include the following: breeding resistant plant strains, developing chemical treatment methods which lessen and prevent damage, modifying growth conditions to minimize exposure, or abandoning the culture of susceptible species for more resistant ones.

Plants could be used as monitors of air pollution because of their sensitivity to a variety of common air contaminants, their minimal cost as compared to expensive monitoring machines, and their ubiquity. Unfortunately, there are a number of disadvantages which have precluded the use of plants as air pollution monitors in all but a few cases.[2] These include the susceptibility of plants to damage from other causes which may be confused with atmospheric contaminants, the difficulty of definitely establishing cause and effect relationships between air pollution episodes and plant response, and the difficulty of quantifying the results obtained from vegetation surveys and plant monitors.

The effects of air pollutants on domesticated animals are usually categorized in terms of responses during episodes of intense exposure or following up on prolonged dosages of airborne toxic substances. The impacts are reflected in lower rates of animal and animal product production, decreased longevity, and increased susceptibility to other environmental stresses.

Effects of air pollution on human health are generally recognized as being short-term acute, or long-term chronic. Short-term effects are associated with atmospheric conditions that interfere with normal bodily functions but do not cause any permanent damage. Acute illness and death due to air pollution factors are rare incidents generally associated with unique atmospheric conditions and high pollutant concentrations. Long-term chronic effects of air pollution are perhaps the most significant and, unfortunately, the most questionable problem associated with human exposure to air pollution. Several chronic respiratory diseases are thought to be caused by or aggravated by air pollution, including chronic bronchitis, emphysema, and lung cancer.

Each person inhales 30-35 pounds of air per day. Because we cannot select the quality of air we breathe, the physiological impact of air quality may be considerable. Personal discomforts of individuals residing in locations affected by air pollution include eye irritation and irritation of the upper respiratory system. Individuals with pre-existing conditions of emphysema, asthma, bronchitis, and sinusitis are affected to an even greater extent than a normal individual.

The human body possesses mechanisms to repel and discharge air pollutants. As air pollutants enter the respiratory system, they may, if in the form of droplets or large particulates, be filtered by the hairs in the nostrils. If this barrier is passed, exclusion from the lower respiratory tract may be accomplished by brain impulses which inhibit inhaling of material, a response usually associated with irritating vapor inhalation. If a particulate is encountered, a mucous membrane entraps the particle, which is then moved out of the respiratory tract by cilia. Should an irritant bypass these initial respiratory defense mechanisms, muscle fibers in the lower respiratory tract constrict to prevent passage of the contaminant into the blood stream, causing difficulty in breathing.

When all the primary body defenses fail, direct damage to the respiratory system may result from the stress imposed by air pollutants. Respiratory injuries include the following: destruction of the tissue lining of the upper respiratory tract (epithelial tissue); destruction and atrophying of the tissue which forms the alveoli; the production of cancer and the physical blockage and/or induced contraction of the smaller air passages. All of these injuries result in the reduction of efficient gas transfer through the lungs. Such reduction can raise blood pressure and put a greater strain on the heart. Furthermore, materials taken into the lower respiratory tract may be transferred, through the blood, to other organs of the body where they may adversely affect the functions of other vital processes.

In summary, the effects of air pollution on living receptors are varied and often species specific. As the following sections will demonstrate, adaptation by plants, animals, and man to excessive air contaminants can be costly in terms of controls, economic loss, damage to or loss of life, and degradation of living conditions.

MATERIALS

There is a literature describing pollution impacts on materials and on methods of measuring these impacts; and there is monitoring information for specific air pollutants. Few studies have firmly established the mathematical relationships between specific levels of pollution and specific degrees of damage. One problem is that air may contain more than one type of pollutant, making difficult the isolation of specific causative or catalytic agents — particularly when combinations of pollutants may magnify (synergize) or cancel (antagonize) each other's effects. Another factor is that topographic and meteorologic conditions at a specific site may differ from those at the nearest monitoring station, frustrating the prediction of specific effects at a given location. Other variables which complicate the expected association of air quality and materials damage include the duration of a pollution level, the amount of moisture in the air, the duration of exposure (e.g., an auto parked in a given area), the differences among similar materials (e.g., different types of paint), and the use to which the materials are being put (e.g., electronic equipment). Much of the material which follows is presented in more detail by *The Air Pollution Manual, Part 1* by the American Industrial Hygiene Association,[3] from which we borrowed heavily. In addition to the review of their material impacts, we briefly describe the pollutants at this time.

Nitrogen Oxides (NO_x). Nitrogen oxide air pollutants include NO, NO_2, and N_2O. NO_2, the most common, is a pungent smelling, brownish red gas that comes from motor vehicle exhausts and power plant and factory combustion activities. High concentrations of these three nitrogen oxides cause fabrics to fade and have an adverse effect on paints.

Sulfur Oxides (SO_x). Sulfur oxide pollutants are SO_2 and SO_3. SO_2, the most common urban pollutant is a colorless, pungent gas that comes predominantly from the combustion of sulfur bearing fuels by electricity generating stations and factories. They affect building stone, dyes, paints, textiles, paper, metals, and tanned leather. This is one pollutant with monitoring data which shows specific linear relationships between concentration levels and damage to materials. Most of the damage occurs when sulfur oxides react with atmospheric moisture, forming sulfuric acid. Without water, SO_2 would take much longer to oxidize to SO_4.

Sulfuric acid can etch building materials, irreversibly damaging statues and similar artwork. Sulfur oxides also react with atmospheric moisture and the calcium carbonate in both limestone and marble to form calcium sulfate and gypsum, which are water soluble. Thus, the building surfaces are gradually eroded by rainfall.

Sulfur oxides cause fading in dyed fabrics. Sulfuric acid is directly damaging to nylon and to cellulose based materials such as cotton, linen, rayon, acetate, and paper. Leather cracks and weakens when it absorbs sulfuric acid from the air. Leather also contains small amounts of iron from the tanning process which react with the sulfur oxides to form sulfuric acid.

Pollution caused sulfuric acid has peeled, cracked, and blistered paints on homes and autos. Concentrations of only one to two parts per million are sufficient to lengthen the drying time of paints.

Sulfur dioxide speeds oxidation (rusting) of ferrous metals and has a corrosive effect on them when combined with atmospheric moisture. The second effect can be directly related to the levels of sulfur dioxide. Zinc is used to coat base metals to protect them from normal corrosion, but is also susceptible to this acidic pollution. Nonferrous metals such as aluminum, copper, and silver form a protective tarnish which prevents corrosion. Unfortunately, this coating interferes with the usefulness of the metals. In electronic equipment, for instance, tarnished metal contacts will cause switching malfunctions.

Hydrogen Sulfide. Hydrogen sulfide causes metals to tarnish, interfering with the functioning of electronic equipment. Hydrogen sulfides combine with the lead in house paints to form a black substance known as lead sulfide. If the pollutant is abated, lead sulfide oxidizes into white lead sulfate, permitting some of the original paint color to return. Hydrogen sulfide is one of a group of sulfides and mercaptans with extremely unpleasant odors. Their presence tends to be in the vicinity of hydrocarbon processing facilities such as petroleum, coking coal, and paper processing plants and near improperly treated solid waste and sludge.

Ozone (O₃). Ozone is a colorless gas produced by the reaction of pollutants (e.g., NO_x, hydrocarbons) under sunlight. Ozone is damaging to rubber, microfilm, paints and dyes, and textiles. Stretching makes rubber especially susceptible to ozone, which attacks the double-bonded carbon chain and ages the rubber prematurely by making it brittle. Some synthetic rubbers such as neoprene, butyl, and ethyl-propylene are not affected by ozone.[4] Anti-ozone additives increase costs and can only be used on black rubber. Anti-ozonants recently developed for light colored rubber materials are not as effective.[5]

Ozone is also capable of oxidizing the silver grains on stored microfilm.[6] Like pollutants mentioned previously, ozone fades dyes and causes peeling and cracking of paints. The effect of ozone on fabrics is to shorten the life of cotton, white nylon, and polyester fibers, with cotton becoming more vulnerable when it is wet.[7]

Particulates. Particulates are any solid or liquid particles produced by natural (e.g., wind, fire) or man-made means (e.g., combustion). Particulates affect electronic equipment, paints, fabrics, catalytic converters, stone, clay, and glass. Abrasion is one way in which damage occurs. In the case of electronic equipment, particulates which settle on switching contacts can interfere with conduction. They also speed the rate of metal corrosion in the presence of sulfuric acid. This can be directly correlated with particulate concentration levels. Fly ash particulates contain sulfur oxides which can blister paints and attack fabrics. Damage to fabrics tends to occur first along folds and other stress points, and is exacerbated by the frequency and rigor of cleaning. Lead particulates in auto exhaust can shorten the life of catalytic converters which control the emissions of hydrocarbons and nitrogen oxides from motor vehicles.

Carbon Monoxide. Carbon monoxide is a colorless and odorless gas resulting largely from the incomplete combustion of carbon containing substances. Carbon monoxide does not seem to be damaging to materials. For the most part, CO is stable and reacts only very slowly with ozone to form carbon dioxide.[8] However, the hydroxyl radical, an intermediate in photochemical smog production, may oxidize CO to CO_2 more quickly.[9]

MEASUREMENTS OF DAMAGE

Measurements of materials damage can be expressed as additional repainting or cleaning, shortened product life, increased repair, increase in cleaning time, percentage of the material which has been destroyed, changes in strength, changes in electrical properties, and changes in weight due to corrosion. In some instances, soiling of materials can be directly correlated with measurable amounts of settled dust, or with concentrations of suspended particulates. These are calculated by the reflectance or absorbance measurements of filtered materials.[10] Corrosion products increase the weight of a metal sample over short periods of time, but slough off and decrease the metal's weight after long periods of time. Thus, changes in weight and/or thickness can be measured, as can changes in blending or torsion. Corrosion rates are the most common measurement for metals damage, and these can be directly correlated with sulfur dioxide levels.[11] Statistics on this subject can be obtained from the American Society for Testing and Materials.

The Economic Costs. The impacts of air pollution that have been reviewed may be broadly grouped into health and safety of people, plants, animals, and materials. While the literature sketches the outline of damage caused by air pollution, the complexity of interrelationships among emissions and impacts has limited the development of comprehensive and

conclusive evidence. Nevertheless, some of the evidence has been translated into economic cost.

Temporary upward fluctuations of gaseous and particulate pollutants ac-
companied by abnormal meteorological conditions (inversions) have been
linked to excess deaths in urban areas. In 1967, the direct cost of all
human mortality and morbidity from diseases associated with air pollution, including emphysema, bronchitis, asthma, and lung cancer, was set
at $2 billion annually in the U.S. In 1971, the EPA increased this esti-
mate to $6 billion and, in 1972, raised it again to $9.3 billion, accounting
only for work loss and medical care. Other costs of air pollution include
losses in property value estimated at $8 billion annually plus agricultural
losses and deterioration of material at $7.6 billion annually, or a total of
$24.9 billion of air pollution costs in the United States annually.[12]   These
crude approximations are thought to be a minimum cost, neglecting
aesthetic values, discomfort, and effects of pollutants in combination or at
low levels. The acute hazard of man-made pollutants lies in the fact that
they are not uniformly mixed, but tend to concentrate near their place of
origin—man's industrial and urban living spaces.

This section divides the economic aspects of air pollution into two parts:
(1) the costs of damage and (2) the costs of control.

Cost of Damage. An understanding of how cost impacts are developed is
important. Due to lack of data, economic impacts of air pollution are often
difficult to correlate with specific pollution levels. Thus, the detail found
in economic impact discussions is rather uneven and may include assumptions which are intuitively logical but practically impossible to quantify
and use in analysis. One example found frequently in the literature is the
statement that a direct cost of air pollution is people accepting lower
paying jobs in cities with less pollution. However, the spatial and temporal aspects of such action, including the number of people who make
job-residence decisions solely on the basis of air quality, the length of
time a family will continue to live in an increasingly polluted area, and
the pollutant thresholds which precipitate decisions to move, are hard to
prove or disprove beyond an author's personal feelings on whether or not
this occurs fairly often. If the jobs vacated or refused by people moving to
cleaner cities are filled with new workers, then one hesitates to include
this "cost" among the economic disbenefits. Another problem with
economic quantification is that pollution costs represented by conscious
consumer decisions (e.g., buying a more expensive house in an unpolluted neighborhood) are based on the assumption that individuals are fully
informed about pollution levels—including nonvisible pollutants and in-
sidious effects—and enjoy unfettered mobility. In fact, many of the

economic cost models openly state that the model is based on these assumptions. In reality, of course, this ideal situation is rarely found. In addition, individuals weight the variables differently. Considerations on quality of schools and proximity of park and shopping areas must be traded off against perceived levels of air pollution which exist at the time a home is purchased. Thus, the data gaps and uncertain relationships among variables make formulation of elaborate mathematical models for determining damage costs pointless, and nearly all estimation methods assume a simple linear relationship between the levels of pollution and the cost impacts. Therefore, calculations of empirical economic impacts should always be examined for their appropriateness to the size of the analysis area and the accuracy and practicality of the costs developed.

Health Costs. Barrett and Waddell discuss two studies which estimate health costs.[13] Health losses are represented by demand for medical services, employee sick leave, etc. The percentage of these health losses attributable to pollution is determined and assumed to be constant for each pollution level. The health losses are translated into dollars using costs of medical service, lost wages, etc. The dollar value is then multiplied by the percentage assumed to be due to pollution, thus providing an estimate of the cumulative costs to human health at each pollution level for each pollutant type.

In the Ridker study total national health costs for respiratory system diseases were indicated by costs of treatment, absenteeism, premature death, and premature burial for each disease. Indicators for the above were the per capita value of shipments of related drugs, percent of yearly work days lost multiplied by average annual earnings, future earnings lost (discounted at 5–10 percent) minus present burial costs. (It would appear that the latter would distort the cumulative totals of the other costs.) The proportion of these costs attributed to pollution was 18–20 percent, varying according to age, sex, race, smoking habits, and rural-urban population ratios. However, Ridker could not relate health or cost impacts to specific pollutants.

The Lave-Seskin study focused on respiratory illness, heart disease, and certain types of cancer. Cost indicators were the same as above, except that some medical treatment costs were included, future earnings lost were discounted at 6 percent, and premature burial costs were not used. The percentage of disease attributable to air pollution was different for each disease. Adding the pollution caused costs for all of the diseases, the study concluded that 4.5 percent of national health costs for human morbidity and mortality were attributable to air pollution.

The Ridker and Lave-Seskin studies are two samples of the literature. A recent case study conducted in Portland, Oregon, by Jaksch reports outpatient medical costs.[14]   Carnow's study of the impact of air pollution on patients with acute respiratory problems illustrates the type of detailed study necessary to develop credible estimates of the economic costs of health.[15]

Agriculture and Vegetation. Indicators of direct costs are: lost income due to crops which cannot be harvested, lower crop yields, lower quality crops, extra cultivation, and extra irrigation or fertilizer to maintain crop yield. The costs of planting and cultivating the lost crops can also be added in. Indicators of indirect economic losses are costs of substituting lower value crops, relocation to a nonpolluted area, reforestation, and lost profits. Harvest time is the "fiscal year" for calculating costs. As in the previous discussion, the economic values can then be multiplied by a coefficient representing the proportion of damage attributed to pollution. In the studies discussed by Barrett and Waddell, data were gathered by specialists making field surveys. Crops were categorized as field, flower, fruit, or vegetable, and attempts were made to correlate the damage with specific pollutants.

Visibility and Safety. The costs of reduced visibility can be measured in terms of highway accidents for motor vehicles and extra fuel use and missed connections for airplanes.[16]   Although one could determine the costs of damage during specific pollution episodes, it would be difficult to develop a linear relationship of costs per unit of pollutant. If an accident threshold level for relevant pollutants could be determined, however, frequency of occurrence might provide a cost indicator for damage. Another method might be to establish the increase in percentage of vehicles per hour which are involved in accidents as visibility decreases. The costs of reduced visibility in scenic areas are discussed under aesthetics.

Aesthetics. Economic damages to aesthetic enjoyment include direct pollution damage to sculpture, books, paintings, and other works of art, reduced visibility at scenic sites, and unpleasant odors at recreational areas. Damage to works of art can be measured as loss of value or costs of cleaning them up. Costs to all of the above categories can also be measured as avoidance costs; i.e., how much will people pay to go to another recreation area. Surveys of citizens and income-attendance records at tourist related industries are methods of gathering data on avoidance costs, but avoidance costs would be difficult to calculate if the demand is highly elastic, or if no substitute recreation areas are readily available. Avoidance costs for artwork include microfilming books which have deteriorated due to pollution, and air conditioning.[17]   One of the difficulties in assessing avoidance costs is that much depends on citizen perception of pollution. In the studies which Barrett and Waddell reported on, concern for pollution was directly correlated with economic status, and people were influenced more by high daily levels than by high averages over a month or season.

Litigation. Barrett and Waddell discuss the Havighurst study in Philadelphia as an example of the use of monetary awards in suits against polluters as another means of estimating air pollution damages, especially since the loss of revenue or market value is of primary consideration in determining the amount of money to be awarded. Data problems included the lack of cases in a given area, the fact that legal records may not contain the specific pollution damages or pollutant levels, and the fact that urban dwellers are less likely to use this means of relief than rural dwellers. However, the study concluded that this approach might be used in the future if state and local control agencies acted as clearinghouses to receive reports of pending litigation and to provide air quality data relevant to the cases.

Soiling. Soiling costs can be represented as cleaning frequency, cleaning time, repainting frequency, and shortened product life. Using surveys, one could develop a historical trend, plotting increased annual or per capita cleaning costs against increased pollutant levels. Barrett and Waddell reported on a study in Philadelphia conducted by Booz-Allen with results which showed that low-cost cleaning activities (windows, venetian blinds) were sensitive to high pollution levels, whereas high-cost cleaning activities were not. They also discussed a study of pollution effects on painting frequency. The analysis first calculated regional sales of paint and allied materials, including inflation factors over the period of years which the analysis covered. Labor costs were assumed to be three times the cost of the paints, and the painting job was assumed to be two times the labor cost if given to a contractor. They assumed that contractors did 1/3 of the painting jobs and that 15 percent of the bills were an overstatement. They also attributed 1/3 of the painting costs to air pollution.

Materials. Soiling and avoidance cost methods can be used. Other cost indicators discussed by Barrett and Waddell include direct costs of replacing or protecting parts and plating contacts with precious metals and indirect costs of shutdowns, overdesign, loss of product, inefficiency, explosion, contamination, and air conditioning and purification to avoid pollution contamination of electrical contacts.

The erosion of limestone, marble, clay, etc., and the etching of glass cannot be easily translated into costs, since these items (other than glass) are not replaceable in erected buildings. It is also difficult to estimate the foreshortening of the building's useful life. Thus, damages must be expressed in terms of qualitative judgments regarding the aesthetics of the damaged buildings, which are then translated into reduced property values. Damages can also be expressed as costs of repair, costs of the original materials during construction, or costs of the materials in present day terms.

Another approach is to estimate the percentage of surface damaged and its lost value. Barrett and Waddell reported on a Midwest Research Institute study which attempted to correlate costs with pollution levels in assessing damages to materials. The physical damage was expressed as a percentage between 0 and 100, and the cost of replacing this percentage of materials was calculated. This allowed them to compare the costs of prevention with the costs of restoration. Another method used was to multiply the annual production volume in dollars by the weighted average economic life based on usage, multiplied by the weighted average for the percent of material exposed to pollution. The "in-place" or "as used" value included a labor factor. The economic loss was the economic value times the difference between the pollution value and the in-place value.

Property Values. Property values can be measured by dislocations and variation in median property values over time. [18] But it is difficult to relate the costs to the air pollution level. Air pollution dust and particulates also prevent upgrading of neighborhoods. [19] A recent study reports appraisers' judgment of the effect of air pollution on property values. [20]

Costs of Pollution Control. The costs of abating air pollution may be divided into capital and operation-maintenance for the public and private sectors. The Council on Environmental Quality estimates a total cumulate cost of $166.1 billion (in 1974 dollars) for air pollution control expenditures for the period 1974–1983. [21] Nearly all of this money will come from the private sector. One-third of the total ($55.6 billion) is expected to come from industry. Much of this will be used for the following types of pollution control equipment: (1) mechanical (e.g., settling chambers, inertial separators, and cyclones) which have efficiencies between 20 and 90 percent, are relatively inexpensive, and are most efficient at removing 10 micron or larger sized particles; (2) wet scrubbers which are expensive, are 80 to 99.5 percent efficient, and are particularly used for gases, and work best for pollutants in the size classes from submicron to 10 microns; (3) electrostatic precipitators which are expensive, are 60 to 99.5 percent efficient, and are best at ranges of 1 to 10 microns but can go as low as 0.1 and as high as 200 microns; (4) fabric filters which are expensive, have up to 99.9 percent efficiency and have a wide variety of particle ranges; and (5) incinerators and stacks which are extremely expensive and are used to burn and diffuse gases and particles, respectively.

To provide a perspective about the costs of industrial air pollution control, the following comparative estimates are provided. Utility costs are estimated at $34.3 billion (60 percent of industrial costs). Private mobile sources (predominantly automobiles) are projected at $70.2 billion (125 percent of private industrial costs).[22] Another perspective is the fact that the private industrial costs for water pollution control are estimated to be about the same as the private industrial costs for air pollution control. Overall, between 1974 and 1983, industrial costs for air and water pollution control are expected to be about $115 billion.

Another cost which industry has claimed is plant closings and movements. U.S.EPA sponsored studies have reported the alleged closing of 73 plants employing about 13.7 thousand people between January 1971 and June 1975. The major industries affected are primary metals (3 percent of the primary metal industry's labor force), paper products (5 percent of the paper industry's labor force), and chemicals (2 percent of the chemical industry's labor force). The problem of plant closings does not appear to be an important problem when viewed from the national perspective since most of the closings have been of older and inefficient facilities which probably would have been closed in the near future. However, many of the closings are in old, industrial towns that are already economically depressed.[23]

Properties and Origins of Man-Made Pollutants, Especially Industrial

The air pollutants that cause the impacts that have been described above are frequently categorized as belonging to one or more of the following four groups: (1) natural or man-made; (2) primary or secondary; (3) point, line, area; and (4) particulate or gas. This section will review these classifications and then provide a brief perspective on industrial emissions with respect to these classifications.

The natural versus man-made dichotomy is an obvious classification. Natural pollutants include pollen, gas from decaying material, and particulates from forest fires, dust storms, and volcanic eruptions. Man-made pollutants include those from the following processes: combustion, chemical, nuclear, heating, refining, quarrying, mining, and roasting. While the distinction is readily apparent, man's activities may accentuate natural pollutants. For example, serious fires and dust storms may result from man's land use practices. This book is concerned with man-made air pollutants.

With respect to origin, pollutants may be classified as primary or secondary. Primary pollutants such as particulates, sulfur dioxide, hydrocarbons, oxides of nitrogen, and carbon monoxide are emitted directly into the atmosphere. Secondary pollutants such as ozone and peroxyacetyl nitrate (PAN) are formed by atmospheric chemical reactions. This volume is mostly concerned with the primary pollutants, specifically particulates and sulfur dioxide which are emitted by industries. A second concern will be with emissions from autos, trucks, and space heating.

Man-made pollutants may be characterized as to their source: point, line, or area. Point sources are easily identifiable sources of air emissions such as industries and electric generating stations. Shopping centers, stadiums, railroad stations and other loci of activity do not directly emit major quantities of pollutants, but indirectly serve as point sources by attracting large masses of automobiles. Accordingly, they are called indirect point sources.

Line sources form strands of pollutants along highways from motor vehicles, and along railroad lines from oil, diesel, and coal fired trains. Area sources are clusters of relatively small air emission sources such as home space heaters and small parking lots. Area sources are so numerous that they cannot be pinpointed.

The fourth common classification is based on particle size. The standard particle size unit is the micron. A micron is a unit of length equal to one one-millionth of a meter. It is usually abbreviated as u. Air pollutants may be classified into the two general categories of particulates and gases. Particulates consist of solid and liquid particles which will remain suspended in the air for a period of time which varies inversely with particle size. Particles greater than 50 microns such as some sprays and dusts quickly settle out. Particles of between 0.01 and 50 microns are called aerosols. Aerosols consist of colloidal suspensions of particles in gases which are not large enough to quickly settle out under the influence of gravity. As a result aerosols tend to remain suspended for relatively long periods of time.

The major aerosols are dust, fumes, mist, and smoke. Dusts are solids such as coal, cement, ashes, sawdust and sand, which are normally 1 micron or greater in size. Mists (usually 0.05 to 1 micron) are formed by chemical reactions of particles with water vapor. For example, water vapor and oxides of sulfur reactions lead to the formation of sulfuric acid. Fumes are particulates formed by associated chemical processes (condensation, distillation, calcination, sublimation, and others) which produce a wide variety of particles of the general size range 0.03 to 0.30 microns.

Fumes are perhaps the most serious industrial pollution problem for two reasons. First, particles of the 0.05 to 2.0 micron range are difficult to remove economically.[24] Second, in addition to the obvious odor problem associated with fumes, is the fact that fumes contain many materials assumed to be toxic and carcinogenic agents such as aromatic hydrocarbons and amines.

Finally, smoke (0.05 to to 1 micron) is formed by the incomplete burning of hydrocarbons. This book will focus on particulates because of their association with stationary pollution sources.

Gases range in size from about 0.0001 to about 0.001 microns. The most common and important gaseous pollutants in urban regions are carbon monoxide, hydrocarbons, oxides of sulfur, oxides of nitrogen, carbon dioxide, and ozone.

Carbon monoxide levels appear to be directly correlated with automobile traffic. Hydrocarbons enter the earth's atmosphere from a wide variety of urban sources including evaporation of fuels and solvents, petroleum refining processes, and incomplete combustion of organic fuels. Hydrocarbons are of particular interest as a factor in the formation of ozone from nitrogen oxides and sunlight. Urban air has about 0.5-1.0 ppm total organics which includes over 80 distinct molecular species such as benzene, ethanol, chlorinated hydrocarbons, and methane, the largest component.

SO_2 is the most common primary sulfur oxide pollutant found in the atmosphere. SO_2 is of great significance in this study because of the enormous quantities emitted into the atmosphere by heat producing machines and power plants using high sulfur coal and other sulfurous fossil fuels. SO_3 is formed in a secondary reaction and later joins with water vapor to form a dangerous sulfuric acid (H_2SO_4) aerosol.

Man-made NO_x is chiefly the product of fuel combustion in furnaces and engines. In the United States, better than half of all the NO_x pollution comes from point sources such as utility boilers and industrial furnaces and processes. As a consequence of its origin, the distribution of NO_x closely follows population concentrations, with the majority of emissions occurring in urban centers.

Reactions among some of the primary pollutants just discussed form secondary pollutants called photochemical oxidants. The reactions involve sunlight, nitrogen oxides, ozone, oxygen, and reactive hydrocarbons. The nitric oxides and various hydrocarbons involved are attributed to motor vehicle fuel combustion, but in some regions the majority may be emitted by industrial processes. Olefins are the hydrocarbons which enter into the photochemical reactions, but parafin as well as aromatic and napthene hydrocarbons can also be involved, though to a lesser extent. Methane hydrocarbons are not involved. Natural sources of photochemical pollutants are terpenes, a reactive hydrocarbon emitted from needle bearing trees and other types of plants at an estimated rate of 55,000 tons per day.[25]

Nitric oxide (NO) emissions come into contact with oxygen (O_2) molecules and form nitrogen dioxide (NO_2). NO_2 absorbs sunlight until it "photodissociates" into NO and O. The O atoms quickly attach themselves to O_2 molecules, forming ozone (O_3). The ozone then aids in oxidizing NO to NO_2. This whole process takes about three to four hours and prevents ozone from reaching toxic concentrations.[26] Oxyacyl and peroxyacyl also react with the NO_2 to form peroxyacetyl nitrate (PAN) which irritates plant tissues and animal membranes.

Carbon monoxide and particulates, when present, both speed the reactions. Sulfur dioxide may slow the formation of PAN by reacting with ozone, but it may also oxidize into hygroscopic sulfate particles which block visibility and cause other types of damage.

During the time it takes for peak concentrations to form, the pollution mass may drift into nearby suburban areas. A study by the Interstate Sanitation Commission traced auto emissions in the Philadelphia-Camden region to high ozone readings in the New Jersey-New York-Connecticut air quality region. A followup study traced the movements of oxidants from Michigan, Ohio, and other midwestern centers to the New York-New Jersey-Connecticut area.[27] Clearly, the photochemical oxidant problem is an inter-regional one.

Overall, SO_2 and particulates are the major pollutants directly associated with industrial sources. The specific extent to which all of the pollutants are directly related to industry will be reviewed in the following section.

THE ROLE OF INDUSTRIAL EMISSIONS

Between 1940 and 1970, nationwide emissions of the six regulated air pollutants grew substantially: particulates, + 15 percent; SO_2, + 50 percent; CO and hydrocarbons, > 100 percent; and NO_2, >400 percent.[28] Since the passage of the Clean Air Act in 1970, the increase has been halted. Between 1970 and 1974, particulates were down 29 percent (to 19.5 million tons per year (mtpy)); SO_2 was down 8 percent (31.4 mtpy); CO dropped 12 percent (94.6 mtpy); hydrocarbons dropped 5 percent (30.4 mtpy); and nitrogen oxides were up 10 percent (22.5 mtpy).

Industrial pollution abatement has been important in the reversing of the disturbing three-decade trend and the possible continuation of the reversal into the future. Industry's water effluent emissions were responsible for the vast majority of BODs and total suspended solid effluent discharges in addition to hazardous discharges. Industry's relative role in air emissions is not as great as it is in water pollution (Exhibit 1), but is nevertheless important.

EXHIBIT 1
ESTIMATED EMISSIONS OF AIR POLLUTANTS, BY WEIGHT, NATIONWIDE 1971 (IN MILLIONS OF TONS PER YEAR)

Source of Emissions	CO	%	Parti-culates	%	SO_2	%	HC	%	NO_x	%
Industry	11.4	11	13.5	50	5.1	16	5.6	21	0.2	1
Other	88.8	89	13.5	50	27.5	84	21.0	79	21.8	99
Total	100.2	100	27.0	100	32.6	100	26.6	100	22.0	100

SOURCE: Fourth Annual Report of the CEQ, Washington, D.C.: U.S.G.P.O., September 1973, p. 266.

Industry is responsible for half of the particulate discharges and much smaller portions of the other regulated parameters. While industrial discharges do not appear to be the most important source of emissions, one must bear in mind that the particulate emissions include toxic particles. In addition, in some urban-industrial areas, industrial emissions account for a larger proportion of emissions. For example, industrial fuel and process emissions accounted for between 40 and 52 percent of total particulate and SO_2 emissions in the city of Philadelphia in the years 1962, 1966, and 1971.[29]

McCutchen concludes that for the near future industrial source emission controls will take on added importance because of the difficulty of applying auto emission controls.[30] If motor vehicle emission standards continue to be postponed, stringent stationary source emission controls will be necessary to prevent significant air quality degradation. Even if the 1970 motor vehicle regulations had been put into effect by 1977, careful siting and emission control of stationary sources would have been necessary.

Summarizing, the first two parts of this chapter reviewed the characteristics, sources, and impacts of air pollutants. The final section of this overview considers air pollution management.

Managing the Ambient Air Environment: Air Quality Standards and Emission Standards

This section considers legal and administrative actions aimed at controlling air emissions. Air resources management consists of choosing a set of options for (a) setting standards, (b) implementing and enforcing standards, and (c) financing the air quality program. Measuring the impacts of industrial location decisions involves applying the standards to the project.

AIR QUALITY AND EMISSION STANDARDS

In the following discussion, two types of air quality standards are discussed: one for ambient air, the other for emissions.

Ambient air quality standards define the maximum background level to which each pollutant may accumulate, regardless of source. Ambient air quality standards involve the concentration level of a pollutant, the length of time during which this concentration level exists, and the number of times it occurs. Since the "standard" is an average concentration level over a given period of time, a fluctuating pollutant level may temporarily exceed the legal level during the averaging period. Averaging times vary from one hour to one year.

Emission standards refer to a maximum emission volume or concentration of a pollutant from a specific source. They typically take three forms: (1) emission rate per unit of a product, (2) specification of process or control equipment, and (3) specification of type of product used in the process (e.g., sulfur levels in fuels). Although they are a means of achieving ambient standards, one cannot readily establish direct causality between reduced emissions and reduced ambient levels of pollution. This is because ambient air quality is very much dependent upon climate, topography, and atmospheric conditions. Thus, emission standards are educated guesses for achieving ambient air quality standards.

Air quality standards should not only reflect health and welfare, but also weigh present and projected land uses, costs, and the technological state-of-the-art. Present land uses are important considerations because some receptors (hospitals, recreation areas) are more sensitive to pollution impacts than others. Future land uses should be considered because space heating devices in additional homes and apartments can add significantly to background levels of pollution. Costs are a consideration because the marginal costs for reducing additional increments of nonhazardous pollutant emissions may be unreasonably high as 100 percent capture of potential emissions is approached. Setting standards which cannot possibly be achieved using state-of-the-art technology by a given deadline will result in deadline extensions, legal confrontations, and exceptions which render the program a failure. A more enforceable set of standards can produce a more steady progress toward improved air quality.

IMPLEMENTATION

Implementation procedures are actions designed to achieve and maintain air quality standards. In this discussion, they are divided into two categories: (1) land use controls which influence the location of activities and (2) direct source controls which influence pollution related activities, regardless of their location.

The first approach relies on the predictive skill and political acumen of government officials to achieve air quality standards. Measures include zoning, fiscal-economic sanctions, moratoria, and preconstruction review. Roberts and associates are pessimistic about achieving air quality standards with land use controls, since these methods have not been wholly effective in achieving other community planning objectives.[31] Land use controls are particularly unpredictable in their effect because atmospheric conditions may cause contaminants to drift into other areas.

Direct source controls rely upon available technology and the compliance of courts and individuals to achieve federal ambient air quality standards. Measures include control hardware designed to clean or capture the emissions, permits to emit, rationing of resources, bans on particular activities (e.g., burning of leaves), operating regulations, stack height regulations, redesign of engines and product processes, regulation of fuel content, and substitution or alteration of materials (recycled steel and aluminum scraps, for example, create less air pollution during smelting operations than do virgin ores).

Since contaminants are never really removed from the environment but are simply shifted from one medium to another, there are tradeoffs involved in selecting among direct control measures. Sulfur, for instance, can be removed from stack emissions, but the market for sulfur often will not absorb the quantities which are thus recaptured, and it often must be dumped somewhere. Wet scrubbers, which clean stack emissions, merely transfer the contaminants from air to water.

Monitoring is an implementation procedure which threatens a negative consequence for the violator—fines, withdrawal of funds, jail terms, injunctions, or sealing of equipment.

Implementation and enforcement usually take place at the lowest level of government capable of efficiently dealing with the problem. This means that the geographic control level requires an economic base capable of supporting the personnel and equipment and enough pollution sources to justify the expense. Large cities could support their own air pollution agencies; but in other areas a county, regional, or state agency would be more efficient. Interstate compacts are also possible for establishing a control level, but they require congressional approval, and the scope of their authority is unclear, given the fact that the federal government has preempted jurisidiction over interstate air pollution problems.[32] One suggestion has been to establish air "basins," each of which has an air mass with the same flow pattern as control regions.

FINANCING

Methods of financing include taxes, grants, matching funds, user fees, bonds, etc. Different aspects of the air quality program may have to be separately financed, since funds for research, planning, training, demonstration projects, capital construction, and operations are spread among different laws.

GOVERNMENT LEVELS OF AUTHORITY

Federal Level. Originally, the federal role was small. Air pollution activities handled by the Department of the Interior's Bureau of Mines reflected early concerns over pollution by coal dust and fuel combustion particulates.

The Air Pollution Control Act of 1955 (Public Law 159) was the beginning of a growing federal involvement. It assigned research, technical assistance and training programs to the Public Health Service within the Department of Health, Education and Welfare (HEW). Five years later, the Public Health Service established the division of air pollution and delved into legal, administrative, economic and social areas. At that point, the purpose of the federal government's effort was to provide information and technical assistance to air pollution programs at lower levels of government.

The Clean Air Act of 1963 (Public Law 88-206) provided the Public Health Service with authority over interstate air pollution problems and federal sources of pollution, filling in obvious jurisdictional gaps without usurping any state or local powers. Control and abatement programs were emphasized.

With the Clean Air Act Amendments and Solid Waste Disposal Act of 1965, the federal government began setting emission standards and controlling more categories of sources. Provisions included: (1) emission standards for new motor vehicles, (2) control over sources of international air pollution which originate in the U.S., (3) providing advice on intrastate problems of substantial significance, (4) development of air quality criteria, (5) requiring states and local agencies to develop air quality control regions and air quality standards based on the air quality criteria, and (6) requiring that state and local agencies develop a compliance timetable.

Two sets of motor vehicle emission standards emerged from HEW after the 1965 act: (1) crankcase standards for new autos and motor vehicles under a half ton to prevent evaporation of oil—a source of 25 percent of auto pollution,[33] and (2) exhaust standards for hydrocarbons and carbon monoxide—one set of standards for light duty engines and a more permissive set for heavy duty engines.[34]

The foregoing did not preclude state and local governments from setting additional standards more stringent than the federal ones. A major purpose of the Air Quality Act of 1967, however, was to prevent the states (except California) from establishing their own emission standards for new motor vehicles. That is, the federal government "preempted the field" in regard to emission standards for new motor vehicles. In addition, manufacturers were to provide HEW with information on fuel additives.

The 1970 Amendments to the Clean Air Act established the Environmental Protection Agency, giving it authority to establish standards and *require the states* to develop implementation plans for those standards by the middle of 1972. Congress gave EPA control over emissions from new stationary sources to prevent polluting industries from migrating to unpolluted states where standards might be more lax.[35] In anticipation of pressure from the automobile industry, Congress did not delegate the setting of auto emissions to EPA, but set those regulations itself. Also, the field of auto and aircraft emission standards was specifically preempted at the federal level so that manufacturers would not have to contend with differing standards among the states.[36] Another feature of the act was the requirement that auto manufacturers provide warranties of 5 years or 50,000 miles for their pollution devices.[37]

Ambient air is the atmosphere to which the general public has access and which is outside of buildings. Two sets of ambient air quality standards resulted from the 1970 Clean Air Act Amendments: primary standards to protect public health, and more stringent, secondary standards to protect public welfare. Public welfare includes impacts on property, materials, climate, economic value and personal comfort. Only six pollutants—sulfur dioxide, nitrogen oxides, carbon monoxide, particulates, nonmethane hydrocarbons, and photochemical oxidants—are covered by these ambient air quality standards. All six have threshold levels denoting concentrations which cause adverse impacts on public health and welfare. The standards (Exhibit 2) are set at levels low enough to avoid "any adverse physiological change," with "modest" safety margins.[38]

The Clean Air Act of 1970 originally set mid-1975 as the deadline for meeting the primary air quality standards, with possible extensions to 1978. Secondary standards were to be met at some later date. Former EPA administrator, Russell Train, reported in May 1975 that air quality had been improved but that many air quality regions would not meet the primary standards.[39] For example, while auto emissions were down 67 percent from cars built in 1970, the 90 percent reduction mandated by Congress had not been met. Of the approximately 20,000 major stationary sources, more than three-fourths had met the emissions standards or were following a compliance schedule. Nevertheless, 153 of the 247 air quality control regions were expected not to meet the ambient standards for one or more parameters: 59 on SO₂; 79 on photochemical oxidants; 69 on CO; and 16 on NO_x.

Many air contaminants which are toxic are covered by laws on hazardous substances, rather than by ambient air quality standards, but are still under the jurisdiction of EPA. So far only four hazardous pollutants have been subject to regulation: asbestos, beryllium, mercury, and vinyl chloride. EPA is now in the process of moving toward the regulation of arsenic, cadmium, polycyclic organic materials (by late 1978), and radioactive pollutants (by late 1979). Additional information about toxics will be presented in the solid waste chapter.

EXHIBIT 2
Ambient Air Quality Standards

Pollutant	Averaging Time	Standards	
		Primary	Secondary
Total Suspended Particulates	Annual Geom. Mean	75ug/m³	60ug/m³
	24 hr.*	260ug/m³	150ug/m³
SO₂	Annual Average	80ug/m³ (0.03 ppm)	60ug/m³ (0.02 ppm)
	24 hr.*	365 ug/m³ (0.14 ppm)	260ug/m³ (0.10 ppm)
	3 hr.*	—	1300ug/m³ (0.5 ppm)
CO	8 hr.*	10,000ug/(m)³** (9 ppm)	Same as primary std.
	1 hr.*	40,000ug/m³ (35 ppm)	
Nonmethane Hydrocarbons	3 hr.* (6-9 am)	160ug/m³ (0.24 ppm)	—
NO₂	Annual Average	100ug/m³ (0.05 ppm)	—
Photochemical Oxidants	1 hr.*	160ug/m³ (0.08 ppm)	—

NOTES: *Not to be exceeded more than once a year.
   **10,000ug/m³ = 10 mg/m³

Some air contaminants, however, escape coverage by both sets of laws. Odors are categorized by EPA as "noncriteria" pollutants and thus are not covered by federal legislation.[40]   Particulate emissions tend to be restricted in terms of their concentration levels, but without regard for their specific chemical composition—particulates may be composed of carbon, silica, sulfates, lead, rubber, metal dust, lime, and other substances which vary in their impacts at a given level of concentration. Holmes and others note in their EPA "White Paper" that reactive hydrocarbon emissions are regulated while the less reactive, but not inert, hydrocarbons are ignored.[41] And pollutants from natural sources, such as volcanoes and forest fires, obviously cannot be controlled by legislation.

It is important to note that the foregoing laws refer to pollution of public air space and not to air contaminants related to a person's work space. Workplace hazards are covered under HEW's National Institute for Occupational Safety and Health (NIOSH), which was established under a 1970 act, and the Occupational Safety and Health Administration (OSHA). NIOSH researches workplace hazards and suggests safe limits for air contaminants, while OSHA sets the standards.[42]

In 1973, pollution from indirect sources became the focus of federal action. States were required to include indirect sources of pollution in their implementation plans and to resubmit their implementation plans with these revisions. Indirect pollution sources which were to be included were: (1) new highway sections with 20,000 vehicles per day or more; (2) new airports with 50,000 or more plane operations per year; (3) new parking areas with 1,000 or more spaces in urban areas or 2,000 or more spaces in nonurban areas; and (4) any indirect sources constructed or modified after 1974.[43] However, in 1974 and 1975 the indirect source regulations were delayed and modified. Parking facilities and shopping centers were eliminated from the program, and implementation of the program was delayed.

As a result of fuel shortages, the 1974 Energy Supply and Environmental Coordination Act was created as a set of amendments to the Clean Air Act. The apparent purpose of the act was to enable the U.S. to switch to an alternative energy source—coal—in the event of a petroleum and gas shortage. To this end, it (1) allows EPA to temporarily suspend emission standards for stationary sources which cannot obtain clean fuels, (2) allows EPA to suspend a stationary source's fuel allocation and to prohibit major fuel users from burning gas or petroleum, (3) encourages electric power plants to burn coal and allows long-term extension of deadlines for sources forced to use coal, (4) allows EPA to override state programs and permit the use of less effective emission controls, (5) delays the deadlines for auto emissions, (6) allows EPA to require review of state implementation plans to ensure consistency with the 1974 act, and (7) states that no action taken under the Clean Air Act shall be subject to the National Environmental Policy Act.[44]

Finally, it is important to note that a 1972 lower court ruling, which was upheld by the U.S. Supreme Court in August 1974, prohibits EPA from approving a state plan which allows air in clean areas to significantly deteriorate. All regions were classified into three types: (1) class 1—air protected at existing levels; (2) class 2—moderate deterioration permitted; and (3) class 3—deterioration permitted up to and above the national air quality standards. Allowable increases in particulates and SO_2 were specified and have been modified by the 1977 amendments (Exhibit 3). All states in the country were put into class 2, subject to changes by the governors of their states.

The Clean Air Act Amendments of 1977 adopted the class 1,2,3 trichotomy with a few modifications. Class 1 areas include national parks and wilderness areas over 5,000 acres. They are protected from most development. The new law, however, does allow the governor of a state to permit industrial violations of sulfur dioxide emission standards (not for particulates) for up to eighteen days (the 24-hour maximum standard) if the secretary of the Department of the Interior approves. If not, the president has ninety days to make the decision.

As an outgrowth of the nondegradation issue, in early 1977, EPA introduced a new "offset" policy in the form of a ruling which, like the class 1-3 trichotomy, may have had an extremely important impact on new industrial siting in urban-industrial regions. The new policy would allow some industrial expansion in highly polluted areas. For this expansion to take place, other sources have to compensate for the proposed new emissions by reducing existing discharges. New plants must use the best technology available and must receive EPA approval of a plan for reducing discharges from their existing facilities prior to building the new facility. EPA held public hearings on this ruling.

The 1977 amendments used this offset approach in reaching a compromise. The 1970 act required the attainment of primary standards by 1977. The 1977 amendments extend the deadline for meeting the primary standards to 1982 and to 1987 in areas that are particularly dependent on the auto.

While postponing the 1977 deadline, the 1977 amendments allow nonattainment areas to impose standards stricter than the federal requirements. In addition, industrial growth in non-attainment areas will be permitted only if emissions from other sources are proportionally reduced and progress is being made toward the 1982 standards.

To summarize, in regard to clean air, establishment of air quality standards is currently the primary responsibility of the federal government, which sets minimum ambient air quality standards for the six major pollutants; sets minimum emission standards for hazardous substances and new point sources; and retains exclusive control over emission standards

EXHIBIT 3
ALLOWABLE INCREASES FOR CLASS 1, CLASS 2, AND
CLASS 3 REGIONS*

Allowable Increases	Class 1	Class 2	Class 3
	(ug/m³)	(ug/m³)	(ug/m³)
Particulate matter:			
Annual geometric mean	5	19	37
24-hr. maximum	10	37	75
Sulfur dioxide:			
Annual arithmetic mean	2	20	40
24-hr. maximum	5	91	182
3-hr. maximum	25	512	700

SOURCE: Federal Register, Vol. 39, no. 235, Part 3, December 5, 1974, modified by the amendments of 1977.

for motor vehicles (except in California) and aircraft. However, there are no standards for odors. Emission standards and compliance deadlines may be suspended or altered in order to accommodate a shift to coal as a substitute for petroleum and gas if another energy crisis should occur.

The Limited Federal Role in Implementation. It is economically inefficient for the federal government to become involved in the day-to-day specifics of implementing and enforcing the standards. Therefore, the federal role in implementation is primarily research, approval of state plans, technical assistance, and dissemination of information—centralized functions which take advantage of economies of scale.[45] A few implementation procedures are appropriate to the federal level. Most activities are centered within EPA, but HEW and the Federal Highway Administration (FHWA) also have some programs.[46] These will be briefly summarized.

With the exception of California, federal control of emission standards for new cars in the 1965 act prevents manufacturers from dealing with varying state standards, but was not intended to be the sole method of dealing with auto pollution. New car turnover may not occur quickly enough to achieve ambient air quality standards, and air quality may even get worse before a significant number of old autos have been replaced. Indeed, the 90 percent emissions reduction for CO, HC, and NO$_x$ mandated by the 1970 act has been changed. The newest set of revised emission standards were forthcoming from the 1977 amendments. The 1981-model cars must cut hydrocarbons to 0.41 grams per mile from the present 1.5, carbon monoxide from 15 to 3.4, and nitrogen oxide from 2 to 1.

EPA may, however, freeze the CO standard at 7 (technology not available) and can grant a four-year waiver for NO_x standards to spur development of diesels and other more fuel efficient engines.

With the 1967 Air Quality Act, the secretary of HEW could seek immediate injunctions if any source emissions constituted an "imminent and substantial endangerment to the health of persons." The secretary could also bring violators of the standards in any air quality control region to court.[47]

The 1970 act provides indirect enforcement power by prohibiting federal agencies from obtaining goods, materials, or services from a source which has been convicted of intentional violation of emission standards. And a 1971 presidential order prohibits federal financial assistance to facilities not complying with the standards.[48]

The 1970 Highway Act requires highway construction to be compatible with the Clean Air Act and state implementation plans. In 1973, the FHWA air quality guidelines carried this further by setting forth procedures for constructing highways so as to comply with the 1970 Clean Air Act.

In 1974, HUD's regulations and guidelines pursuant to the Housing and Urban Development Act of 1974 covered the air quality impacts of housing projects and their effects on the air quality standards. Finally, the federal government also can provide accelerated depreciation for capital investments to industries installing pollution control equipment.

Some areas of controversy and opposition occur among different agencies when powers are fragmented. For instance, EPA has difficulty implementing some of its standards because the Department of Commerce represents the views of the mining and fuel industries. The Office of Management and Budget must review EPA proposals and clear them with other agencies.[49]

Penalties for breaking the law in regard to warranties for automotive pollution control devices are fines of up to $25,000 per day and/or one year imprisonment, for first offenses. EPA has recently used this law against several auto manufacturers. For second offenses, these penalties are doubled.[50] If EPA fails to perform its legal duties, the federal government itself can be sued.[51]

State Level. The Clean Air Act of 1970 set forth the need for a federal effort to attain cleaner air. The states retained the primary responsibility for implementing the effort. States may set stricter ambient air quality standards for additional pollutants, and may set standards to control odors. Basically the main role of the states has become one of implementing the federal ambient air quality standards. The states must submit their implementation plans for EPA approval.

Since the states must prevent the violation of primary and secondary ambient air quality standards within their borders, they have slowly been impinging on local level jurisdictional powers. Land use controls are the domain of local governments, but states can regulate development of statewide interest, such as water, sewer, and energy facilities, airports, ground transportation systems, and new communities.[52] States also may prevent the construction, modification, or operation of sources whose emissions are incompatible with the attainment or maintenance of national ambient air quality standards.[53]

For transportation (line) sources, one control strategy is to reduce emissions per mile. Emission inspection programs can aid the implementation of both state and federal auto emission standards. Additional procedures include standards for installing motor vehicle control devices,[54] inspection and maintenance programs, and requiring control devices on older model vehicles.[55] Another, less direct strategy is to reduce vehicle miles. This can be done through traffic pattern changes and encouragement of car pooling and public transportation. Similarly, a strategy of reducing emissions per passenger involves the encouragement of mass transit. Buses and rail rapid transit, for instance, have fewer emissions per passenger mile than autos.[56] Gas rationing and high fuel taxes also reduce vehicle miles, but may not significantly decrease auto use during critical rush hour periods. Elimination of leaded gasoline is another method. Instead of forcing all cars to use retrofit devices, it is possible to effect a more gradual change by requiring the changes only on new cars, which will gradually replace the older ones.

Some states provide financial assistance and/or accelerated depreciation for pollution control.[57] The emission tax is another type of economic control, but is not very popular with industry. Emission taxes are an advantage in that polluters pay in proportion to the contaminants they contribute, but the disadvantage is that firms feel it is unfair to pay for both the expensive control equipment and the remaining emissions. Emission taxes may also subordinate clean air to the purchasing power of large industries.

Permit systems have been successfully used and seem to afford a great deal of information, if not control over polluters. Permits may be required for plant construction and installation or repair of equipment. In addition, permit fees are a source of revenue. A permit authority should be able to specify the hardware to be used by each source. The Bay Area Pollution Control District in California indicates the problem of not being able to specify the hardware: numerous performance checks are necessary because the type of control technique being used is unknown.[58]

Some controversy centers around the fact that a plant's emissions may be acceptable at one location but unacceptable in an area where atmospheric or topographic conditions hinder the dispersion of the pollution. Industries consider these site specific differences unfair since one plant will have to install expensive equipment and another will not. Forecast modeling has been another source of controversy because industries resent having to purchase expensive equipment on the basis of predicted emissions rather than actual ones.[59]   Contention occurs over the equity of this procedure, as well as over the type of forecasting models used.

States can enforce air pollution laws through their police powers to protect public health, safety, and welfare. Information on each state's laws can be obtained from the state capitol, the U.S.EPA regional office, and the Internal Revenue Service. *Chemical Engineering* prints an annual update of state laws.

Some financing is available from the federal government. The 1963 Clean Air Act provided for matching grants to state and local agencies in order to establish or strengthen air pollution programs. The Air Quality Act of 1967 authorized HEW to provide grants to state air pollution control agencies for developing motor vehicle inspection and emission testing programs; the law also expanded planning grants for state and local programs.[60]

One of the most interesting federal-state issues has been the granting of variances to stationary dischargers by the states. The 1970 Clean Air Act called for the achievement of the ambient air quality standards by 1975, or by 1977, with a two year extension. When it became apparent that extensions were necessary for some emitters, states issued variances. EPA's position was that the variances were revisions of the state implementation plans.[61]

EPA's position on variances was challenged. In April 1975, the U.S. Supreme Court ruled that if the state's plan achieves and maintains the ambient air standards, then the EPA cannot intercede against a state's timing and enforcement process.

The New Jersey glass industry provides an interesting example of a variance procedure.

> The state's strategy for dealing with air pollution in New Jersey is, in general, directed at gross classifications of air contaminants, for example, particles from manufacturing processes, rather than specific substances. This is an acceptable method for dealing with air contamination on a broad scale. Moreover, no regulation of this type can be designed to adequately anticipate each and every situation which might arise.[62]

The glass industry is one of the situations in which the state of New Jersey believes the general procedure is inadequate. Briefly, the New Jersey Department of Environmental Protection has proposed a variance designed to encourage the use of recycled glass in glass melting operations. In the course of promulgating this variance, the DEP will change its particulate emissions policy for glass furnaces from a grain loadings or control efficiency basis to a production weight method.

The present particulate emissions from New Jersey glass furnaces are 2,800 tons per year. The existing grain loaders and control efficiency standards would reduce emissions to 1,100 tons per year. The revised standard would permit the emission of 1,800 tons per year. The 700 tons of emissions are being traded for additional cycling of recovered glass and, more important, for the removal of the threat that the New Jersey glass industry will leave the state because the current state emission standards are more restrictive than those of neighboring states.

Intermediate Levels. As mentioned previously, the air flow pattern of a particular air mass may form a natural air basin which is better suited for pollution control programs than arbitrary political boundaries. Regional area agencies are most effective when they have some enforcement power over all communities in their jurisdiction. If participation is voluntary, it will be difficult to achieve standards, since pollution does not recognize city boundaries. An administrative aid to implementation and enforcement is the formation of interstate compacts. These need the approval of Congress, unless they are formed solely for the purpose of research.[63] Since these compacts may span several states, it is advisable to include authorization to use federal courts for prosecuting a state which fails to live up to the contract.[64] The scope of authority of such compacts may be rather narrow because the federal government has given itself authority over interstate pollution problems.

Yet in some regions the pollution problems defy single-state solutions. The most obvious example is photochemical oxidants. The previously mentioned Interstate Sanitation Commission study traced photochemical oxidant problems from the midwestern states to the Philadelphia-New York-New Jersey-Connecticut region, and within the New York region traced the problems from Philadelphia to Connecticut.[65] Southern New Jersey farmers claim that ozone has caused $1 million in crop damages during 1975 and 1976.[66] The same article reported that the environmental heads of thirteen states from Maine to Virginia will try to study the hydrocarbon emission issue as an interstate problem.

Local Levels. Local governments may create air pollution standards more stringent than those of the federal government, but standards more stringent than those of the state will probably be invalidated by the courts.[67] The scope of local power for setting standards depends upon whether the municipality bases its authority on common law, police power, or specific enabling legislation.

Under common law, municipalities could abate smoke and other emissions which constitute a nuisance. However, common law definitions previously did not permit smoke to be declared a nuisance, per se, so cases had to be decided individually on the basis of damages caused by the emissions. The Ringlemann Smoke Chart was used as a measure of opacity in setting smoke standards, but no other types of standards could be set. Current legal interpretations allow cities to declare emissions a nuisance at common law.

Otherwise, municipalities have only those powers which have been delegated to them by the states. The statutory police powers usually delegated to localities by the states provide authority to protect public health, safety, and welfare. Police powers cover only the right to abate odors, smoke, dust, and other nuisance emissions which are visible. Invisible pollutants such as carbon monoxide or ozone are more dangerous and are not covered under police powers.[68] However, the current trend is to use police powers for controlling pollutant problems other than nuisance emissions. There is also a trend to cover air pollution which not only causes inevitable disease and damage, but also creates conditions hazardous or perilous to public health.[69]

Specific enabling legislation defines the communities' authority to set standards and control different types of pollutants. Although local governments have the smallest role in setting air quality standards, they have the greatest range of options for implementation.

Local Mobile Sources. One land use control for dealing with motor vehicle traffic is to ban autos or parking in center city areas. However, the administrative structure for enforcing the law and granting exceptions may be expensive, and this solution tends to be unpopular with the public. A status quo measure of disallowing construction of any new parking lots might be more feasible.

Cities cannot set automobile emissions standards, but they can set certain other types of performance standards to aid in achieving ambient air quality standards. A New York City regulation, for instance, prohibits the operation of a motor vehicle at an idle for more than three minutes, except under special conditions. Another New York City regulation prohibits a motor vehicle from emitting visible smoke or fumes for more than ten seconds while idling, or for more than ninety yards while moving.[70] Cities can also require that control hardware, such as catalytic converters, be installed on certain categories of vehicles within city boundaries. These include public vehicles (such as taxicabs) and vehicles owned and operated by the city.[71] A third control is to regulate the lead and phosphorous content of gasoline sold within the town boundaries.[72] Various direct and indirect methods of reducing auto use have uncertain results. High parking charges or taxes may discourage people from bringing their cars into the city, assuming these measures are coupled with a positive mass transit program. High fuel taxes and gas rationing may not produce the desired effect, as discussed under state level options.

Point and Area Sources. Some methods of influencing location of activities are designed to prevent deterioration of air quality in clean areas. Special taxes and preferential assessments can reduce development pressures, giving owners a low tax rate as long as the land is left undeveloped or used for low intensity purposes. As a followup measure, conversion penalties require owners to return their tax benefits if their land is developed within a specified number of years.

In regard to residential development, residential density zoning may limit the burden created by space heating devices in homes, as well as the burden which would be created by auto ownership from additional residents. Emission density zoning is a variant on this. The jurisdictional emissions quota, for instance, involves restricting the emissions within a given area, with allowable emissions allocated to the point sources in the area.[73] Unit area emission quotas, as another example, restrict the allowable emissions from the land itself. For instance, a unit area quota, based on tons per acre, forces heavier polluters to settle on larger lots of land, which serves as a sort of additional buffer between the industry and the receptors.

Transfer of development rights occurs when land is broken into segments which all have development rights of equal intensity. However, the parcels will not be developed equally. For example, those who want to build higher structures can purchase the rights from other owners who do not want to use all of their development rights. This provides a balance between open space with clean air and intensive development. More recently, the concept of transfer of emission rights has been discussed. In transfer of emission rights, parcels would be zoned for the same tons per acre of pollutant emissions, and owners could sell part or all of their rights (in tons per acre) to an industry or other developer. Another locational restriction, the construction moratorium, is probably not going to be upheld by the courts in the instance of air pollution for anything more than a short term solution than it has been for sewerage and water treatment.

For more direct controls, the city can regulate the sulfur content of fuel used in boilers; prohibit open burning; prohibit people from storing, transporting, or handling materials in a manner which creates airborne pollutants; and require special training for equipment operators.[74] A permit system can be effectively used at local levels, and the permit fees are a source of revenue. Permits can be required for construction or operation of industrial plants and for installation or alteration of fuel burning equipment in industrial facilities and apartment complexes.[75] Emissions taxes, as discussed under state level options, are controversial to both industrialists and environmentalists. A more positive type of economic incentive is to allow industries accelerated depreciation on capital investment of pollution control equipment or preferential assessments.

Enforcement measures which are weak or lacking in money or manpower can seriously undermine air pollution legislation. Thus, local level ordinances should also provide for enforcement.[76] In Chicago, for instance, inspectors and investigators have patrolled the city and can issue tickets to violators. Duties can include inspection of fuel and refuse burning equipment after installation or mandatory repair work, sealing of substandard equipment, etc.[77]

Air pollution violations may be handled as violations of an ordinance, misdemeanors, or criminal cases. In the latter case, all Fourth Amendment rights apply, including arraignment, trial, and search warrants.[78] Penalties may include fines and jail sentences. Fines and jail terms are effective only if the penalties are more expensive than installing and maintaining pollution abatement equipment and if conviction of violators can be obtained.

One problem with obtaining a conviction, at least in the past, has been that vague, poorly written municipal ordinances were not upheld by the courts.[79] Similarly, courts will not uphold an ordinance which they deem arbitrary and unreasonable—such as one which sets unrealistic compliance deadlines or demands performance standards which are not possible with existing technology. It is advisable to write "severability clauses" into a statute. This means that if some parts of a statute are invalidated, the rest of it will remain in force.[80] There is an interesting "catch-22" in regard to conviction. A polluter cannot use the lack of suitable abatement methods as a defense, but is not likely to be convicted unless the plaintiffs can prove that the best available methods were not used.[81]

Private citizens who are burdened by a polluter may bring the offender into civil court. It is important to note than any "person" is entitled to sue an air pollution offender. This term refers to a government, public or private corporation, firm or partnership, or ordinary citizen.[82] Other environmental laws specify that any "citizen" can sue, and this means that one must be able to prove "standing" via a particular level of economic loss or other special damages. Bases for citizen suits are usually economic damages, health damages, or infringement of property rights. However, if the potential damages are known, citizens can have the pollution abated before the damage occurs.[83]   Presumably, this refers to suits brought in criminal courts, because Lewin notes that civil suits can only be used for damage which has already occurred, and not for abating potential dangers.[84]   Injunctive relief from a polluter is time consuming since there must be a full hearing, and preliminary injunctions are granted only if imminent danger can be proved to health or property.[85]   Although courts will provide injunctive relief when necessary, they will rule against laws which appear to be clearly inequitable to the firm, such as unrealistic compliance deadlines.[86]

The first three sections of this chapter have overviewed air quality management. Their goal was to introduce the reader to the characteristics, sources, and impacts of the pollutants and to the complex legal and administrative structures which try to abate them.

Obtaining and Using Emissions and Ambient Air Data

These sections set the stage for the practical step of obtaining and using air quality and emissions data.

EMISSIONS INFORMATION

The initial step in determining the air quality impact of industrial development is to determine the quantities of emissions from the facilities. The relevant air emissions literature may be divided into three types.

1. Information about the discharges of specific industrial processes
2. Coefficients for general groups of industries
3. Coefficients designed to measure emissions from activities related to new industrial development such as automobile emissions, space heating, and solid waste disposal.

Specific Industrial Processes. One of the outgrowths of the Clean Air Act Amendments of 1970 was that any *new or modified* stationary source belonging to particular industrial groups would have to use the best available control technologies. In December, 1971, the U.S.EPA promulgated new-source air emissions standards for five industries (initially proposed date listed).

1. Fossil fuel fired steam generators (8/17/71)
2. Incinerators (8/17/71)
3. Portland cement plants (8/17/71)
4. Nitric acid plants (8/17/71)
5. Sulfuric acid plants (8/17/71)

Between mid-1973 and early 1976, new-source performance standards were proposed and promulgated for nineteen other industries.

6. Asphalt concrete plants (6/11/73)
7. Petroleum refineries (6/11/73)
8. Storage of petroleum liquids (6/11/73)
9. Secondary lead smelters (6/11/73)
10. Secondary brass and bronze ingots (6/11/73)
11. Iron and steel (6/11/73)
12. Sewage treatment plants (6/11/73)
13. Copper primary smelters (10/16/74)
14. Zinc primary smelters (10/16/74)
15. Primary lead smelters (10/16/74)
16. Primary aluminum plants (10/23/74)
17. Wet process phosphoric acid plants (10/22/74)
18. Superphosphoric acid plants (10/22/74)
19. Diammonium phosphate plants (10/22/74)
20. Triple superphosphate plants (10/22/74)
21. Granular triple superphospate plants (10/22/74)
22. Coal preparation plants (10/24/74)
23. Ferroalloy production (10/21/74)
24. Electric arc furnaces (10/21/74)

As of early 1976, the emissions of these twenty-four industries were regulated at the federal scale. McCutchen expects potentially an additional 100 source standards.[87] While the 1977 amendments granted up to three extensions for existing plants to meet emission standards (especially plants converting to coal as a fuel), new plants are required to install the best available technology, irrespective of the relative cleanliness of the fuel, and to use continuous emissions control equipment.

The new source performance standards (NSPS), like their water emissions counterparts, are quite detailed. The NSPS for electric arc furnaces, one of the industries in the case study, will be briefly reviewed as an illustration. The standards for this portion of the steel industry were published in the *Federal Register* on September 23, 1975. The background documents had been published a year earlier.[88] The major controls relate to the control device, the shop, and the dust handling equipment.

> Emissions from the control device are limited to less than 12 mg/dscm (0.0052 gr/dscf) and 3 percent opacity. Furnace emissions escaping capture by the collection system and exiting from the shop are limited to zero percent opacity, but emissions greater than this level are allowed during charging periods and tapping periods. Emissions from the dust-handling equipment are limited to less than 10 percent opacity.[89]

These specific standards are based on a detailed study of the industry. The major pollutants are particulates. The literature suggests that, without controls, thirty pounds of particulates are emitted per ton of carbon steel and fifteen pounds are emitted per ton of alloy steel. The 12 mg/dscm (milligrams per dry standard cubic meter) emission standard assumes one of two control technologies: (1) a fabric filter collection system or (2) a combination of a direct shell evacuation-canopy hood system.

Assuming a plant carbon steel furnace capacity of 300 tons, uncontrolled emissions would be about 30 pounds per ton. A direct shell evacuation system would reduce emissions to about 3.05 pounds per ton. The addition of buildings, evacuation or canopy hoods, and a closed roof would reduce the emissions to about 0.359 pounds per ton. The 12 mg/dscm requirement is, in essence, close to a 99 percent particulate control emission standard.

The electric arc process also produces gases. Carbon monoxide is produced by the reaction of the carbon electrodes or carbon in the steel with the oxygen blown into the furnace or with the iron oxides. Carbon monoxide production is estimated as high as 6 pounds per ton of steel produced. While CO emissions are not regulated, the control systems outlined here were measured as reducing emissions from 6 to between 0.54 and 1.39 pounds per ton of steel. Small amounts of NO_x, SO_x, and fluoride are produced.

The other emission standards for the electric arc furnaces are detailed in the development documents. Overall, this brief description demonstrates that if the industry of interest to the reader has a new-source performance standard, EPA will supply the user with ample emissions data.

Emission Coefficients for General Industrial Group Information. If the industries of interest are not included in the NSPS groups, the second useful source of data is the U.S. EPA publication *Compilation of Air Pollutant Emission Factors* (AP-42).[90] This publication, which is frequently revised, reports uncontrolled combustion sources, solid waste disposal equipment, mobile combustion sources, sources of evaporation, and industrial processes.

The industrial process data is at the four-digit SIC code level. The process is briefly described, average emissions per unit of production are given, and references are provided.

To help the user judge the validity of the coefficients, each process is ranked A, B, C, D, or E. An A ranking means that the coefficient is excellent; B is above average; C is average; D is below average; and E is considered poor. Overall, the AP-42 publication is useful for regional planning studies in which a relatively large number of industrial processes are being considered.

A third source of specific industrial emissions data is the permit requirements of state laws. Most state emissions laws aim at controlling par-

210 A Primer on Industrial Environmental Impact

ticulate and SO₂ pollution. The New Jersey laws will be briefly reviewed as an illustration. With respect to particulate emissions from fuel combustion, the rates in Exhibit 4 are used.

With respect to particulates from other stationary sources, 99 percent capture of uncontrolled emissions is the rule, though variances may be granted for glass furnaces. For example, a plant which produces tin and lead alloys feeds two tons of scrap tin, solder, and lead into its melting furnaces per hour. Without controls, the facility would produce 7 pounds of tin oxides per hour and three pounds of lead oxides. With bag house controls the emission rates are 0.07 pounds of tin oxides and 0.03 pounds of lead oxides.

There are also state of New Jersey regulations for smoke emissions from stationary sources. No smoke or appearance which is darker than number 1 on the Ringlemann Smoke Chart or greater than 20 percent opacity, exclusive of water vapor, is to be emitted from stationary engines for a period of more than ten seconds.

Sulfur dioxide emissions from fuel combustion are controlled by specifying the fuel content of the fuel (Exhibit 5).

Some perspectives on the federal and state emissions regulations are available by examining emissions data from existing industries. The availability of state data is quite variable and can be determined only by phone calls to the appropriate state agency and regional U.S.EPA office. Again, New Jersey will serve as an illustration.

The state began a permit program in 1967. All industries which have been constructed since 1967 or have changed their processes since 1967 should have filed a permit with the N.J.DEP. Those industrial processes which were constructed before 1967 and which have remained the same have no available record unless citizen complaints were filed. If the complaints were serious, the N.J.DEP sent an inspector who obtained data about the emissions. Since about 90 percent of the complaints are about volatile organic chemicals, many of these plants have been studied, even if they predate the 1967 permit program.

While most of the important processes have submitted data, officials have indicated that the reports are not readily accessible and that some of the early tests leave a good deal to be desired. State officials look to the national emissions data inventory being compiled by the U.S.EPA and the state to pull these data together into a computerized form.[91]

A call to your state agency will help you determine whether your state has readily available industrial prototype data. County planning boards and large universities sometimes have personnel who can further advise you about other sources of emissions data and the adequacy of available data. Other possible sources of data include reports of the Occupational

EXHIBIT 4

NEW JERSEY STANDARDS FOR EMISSION OF PARTICLES
FROM HEAT PRODUCING FACILITIES

Heat Input Rate (Million BTU's per hour)[a]	Maximum Allowable Emission Rate
1	0.6 lbs/hr.
10	6
20	8
30	9
40	10
50	11
60	12
70	13
80	14
90	14.5
100	15
120	16.5
140	17.5
160	18.5
180	19.3
200	20
400	40
600	60
800	80
1000	100
2000	200
etc.	etc.

SOURCE: New Jersey Administrative Code 7:27.
NOTE: [a]In-between values are to be interpolated.

EXHIBIT 5

LIMITS ON SULFUR CONTENT OF FUEL OILS

Grade of Fuel	Percent Sulfur by Weight
No. 2 & lighter	0.2
No. 2	0.3
No. 5, no. 6 & heavier	0.3

SOURCE: New Jersey Administrative Code 7:27.

Safety and Health Administration, the U.S. Bureau of Mines, and stack effluent reports from fire departments.

Once process specific information has been gathered, turn to the recently published EPA compilation of land use based emission factors.[92] Exhibit 6 summarizes fuel combustion emissions at the two-digit SIC code level. Exhibits 7, 8, 9, and 10 are reproduced from the EPA publication to provide the background data for these exhibits. Before Exhibit 6 is used, the potential user should be sure that the national numbers in Exhibits 7–10, upon which Exhibit 6 is based, are reasonable estimates of regional characteristics. The U.S. Bureau of the Census report on fuels and electric energy consumed should be consulted to determine the extent of regional differences.[93]

If your community-county-regional goal is both to plan for industrial development and to maintain or improve air quality, then a careful analysis of existing stationary sources, including the evaluation of the accuracy of the stack samples, is necessary. The St. Louis and California regions have done a good deal of work in the development of inventory source procedures and estimating emissions.[94]   Other important references are volume 10 of the U.S.EPA *Guidelines for Air Quality Maintenance Planning and Analysis: Reviewing New Stationary Sources* and the fourth supplement (January, 1975) of AP-42 which discusses the relationship between emission factors and new-source performance standards.[95]

One important addition to the industrial emissions information literature which should be expected in the near future is characterization and regulation of emission variability.[96] To obtain these data, surveys of individual processes will have to be studied for uniformity during a day, a week, or a season and with respect to the best use of air pollution control equipment.

Summarizing, the new-source performance standards, the AP-42 publication, and state regulations and emissions information provide a basis for estimating emissions per unit of output at the four-digit SIC code level. These data are to be multiplied by estimates of economic output as previously explained in the water resources chapter.

In addition to knowing the amount of contaminants to be emitted, it is important to be able to offer alternatives to a company's plans about the emission rate, the exit velocity of the pollutants, the exit temperature of the pollutants, and the height and diameter of the exit stack. A state agency or consultant should be able to help with emission exit data.

Emissions from Activities Related to Industrial Development. Major industrial developments add people, automobile and truck traffic, fuel combustion, and other emission sources. If the development of a similar de-

EXHIBIT 6
ESTIMATED NATIONAL INDUSTRIAL LAND USE BASED EMISSIONS FACTORS BY TWO-DIGIT 1967 STANDARD INDUSTRIAL CLASSIFICATION CODE

pounds of pollutant (or kWh of electricity) per floor area sq.ft.year

SIC Code	Particulates	SO_x	CO	HC	NO_x	Joule[a]
20	.64	.50	.013	.0033	.13	38
21	1.22	1.02	.025	.014	.23	48
22	.58	.54	.014	.0081	.14	68
23	.06	.04	.0014	.00084	.015	16
24	.06	.07	.0034	.0023	.045	22
25	.11	.08	.0022	.0012	.021	14
26	3.12	3.09	.069	.040	.69	85
27	.01	.02	.00068	.00048	.0095	25
28	.10	.46	.011	.0081	.16	181
29	1.06	2.78	.055	.038	.73	426
30	.51	.38	.010	.0058	.097	50
31	.17	.17	.0047	.0029	.052	18
32	4.03	2.67	.72	.038	.61	78
33	3.06	2.38	.061	.034	.57	297
34	.14	.12	.0035	.0021	.036	33
35	.22	.18	.0047	.0027	.046	31
36	.22	.20	.0053	.0032	.056	56
37	.68	.48	.013	.0068	.11	54
38	.95	.70	.018	.0095	.15	38
19 & 39	.08	.13	.0035	.0024	.044	31

NOTES: The following are assumed: 2% sulfur in coal; 10% ash in coal; 0.2% sulfur in distillate oil; 1.75% sulfur in residual oil.
1967 SIC codes are used because of data availability. The 1972 SIC code manual provides conversions between 1967 and 1972 codes.
[a]1 Kilowatt hour = 3.6 × 10⁶ joules.
SOURCE: U.S.EPA, *Growth Effects of Major Land Use Projects: Volume 2—Compilation of Land Use Based Emission Factors*, EPA-450/3-76-012-b (Research Triangle Park, North Carolina: September, 1976), p. 2-14.

velopment has been expected by state officials, it will have been incorporated into the state air quality maintenance plan. If the proposed development exceeds the size factored into the air quality maintenance plan, then supplementary calculations are necessary.

These calculations occur in five parts: (1) residential fuel combustion emissions, (2) residential motor vehicle emissions, (3) truck emissions,

EXHIBIT 7
ESTIMATED BUILDING FLOOR AREA PER EMPLOYEE
BY TWO DIGIT 1967 STANDARD INDUSTRIAL
CLASSIFICATION CODE

SIC Code	Name	Square Feet per Employee
19	Ordnance and Accessories	206
20	Food and Kindred Products	598
21	Tobacco Manufacturers	282
22	Textile Mill Products	403
23	Apparel	263
24	Lumber and wood products	796
25	Furniture and Fixtures	628
26	Paper and Allied Products	649
27	Printing, Publishing, and Allied Industries	363
28	Chemicals and Allied Products	649
29	Petroleum Refining and Related Industries	394
30	Rubber and Miscellaneous Plastics	604
31	Leather and Leather Products	345
32	Stone, Clay, and Glass Products	545
33	Primary Metal Industries	352
34	Fabricated Metal Products	476
35	Machinery	418
36	Electrical Machinery	255
37	Transportation Equipment	313
38	Instruments	253
39	Miscellaneous Manufacturing Industries	426

SOURCE: U.S.EPA, Report no. EPA-450/3-76-012-b, September, 1976, p. 3-52.

(4) commercial and institutional emissions, and (5) solid waste disposal emissions.

Residential fuel combustion emissions involve estimating the resident population or number of dwelling units, and classifying these units into types—for example, all-electric as opposed to fossil fuel (gas or oil) homes. We have prepared some coefficients for New Jersey which appear in Exhibit 12. They were derived from local electric utility company records, the AP-42 publication, and local records on climatic data. The most accurate method of determining annual fuel consumption, which is the basis for emissions, is the heat loss method. The heat loss of a dwelling unit varies with the type of materials used in construction, the surface area exposed to the environment, and inside and outside air tempera-

EXHIBIT 8
MEAN 1971 FUEL CONSUMPTION PER EMPLOYEE
BY 1967 STANDARD INDUSTRIAL CLASSIFICATION CODE

SIC Code	Distillate Oil (barrels per employee)	Residual Oil (barrels per employee)	Coal (tons per employee)	Gas (Mcf per employee)	Electricity (10^3 kWh per employee)
20	7.04	6.38	2.88	.31	22.91
21	3.00	7.49	2.58	.06	13.55
22	5.13	7.23	1.70	.11	27.52
23	.72	.16	.11	.01	4.18
24	10.38	1.64	.35	.13	17.57
25	1.33	.83	.52	.04	9.05
26	15.97	73.59	14.94	.75	55.39
27	.87	.40	.02	.04	9.15
28	17.44	22.45	.22	1.68	117.37
29	22.94	75.75	2.54	9.35	167.66
30	5.34	4.37	2.29	.14	30.17
31	2.53	2.12	.42	.03	6.24
32	19.10	14.44	16.66	1.21	42.65
33	13.66	17.93	8.09	.94	104.68
34	2.31	1.48	.51	.12	15.87
35	1.82	1.59	.70	.09	12.80
36	1.64	1.52	.41	.06	14.21
37	2.01	2.16	1.61	.09	16.95
38	1.59	3.05	1.83	.04	9.50
39 & 19	2.55	2.24	.20	.06	10.65

SOURCE: U.S. EPA Report no. EPA - 450/3-76-012-b, September, 1976, p. 3-53.

EXHIBIT 9

MEAN 1971 FUEL CONSUMPTION FOR HEAT AND POWER PER BUILDING FLOOR AREA,
BY TWO DIGIT 1967 STANDARD INDUSTRIAL CLASSIFICATION CODE

SIC Code	Distillate Oil (gals/sq.ft.)	Residual Oil (gals/sq.ft.)	Coal (lbs/sq.ft.)	Gas (cf/sq.ft.)	Electricity (kWh/sq.ft.)
20	0.49	.45	9.63	.52	38.32
21	.45	1.12	18.32	.21	48.03
22	.53	.75	8.46	.27	68.28
23	.10	.03	.85	.04	15.89
24	.55	.09	.87	.17	22.08
25	.09	.06	1.65	.07	14.41
26	1.03	4.76	46.03	1.16	85.34
27	.10	.05	.09	.10	25.20
28	1.13	1.45	.69	2.59	180.84
29	2.45	8.08	12.88	23.74	425.53
30	.37	.30	7.58	.23	49.95
31	.31	.26	2.45	.09	18.09
32	1.47	1.11	61.15	2.22	78.27
33	1.63	2.14	45.98	2.68	297.40
34	.20	.13	2.13	.26	33.34
35	.18	.16	3.33	.21	30.63
36	.28	.25	3.24	.25	55.71
37	.27	.29	10.29	.28	54.16
38	.26	.51	14.43	.16	37.56
19 & 39	.32	.28	1.18	.18	31.23

SOURCE: U.S. EPA Report no. EPA - 450/3-76-012-b, September, 1976, p. 3-54.

EXHIBIT 10
INDUSTRIAL EMISSION FACTORS

Fuel	Units	Particulates	SO_x	CO	HC	NO_x
Bituminous Coal	lb/ton	13	385	2	1	15
Natural Gas	lb/10^6 cf	10	0.6	17	3	180
Distillate Oil	lb/1,000 gal.	15	1445	4	3	60
Residual Oil	lb/1,000 gal.	23	1575	4	3	60

SOURCE: U.S.EPA, Report no. EPA - 450/3-76-012-b, September, 1976, p. 3-55.

EXHIBIT 11
AUTOMOBILE EMISSIONS, GRAMS/MILE

Pollutant	Pre-1968 cars dominate	Mixture of pre- and post- 1968 cars	Post- 1975 cars dominate	Long-range planning, assuming 1977 CAAA*
CO	80	30	15	3.4 -7.0
HC	8	3.5	1.5	0.41-1.5
NO_x	3.5	3.3	3.1	1.0 -2.0
SO_2	0.2	0.18	0.15	0.10-0.2
Particulates	0.3	0.27	0.20	0.15-0.3

*CAAA—Clean Air Act Amendments of 1977.

tures. Heat loss calculations can be rather difficult to make. Engineers and local fuel oil dealers can be of assistance in providing estimates of oil and gas based on heat loss factors.

Domestic consumption of electricity for heating of all-electric homes and for lighting, etc., will result in point source emissions at the generating station where the electricity is generated. The existence of a complicated network for electricity transmission between states and regions makes it virtually impossible to deduce where a given amount of electricity is being generated or what fuel is used to generate it. Nevertheless, Exhibit 13 presents some first-cut estimates, assuming that the electricity will be generated by fuel oil combustion.

EXHIBIT 12

Annual Emissions from Domestic Combustion of Fossil Fuel for Heating Based on New Jersey Data[j]

Unit Heat Category	Pollutant Emission (lbs/year)							
	TSP	SO$_2$[a]	SO$_3$	CO	HC	NO$_2$	Aldehydes	CH$_4$ (Methane)
Single Family								
Oil[b]	14.65-33.65	62.41-143.35	0.88-2.02	7.33-16.83	4.40-10.10	17.58-40.38	2.93-6.73	—
Gas[c]	3.71-8.53	.12-.27	—	3.91-8.97	—	15.63-35.90	—	1.56-3.59
Townhouse								
Oil[d]	6.80-13.78	28.97-58.70	0.41-0.83	3.40-6.89	2.04-4.13	8.16-16.54	1.36-2.76	—
Gas[e]	1.72-3.50	.05-.11	—	1.81-3.68	—	7.25-14.72	—	.725-1.47
Garden Apt.								
Oil[f]	6.00-12.17	25.56-51.84	0.36-0.73	3.00-6.09	1.80-3.65	7.20-14.60	1.20-2.43	—
Gas[g]	1.52-3.08	.05-.10	—	1.60-3.25	—	6.40-12.98	—	.64-1.30

EXHIBIT 12 (continued)

ANNUAL EMISSIONS FROM DOMESTIC COMBUSTION OF FOSSIL FUEL FOR HEATING BASED ON NEW JERSEY DATA[j]

Pollutant Emission (lbs/year)

Unit Heat Category	TSP	SO₂[a]	SO₃	CO	HC	NO₂	Alde-hydes	CH₄ (Meth-ane)
High Rise								
Oil[h]	8.98- 11.45	38.25- 48.78	0.54- 0.69	4.49- 5.73	2.69- 3.43	10.78- 13.74	1.80- 2.29	— —
Gas[i]	2.28- 2.90	.07- .09	— —	2.39- 3.05	— —	9.58- 12.21	— —	.96- 1.22

NOTES: [a]Assumes sulfur content of 0.3 percent.
[b]Based on No. 2 oil consumption of 1,465 to 3,365 gallons per year.
[c]Based on natural gas consumption of 195-449 10³ ft.³ per year.
[d]Based on oil consumption of between 680 and 1,378 gallons per year.
[e]Based on natural gas consumption of between 91 and 184 10³ ft.³ per year.
[f]Based on oil consumption of between 600 and 1,217 gallons per year.
[g]Based on natural gas consumption of between 80 and 162 10³ ft.³ per year.
[h]Based on oil consumption of between 898 and 1,145 gallons per year.
[i]Based on natural gas consumption of between 120 and 153 10³ ft.³ per year.
[j]This includes fuel consumed for heat and hot water in single-family, townhouse, and garden apartment units. The high consumption data for high rises includes fuel consumed for air conditioners. If the high rise being evaluated does not have an air conditioning system of this type, it is suggested that the high value be reduced by a factor of two, thus making the previous low value the high value.

Depending upon the type of dwelling unit and the source of home heating fuel, the number of estimated dwelling units is multiplied by the estimates in Exhibits 12 and 13. Note, however, that these estimates are specific to the study area and would have to be recalculated for different study regions.

Residential motor vehicle emissions require estimating the number of motor vehicles and the vehicle miles traveled and multiplying these by motor vehicle emission factors in the AP-42 publication. The AP-42 publication includes estimates for vehicles of different age and coefficients for operations at different altitudes and speeds. Our best estimates of automobile emissions are presented below (Exhibit 11). They were derived by taking various combinations of automobile mixes. If you are estimating motor vehicle emissions, be sure that you have the latest AP-42 volume. Carbon monoxide will probably be the biggest problem. A recent report by Environmental Research and Technology discusses methods of estimating the impact of land use on carbon monoxide.[97]

If the size of the development generates secondary development, it may be necessary to estimate auto emissions at *indirect sources* such as airports, railroad terminals, port facilities, stadiums, and other facilities which draw large traffic volumes.[98]

If the industrial facilities are likely to utilize many trucks for bringing in materials and delivering products, then *truck emission* calculations should be made. The case study includes such calculations. Commercial facilities and institutions (schools, offices, and others) cause emissions on-site or at generating stations for space heating and lighting, heating of water, and other uses. Finally, if the region uses *incinerators* or other *energy recovery facilities*, some additional emissions may result from a large, new development.

Next, we recommend the following studies for long-range emissions planning. The U.S.EPA *Guidelines for Air Quality Maintenance Planning and Analysis, Allocating Projected Emissions to Sub-County Areas* is available from the agency.[99] A second publication, the Consroe study, compares four emissions projection methodologies (the regional emissions projection system, the plan revision management system, the attainment study, and the air quality maintenance plan) for the St. Louis region and three other reports dealing with the interface of land use and air pollution.[100] Finally, the previously mentioned EPA land use based emission factors study reports national emission factors for the following nonindustrial land uses: single-family residential; mobile home; low-rise and high-

EXHIBIT 13
ANNUAL EMISSIONS AT POWER PLANT RESULTING FROM
ELECTRICAL CONSUMPTION OF ONE RESIDENTIAL
CUSTOMER, LBS./YEAR
BASED ON NEW JERSEY DATA

| | Customer Type | | | |
| | All Electric | | | Avg. |
Pollutant	Single Family[b]	Condo-minium[c]	Apart-ment[d]	Customer for Lighting, etc.[e]
Particulates	12.70	10.60	9.30	5.30
SO$_2$[a]	74.80	62.70	54.60	31.40
SO$_3$	0.95	0.79	0.69	0.40
CO	4.80	4.00	3.80	2.00
HC	3.20	2.70	2.30	1.30
NO$_2$	166.70	139.70	121.70	70.10
Aldehydes	1.60	1.30	1.20	0.67

NOTES: [a]No. 6 fuel oil.
[b]Assumes 1,588 gallons per year burned at generating station.
[c]1,330.5 gal./yr.
[d]1,158.8 gal./yr.
[e]667.6 gal./yr.

rise multifamily; retail, warehouse, wholesaling establishments; office buildings; hospitals; cultural, church, and school buildings.[101] Note once again, however, that the U.S.EPA report contains nationally based figures.

In conclusion, while they reside in many different volumes, the U.S.EPA has developed methods and coefficients that will allow rough estimates of the likely emissions resulting from industrial and related commercial, institutional, and residential developments.

AMBIENT AIR QUALITY MONITORING

There are more than 6,000 air monitoring stations in the United States.[102] Most of these stations are operated by state and local agencies. They transmit their data quarterly to the U.S.EPA National Aerometric Data Bank at Research Triangle Park, North Carolina. The data are analyzed and summary reports are prepared.

Exhibit 14 reports the number of monitoring stations by pollutant.

Total suspended particulates (TSP) are measured extensively by high-volume samplers. While suspended particulates are monitored more than any gaseous pollutant, the TSP parameter falls short of providing desired information about the constituents of the particulates. More information about aerosols and carcinogenic agents is important.

Sulfur dioxide is also extensively measured. Some monitoring of carbon monoxide and oxidants occurs. The monitoring of carbon monoxide, a local automobile related problem, has received a good deal of attention.[103] Oxidants, on the other hand, are an inter-regional problem and accordingly require special attention if the most informative urban, suburban, and rural monitoring sites are to be selected.

There has been very little sampling of hydrocarbons and nitrogen oxides. Most of the sampling of these parameters is associated with their relationship to oxidants.

As in the case of the emissions data, some of the ambient data are of dubious quality. EPA defines *valid* data from a particulates monitoring station as data which "consists of at least 75 percent of all scheduled hourly or 24-hour samples during each of a year's four calendar quarters. Minimal data from a monitoring station must consist of at least three 24-hour samples or 400 hourly values in a given year."[104] With respect to the gaseous parameters, many of the data have been collected with unacceptable methods and without adequate calibration of instruments or measured without proper lab procedures.

In recent years a good deal of attention has been given to upgrading state programs. The state of New Jersey's program is typical. The state has sixty high-volume particulate sampling sites. Most of these are found in densely developed areas. Twenty-two other stations continuously record carbon monoxide and SO_2 at the averaging times required by the ambient standards. The same twenty-two stations also monitor smoke-shade, which is an indicator of particulates. Eleven stations record ozone; five record nitrogen dioxide; four monitor nonmethane hydrocarbons, photochemical oxidants, nitrogen oxides, nitric oxides, and aldehydes; and three record carbon dioxide. Some of the particulate data extend back to the mid-1950s. Most of the data, however, were not recorded until the 1970s.

Overall, the state of New Jersey monitors the required parameters and reports the data. However, with the exception of particulates, there are few sites and the data do not go back very far. Rural areas have little or no data. Furthermore, other parameters are monitored which are not tied to a standard.

EXHIBIT 14
MONITORING STATIONS WHICH REPORTED AT LEAST
MINIMAL DATA, 1970-74

Parameter	1970	1974
Suspended Particulates	1,283	3,683
Sulfur Dioxide	403	2,145
Carbon Monoxide	73	316
Oxidants	51	330

SOURCE: CEQ, *Sixth Annual Report of the Council on Environmental Quality* (Washington, D.C.: U.S.G.P.O., 1975), p. 308.

On the local and site-specific scales, the availability of ambient data will probably depend upon the nature of the community. Communities which suffer from air quality and odor problems are likely to have monitoring sites near major stationary and mobile sources. In addition to federal, state, and county sources, the following are possible data sources:

1. Air pollution episode data in local boards of health
2. National resource inventory data from local environmental commissions
3. Local environmental clubs such as the Sierra Club or high school or college clubs
4. Environmental impact statements prepared for industrial commissions or industries wanting to locate in the area
5. Environmental impact statements prepared for planning boards
6. Private consulting firms' studies and EISs
7. Inspection reports fron environmental departments in localities

Site-Specific Monitoring. If reliable monitoring data are available, they should be used. If, however, the only monitoring data are old and/or are for a site that has a very different land use pattern from your project site, then some on-site monitoring will be required.

To determine if the data at an air monitoring station are a satisfactory substitute for on-site monitoring, one must consider the nature of the pollutant(s), meteorology, and local land use patterns. With respect to emitted and regulated pollutants, suspended particulates are closest to a regional pollutant, carbon monoxide is the most localized pollutant. In order to use monitoring station data for carbon monoxide, one has to make a convincing argument that traffic flows and land use at the monitoring station and project sites are quite similar. To a lesser extent, the same generalization is true of the other gaseous pollutants.

An examination of suspended particulate data frequently suggests less variation among monitoring stations. Accordingly, assuming that the project site does not differ greatly from the monitoring station site(s) in pollutant sources, one should be able to estimate data at the project site from monitoring station data. A literature search was conducted to discover any guidelines and mathematical formulas which have been developed to estimate ambient TSP levels using nearby monitoring stations when no data are available at the site. During conversations in February, 1976, U.S.EPA officials at Research Triangle Park informed us that a formula was being tested for suspended particulates. The formula divides the concentration at each monitoring site by the square of the distance from the monitor to the location being estimated, sums the results, and then divides this sum by the sum of one over the square of the same distances.

For example, assume that four surrounding monitors are selected. We label them A, B,C, and D. The distance from monitor to site is measured on a map and labeled 1,2,3, and 4 to correspond to each monitor. The formula is as follows:

$$C_s = \frac{\dfrac{C_A}{d_1{}^2} + \dfrac{C_B}{d_2{}^2} + \dfrac{C_C}{d_3{}^2} + \dfrac{C_D}{d_4{}^2}}{\dfrac{1}{d_1{}^2} + \dfrac{1}{d_2{}^2} + \dfrac{1}{d_3{}^2} + \dfrac{1}{d_4{}^2}}$$

Where: C_s = Unknown TSP concentration at the site.

C_A = TSP concentration at monitor A.
C_B = TSP concentration at monitor B.
C_C = TSP concentration at monitor C.
C_D = TSP concentration at monitor D.
d_1 = Distance in miles from monitor A to the site.
d_2 = Distance in miles from monitor B to the site.
d_3 = Distance in miles from monitor C to the site.
d_4 = Distance in miles from monitor D to the site.

Presented graphically the formula uses data as follows:

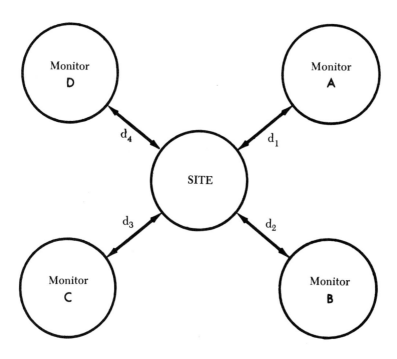

As an illustration, data from four high-volume air samplers in New Jersey were selected. These were at Perth Amboy, Sayreville, South Amboy, and Metuchen. Each monitor is 3.5 miles from the center of the resource recovery park site used as an example in the noise chapter. Using the annual geometric means (in micrograms per cubic meter) as the concentrations for 1975, the calculations are as follows:

Monitor A= Perth Amboy—annual geometric mean= 61.6
Monitor B= Sayreville—annual geometric mean= 57.1
Monitor C= South Amboy—annual geometric mean= 59.3
Monitor D= Metuchen—annual geometric mean= 50.6

(Geometric means are in the form of micrograms per cubic meter.)

$$C_s = \cfrac{\dfrac{61.6}{3.5^2} + \dfrac{57.1}{3.5^2} + \dfrac{59.3}{3.5^2} + \dfrac{50.6}{3.5^2}}{\dfrac{1}{3.5^2} + \dfrac{1}{3.5^2} + \dfrac{1}{3.5^2} + \dfrac{1}{3.5^2}}$$

$$\cfrac{\dfrac{61.6}{12.25} + \dfrac{57.1}{12.25} + \dfrac{59.3}{12.25} + \dfrac{50.6}{12.25}}{\dfrac{1}{12.25} + \dfrac{1}{12.25} + \dfrac{1}{12.25} + \dfrac{1}{12.25}}$$

$$= \frac{5.0286 + 4.6612 + 4.8408 + 4.1306}{0.3265}$$

$$= \frac{18.6612}{0.3265}$$

$$= 57.2$$

Is 57.2 a reasonable estimate for the project site? The four monitoring sites are located at sites that are considerably more developed than the project site. Therefore, 57.2 might be a bit high. Meteorological conditions at the site and the four monitoring stations are not radically different and the distance between the monitors and project site is not far. The estimated ambient level is not close to the 75 ug/m³ primary standard, but is close to the 60 ug/m³ secondary standard. If officials are interested solely in the primary suspended particulate standard, then 57.2 is probably a satisfactory working estimate. If however, 60 ug/m³ is the target standard of interest, then some monitoring will have to be done.

If you can demonstrate that the formula closely predicts other nearby monitoring stations, a better case can be made for this and other estimating procedures which are reviewed in the U.S.EPA *Air Quality Mainte-*

nance Planning and Analysis documents. For example, in our study region we estimated total suspended particulates at two monitoring stations with data from eight monitoring stations with similar meteorological conditions. In one case, the actual TSP concentration was 50.6 ug/m³, the estimated concentration for that site based on four stations which are between 4.5 and 8.0 miles from the site was 55.5 ug/m³. A second monitoring station with an actual annual average of 61.6 ug/m³ was estimated as 57.1 using data from three stations located between 2.5 and 4.5 miles away. In both cases, the differences could be intuitively related to land use differences. When we attempted to apply the formula with monitoring station data taken from sites greater than 15 miles away from the project site, the results were clearly inappropriate. Overall, the total suspended particulates estimation formula is probably a reasonable model for project sites which are close to and have land use and meteorological conditions similar to one or more monitoring stations.

If available monitoring data are inapplicable to the site of interest, then monitoring will be necessary. Air quality monitoring is more complicated than water quality monitoring. The equivalent of the simple, inexpensive water quality sampling kit does exist and is used for testing air quality in mines. However, ambient air quality monitoring requires expensive equipment and a high degree of expertise.

Particulates are sampled with three procedures. A dustfall jar is used to measure the accumulation of solids over a thirty-day period. The dustfall test is not a recognized national particulate measure. Cities like St. Louis, Philadelphia, and Chicago have dustfall standards which predate today's modern sampling equipment.

High-volume samplers, which work like a vacuum cleaner, are used to meet the monitoring requirement for particulates. Tape samplers may be used for particulate sampling. They catch particles on a sticky tape, and the particles are pulled through an instrument which estimates the amount of particulate pollution by analyzing light transmissibility.

Gases are sampled by dissolving or chemically trapping the gas (adsorption or absorption). Grab sampling is possible, but not very reliable. Overall, air quality monitoring requires professional expertise.

The first important monitoring question is choosing the air quality parameters (e.g., CO, SO₂, etc.) to sample. The second question is the length of the monitoring period. After discussions with U.S.EPA personnel we suggest that a monitoring period of twelve days to a year is expected. Ninety days seems to be an acceptable number for many projects. The shorter period is appropriate when a nearby monitoring station with similar land use, meteorological, and terrain characteristics is available. A ninety-day period is preferred. Be sure, however, to examine volume 11 of the *Guidelines for Air Quality Maintenance Planning and Analysis* which deals with air quality monitoring and data analysis.[105] And if you must monitor, be sure that the following three conditions are satisfied: (1) the instrument must be recognized as reliable by air pollution officials; (2) the instrument has been properly calibrated; and (3) the individual doing the monitoring is qualified by training and experience.

The Impact of Emissions on Air Quality

Once industrial processes have produced pollutants which the control devices have not captured, the impact of the pollutants is determined by their dispersal in the atmosphere and subsequent interaction with an exposed population. This section reviews the diffusion of air pollutants.

THE BASIC PROCESSES

The atmosphere is divided into different layers according to height. The troposphere (lower ten kilometers) is the portion of the atmosphere where most pollutants are transported. Atmospheric winds in this lower layer move pollutants in vertical and horizontal directions.

The change in air temperature with changes in atmospheric pressure and hence altitude (known as the adiabatic lapse rate) is a key factor in the transport of air pollutants. Normally, air temperature decreases 5.4°F for every thousand feet in altitude.

When cooler air is above warmer air, the atmosphere is unstable and air pollutants are dispersed. When colder (heavier) air becomes trapped beneath lighter (warmer) air, serious air quality problems may result from this temperature inversion. The air contaminants are trapped and concentrated in the heavy, cold layer beneath the warm air.

Inversions may be classified. Radiation inversions occur at night. The earth's surface is cooled by loss of long-wave radiation. The result is that the air near the ground is cooler than the air above. Air pollutants are trapped in the cool ground layer. Cool fog layers in valleys observed during the morning are visible evidence of radiation inversion.

A subsidence inversion is caused by the sinking of air aloft. As the air mass descends, it becomes compressed and increases in temperature, resulting in a lower layer of cold air being trapped beneath warm upper air. The resulting stability traps pollutants.

Terrain influences the movement of air masses and hence pollutant transport. Wind flows along the axis of valleys due to the presence of cooler air along the slopes flowing downward into the valley during the evening, and warmer air flowing up cooler slopes during the daytime. Shorelines are another geophysical formation which can alter weather. The hot land during the daytime causes the cool water breeze to blow inward. In the evening, the cool land breeze flows outward toward the warmer ocean. These micrometeorological phenomena are extremely significant and should be considered in any air pollution investigation. The three most commonly mentioned local micrometeorological circulation phenomena occur adjacent to lake and sea shores, mountains and valleys, and urban and suburban places.

The frequency and amount of precipitation also affects the pollution concentration. Precipitation acts like a scrubber, removing particles by attracting them on contact.

THE WIND ROSE

Wind speed determines the travel time of a pollutant from its source to a defined receptor and accounts directly for the amount of pollutant diffusion in the windward direction. Therefore, the concentration of any pollutant at any given receptor is inversely proportional to the wind speed. Wind direction will determine in what direction a pollutant will travel and what receptors will be affected at a given time. Wind direction is normally defined by a wind rose, a graphical display of the distribution of wind direction experience at a given location during a defined time period.

The wind rose is a set of wind statistics which describes frequency, direction, force, and speed. The information is depicted graphically in a series of circles representing proportions marked off in quadrants which indicate direction. Wind frequency is added to the graphical wind rose by varying the length of the segments which represent the 16 wind directions: N, NNE, NE, ENE, E, ESE, SE, SSE, S, SSW, SW, WSW, W, WNW, NW, and NNW. The wind rose has five wind stability classes.

The wind rose is imprecise in describing a specific point in a study region because the data used in it are collected at one location in the region and not at each individual location. The data are often a seasonal or a yearly average and are therefore not accurate in accounting for any point in time as required in an ideal representation of atmospheric diffusion. A final limitation of the wind rose is that the wind is only measured in the horizontal plane and is assumed to be identical at any height above the earth's surface.

Local meteorological data are available from a variety of sources. Published summaries and unpublished information about inversion frequencies and general weather conditions are developed by the United States

Weather Service. Local weather bureau officials or the national weather records center can be contacted. Military and commercial interests also collect meteorological data which may be made available.

Special studies can be an excellent source of data. For example, military installations, nuclear electric generating facilities, and sometimes industries will have studies of not only local meteorology, but in addition detailed data on receptor characteristics. In the case of the nuclear electricity generating facility, for example, they will have detailed information about permanent populations out to fifty miles from the reactor site, transient population (e.g., work force, seasonal, schools, motels) ten miles from the site, and special animal and vegetation studies. These data are summarized in regions which are a part of a circular area within a fifty-mile radius centered on the reactor buildings.

MATHEMATICAL MODELS OF POLLUTANT DIFFUSION

No one type of mathematical equation can describe the dynamic motion of the atmosphere and the dispersal of pollutants. One must be satisfied, in most applications, to use average wind rose data and average dispersion distributions. Such simplifications do not necessarily represent actual atmospheric conditions but do make the handling of dispersion information possible in a number of routine applications.

Air pollution models may be divided into three general categories: naive models, environmental control models, and economically based control strategy models. Naive models predict future pollutant concentrations by extrapolating a historical trend or by fitting a regression curve to a historical trend. The weakness of these methods is that they do not take into account either cause-effect relationships or changes in component variables.

Environmental control models attempt to mathematically simulate the cause-effect relationships among emitters and the atmosphere. Outputs from environmental models include pollution concentrations over a given area; the amount of time it will take a pollutant to reach a given geographic point or to disperse; the amount of pollution to be reduced in order to meet ambient air quality standards; future pollution concentrations; and pollution resulting from different levels of industrial development, residential development, and auto ownership.

Environmental control models may use proportional, diffusion, or dispersion techniques. Proportional models are fairly simple. They assume a linear relationship between the causes and effects of pollution. For instance, if one knows how much carbon monoxide is emitted in the county as a whole, then the proportion of that pollutant which will be found in the study area is considered to be equivalent to the proportion of the county's autos which are in the study area. Or the future percentage increase of particulates is the same as the future estimated percentage increase of people.

A simple type of proportional model is the box model. The box model assumes that atmospheric conditions remain constant. Therefore the pollutant covers the area uniformly. The box model can be used for point, line, or area sources. Although proportional models assume a stable atmosphere, it is possible to modify them with weighting techniques which will allow the user to assign individual percentages of the resulting pollutant concentrations to different segments of the study area.

Proportional models can be used to key pollution estimates to almost any measurable or causative variable. For instance, one can derive pollution factors for grams per acre, grams per parking space, grams per capita, grams per 1,000 linear feet of floor space, grams per registered automobile population increases, and dwelling unit increases. Overall, the proportional models are a starting point for analysis.

Diffusion models are much more complex in their simulation of cause-effect relationships. They do not assume a constant relationship among the variables, except for short averaging times, in which they assume that the atmospheric variables which they are using will not change. They may be finite difference models which can take into account the study area's specific topography, photochemical reactions, eddy diffusion, etc. Finite difference models are used over large areas which can be gridded and for which emissions for each cell can be determined.

The most commonly used and simplest diffusion model is the Gaussian plume model, which is used for stack emissions and line sources. Background levels of pollution reflecting area sources must be added in separately. Basically, the Gaussian model approach assumes that the stack plume will move in the direction of the wind, and will spread at right angles to this path according to a Gaussian probability distribution. However, some modelers have used gamma or poisson distributions rather than Gaussian ones.

Another type of environmental model is the atmospheric dispersion model.[106] It assumes that pollutants move through the atmosphere according to eddy motions, rather than molecular diffusion. These relationships are difficult to represent mathematically because of the variability of eddy size and velocities.[107] Dispersion models simulate pollution only from point and line sources. Background concentrations must be added exogenously.

Mathematical simulation and programming models may be used to generate economic efficiency solutions to a pollution problem. For example, they can help determine which control technique is best, given available funding or ambient standards. An illustration of this is the simulation model used by Smith which examined the multimedia (water, air, land) effects of pollution control. Given ambient air and water quality standards, and available sanitary landfill acreages, the Smith model estimated the levels to which air and water discharges would have to be reduced in order to achieve ambient standards, and the necessary increases in landfill areas needed to deal with solid waste deposits.[108]   Other models of this type, focusing on air pollution, are available.[109]

The most ambitious of these combines atmospheric diffusion models, mathematical programming, and emission allocation alternatives.[110] Using Baltimore and Louisville as case studies the EPA has tested the impact of alternative land use patterns on emissions and, in turn, air quality. Ultimately, the goal is to prepare emission quota strategies for political units. The strategies would consist of lids on the total amount of emissions from a specific geographical area. The diffusion models operationalize the implication of winds and terrain on the diffusion of emissions. The mathematical programming models search for the most rewarding land use patterns from an economic perspective, while not permitting undesirable air quality degradation.

With the exception of the box model all of the mathematical diffusion models require a good deal of specialized mathematical knowledge and experience to use effectively. Therefore, we will confine more detailed presentation to the emission density approach, the box model and MARTIK—a readily available diffusion model. References have been provided for those who desire additional contact with this complex literature.[111] The mathematical sections may be skipped.

Emissions Density Approach. The simplest means of relating air quality and land use relies on air emissions information. Air quality models are not used or are used to provide the emissions density constraints. The emissions density approach begins with the local planner being informed by a Federal and/or state agency that emissions in the area are at a specific level and are permitted by nondegradation or other regulations, or by mutual agreement to reach another specific level.

For illustrative purposes, let us assume that a rural, resort county of 500 square miles had particulate emissions of 2,500 tons in 1978. The emissions density is 5 tons per square mile. After conversing with Federal, state and local officials, it has been decided that no more than a 20 percent increase in particulate emissions to 6 tons per square mile should be permitted.

The rural county has an existing electricity generating station. Can a proposed electric arc continuous casting steel mill move to the county without contributing to the violation of the emissions density constraint for particulates?

Four sources of emissions will be considered: industrial processing, electricity generation, and new employee home and automobile-related emissions. The plant is proposed to produce 150,000 tons of output per year. Previously, we found that the best control technology would limit particulate emissions to 0.36 pounds per ton of output. Assuming the adoption of this best technology, the emissions would be 27 tons of particulates [(150,000) (0.36)/2,000]. Without controls, the emissions would be almost 100 times greater!

Electricity will be used at the facility for a variety of purposes. The plant will have about 500 employees. From Exhibit 7 we learn that the size of the facility may be estimated by multiplying the number of employees by 352. The calculation yields 176,000 square feet as the size of the plant. From Exhibit 6 we see that the annual average particulate emission per square foot of floor area is 3.06 pounds. The emissions are estimated to be 269 tons [176,000 × 3.06)/2000]. While we will settle for this estimate for the illustration, in reality electric arc mills are so different from other steel mills that we doubt the above coefficients should be used for all but general planning at the 2-digit SIC code level. Indeed, the industrial coefficients presented earlier in the chapter will always need careful verification when a specific facility is in question.

The third and fourth sources of particulates are due to population migration into the county. We begin with the assumption that all of the 250 production workers and 50 of the 250 white collar workers will move into the county. In addition, using economic multiplier analysis, it is estimated that each of the 500 new jobs will create 5 additional jobs. But only 1,000 of the 2,500 new indirect and induced jobs will require migration into the county. Summarizing, 1,300 of the 3,000 new jobs will be filled by migrants to the county.

The 1,700 local people might change their driving and housing patterns in response to their new jobs. But to simplify the illustration, their changes will be ignored.

The housing and automobile impacts will be focused on the new people. First, an initial assumption is made that half of the 1,300 new workers will live in garden apartments and half in single-family homes, all oil-heated. Family size is estimated at 2.0 persons. From Exhibit 12 we derive the relevant oil home heating coefficients: about 25 pounds for single-family and and 9 pounds for garden apartments. The 1,300 jobs for the migrants will generate about 11 tons of particulates [(650 × 9/2000) + (650 × 25/2000) = 11].

Finally, the automobile emissions of the new migrants are estimated. Vehicle miles traveled are calculated from the following formula:

$$\left(\begin{array}{c} \text{Number of} \\ \text{persons} \end{array} \right) \left(\begin{array}{c} \text{Total passenger} \\ \text{miles per person} \\ \text{per year} \end{array} \right) \left(\begin{array}{c} \text{\% of} \\ \text{passenger miles} \\ \text{by motor vehicle} \end{array} \right)$$

$$\left(\begin{array}{c} \text{number of} \\ \text{passengers} \\ \text{per trip} \end{array} \right) = \left(\begin{array}{c} \text{Vehicle miles} \\ \text{per year} \end{array} \right)$$

Assuming a mean family size of 2 persons, an average of 10,000 miles per person in a rural county, 95 percent of travel by automobile, and 1.72 persons per vehicle trip, the 1,300 new jobs for in-migrants should generate 14.4 million vehicle miles per year, [(2,600)(10,000)(.95)(1/1.72) = 14,360,465]. Assuming particulate emissions of 0.20 grams per vehicle mile (Exhibit 11), the 1,300 new jobs for migrants should cause about 3 tons per year of automobile particulate emissions [(14,360,465)(0.2)/ (914,000 grams per ton) = 3.14].

Summarizing, the proposed new iron and steel plant should raise particulate emissions about 310 tons per year. If particulate emissions in the county remained the same, the emissions density would rise from 5 to 5.62 tons per square mile, a figure approaching the 6 ton density constraint.

In the event that the 6 ton limit was reached, the limit could be pushed back, the steel plant proposal might be rejected, or other emitters might reduce their emissions to allow the steel plant to locate in the county.

The reader should note that the above example has been deliberately simplified. An actual case would consider all pollutants, not just particulates. Officials might choose to focus on the hazardous waste emissions from steel plants in addition to the standard parameters. And as noted above, locally-derived indicators of automobile use, family size, steel plant emissions, and of other factors impacting on emissions should be gathered for the calculations.

The Box Model. The box model is among the least sophisticated of the available models and it is extremely conservative. It is the easiest to use because hand calculations are required. It is especially good for teaching relationships between meteorology, nondegradation, and land use. The box model presented here is not useful for practical planning because it is extremely conservative, had errors in its initial formulation, and in general has been bypassed by newer models.

Allowable pollutant concentration increases are transformed into allow-able increases in pollutant emissions through application of the box model. Existing air quality data in the form of annual mean concentrations of the individual pollutants are used to define the tolerance of an area toward receiving additional emissions. The difference between potential pollutant concentrations (equivalent annual arithmetic mean air quality standards in ug/m^3 and existing pollutant concentrations is compared with anticipated decreased in pollutant concentrations resulting from either imposed emission controls or land use relocation as specified by state pollution control agencies.

The model treats the planning area as one large continuously emitting ground level source having a uniform average emission rate. Spatial varia-tion in terrain and emissions within the area are not accounted for. Model results are expressed as an annual mean allowable increase in emission rates (grams/sec.)

$$E = (C \bullet A)/N$$

where: E is the mean allowable increase in emission rate (ug/sec);

C is the annual mean allowable increase in pollutant concentration (ug/meter^3);

N is the annual mean normalized concentration (sec./meter);

A is the study area of the planning region (meter^2).

A is given by the user, N is obtained from the following formula derived from a graph prepared by Epstein.[112]

$$N = 0.28L + 8 \tag{2}$$

where N is the normalized concentration (sec./m) and L is the longest straight line distance in kilometers through the area. The assumption be-hind equation (2) is that the longer the longest straight line distance rela-tive to the area of the zone, the longer the time period for the dispersion of pollutants from the area. This equation is an *average worst case* as-sumption because the longest axis of a region may not be the axis over which winds flow most of the time. Equation (2) represents average condi-tions. This relationship can be calibrated to the specific meteorological conditions of a geographical region in the United States.[113] The equation should be restricted to values of L of 10 km (6 miles) or more and an area of 64.75 kilometers (25 miles) or more.

The value of C, annual mean allowable increase in pollutants (ug/m^3), is developed by the user.

The box model will be illustrated for TSP, NO$_x$, and SO$_2$ with hypo-thetical data.

1. Pollutant	Ambient Annual Average Concentration in Planning area (ug/m^3)
TSP	70.0
NO$_x$	50.0
SO$_2$	20.0

Step one is derived from monitoring data.

2. Pollutant	Equivalent Annual Arithmetic Mean Air Quality Standards (ug/m^3)
TSP	75.0
NO$_x$	100.0
SO$_2$	80.0

Step two represents primary air quality standards.

3. Initial allowable increases in pollutant concentrations are determined by subtracting the annual average concentrations of the planning area from the equivalent annual average standards.

Pollutant		Initial Allowable Increases (ug/m^3)
TSP	75.0-70.0	5
NO$_x$	100.0-50.0	50
SO$_2$	80.0-20.0	60

4. From the state pollution control agency, it has been learned that existing air quality levels are anticipated to change by 1990 by the following amounts, due to a uniformly applied strategy of emission controls across the state:

Pollutant	Anticipated Decrease in Pollutant Concentration (ug/m$_3$)
TSP	10.0
NO$_x$	25.0
SO$_2$	10.0

Choices at this point in plan design with respect to air quality are:

a) Add the anticipated decreases to the initial allowable increases, which would be designing up to the tolerance of the standards.

$$\text{TSP: } 5 + 10 = 15$$
$$\text{NO}_x\text{: } 50 + 25 = 75$$
$$\text{SO}_2\text{: } 60 + 10 = 70$$

b) Adopt a nondegradation strategy by using the anticipated decreases in concentration as allowable increases: 10 for TSP; 25 for NO_x; and 10 for SO^2.

c) Use the initial allowable increases (5, 50, 60 ug/m^3). Box model analysis is required to translate these allowable concentration increases to corresponding increases in pollutant emissions. We will illustrate the procedure with the 5, 50, and 60 ug/m^2 initial allowable increases.

5. The hypothetical study area has a longest straight line distance of 40 km. Applying this number to equation (2), it is found that the annual average normalized concentration is 19.2 sec/meter. The study area of the planning region is 1,000 km^2. Therefore:

E = (C • A)/N
E = annual mean allowable increase in emission rate (ug/sec);
C = 5,50,60 ug/m^3, annual mean allowable increase (for each pollutant) in pollutant concentration;
N = 19.2 sec/meter from equation (2);
A = 1,000 km^2

Pollutant	Annual Average Allowable Emissions Rate Increase (ug/sec)
TSP: (5.0) × (1,000)/19.2	260
NO_x: (50.0) × (1,000)/19.2	2604
SO_2: (60.0) × (1,000)/19.2	3125

6. To determine total annual increases, multiply by the number of seconds in the year (3.1536 × 10^7 sec/year).

Pollutant	Annual Average Allowable Increase in Emissions (ug) or (g)		
TSP: 2.60 × 31,536,000	8,199,360,000	=	8,199
NO_x: 26.04 × 31,536,000	82,120,000,000	=	82,120
SO_2: 31.25 × 31,536,000	98,550,000,000	=	98,550

7. Next, we allocate portions of the allowable increase to additional transportation activities which are based on national data. For NO_x, 50 percent of the allowable increase is reserved for industry; for SO_2, 0 percent; for CO, 90 percent; for HC, 60 percent; and for TSP, 5 percent.[114] These proportions may be used in the absence of local data.

Pollutant	Annual Average Allowable Increase in Emissions Reserved for Trans.(g)
TSP: (8199) × (0.05)	0.410
NO$_x$: (82120) × (0.5)	41.060
SO$_2$: (98550) × (0.0)	0.000

8. Subtracting these values from the total allowable emissions yields annual average allowable industrial emissions for TSP, NO$_x$, and SO$_2$.

Pollutant	Annual Average Allowable Increase in Industrial Emissions (g)
TSP: (8199) − (410)	7789
NO$_x$: (82120) − (41060)	41060
SO$_2$: (98550) − (00)	98550

Now, one must select a group of industries, commercial, and other activities that do not exceed the annual average allowable increase limits left to stationary sources.

An alternative approach is to test the impact of specific alternative developments. The analyst translates proposed land uses into industrial emissions, electric generating facility emissions, and mobile source emissions. For example, if a petrochemical complex is planned for the region, the initial step involves estimating the emissions from the refinery and related chemical facilities. Second, an employment multiplier is calculated to estimate the number of new jobs created by the complex. These service activities will require additions to electrical generating capacity and produce new sources of truck and automobile emissions. Finally, if new homes are constructed, the residents will produce emissions from generating stations and from their homes for space heating; lighting and other housing related energy needs; and from transportation sources. These new emissions and resultant impacts are compared to estimates derived from continuing past trends in air quality into the future or applying emissions data and the box model to alternative development plans derived from community, county, and state master plans.

The box model is most useful for studying regional environmental planning. Since the box model contains a good deal of temporal and spatial averaging, the air sheds should be relatively large. A minimum size of twenty-five square miles is suggested. And overall we caution the reader again that the box model is conservative and therefore, in our experience when applied in the form above, tends to severely restrict new development. In addition it is relatively archaic in comparison to other models, many of which have been referenced in this section. While we do not recommend its use, the box model, like the DO model presented in the water chapter, is a useful learning device.

The MARTIK Model. MARTIK, TASSIM, APRAC, and other diffusion models stand in strong contrast to the simple box model. We will only discuss MARTIK because it is the one we know best. The MARTIK Model (Martin-Tikvart diffusion modeling program) is an air pollution diffusion model based on a Gaussian distribution where source and meteorological data are manipulated to produce output relative to specified receptor points.[115] Five pollutants may be considered in a single calculation (CO, SO_x, NO_x, HC and particulates) and single wind cases (for example, worst wind conditions) may be calculated in addition to or instead of long-term meteorological averages.

In the MARTIK model sources may be point, line, or area. A point source refers to a steady emission rate in grams per second from one single point; a line source is described as a straight line segment at constant height with an emission rate being given in mean density (grams per meter square/second); and an area source is designated as a rectangular region with axes oriented in east-west and north-south arrangements at constant height with emissions for the sources distributed as a mean density (grams per meter squared/second). Up to one hundred receptor points may be specified, and the horizontal coordinates and height above the reference plane are given for each. In addition, a background and calibration scale factor may be supplied for each receptor for each of the pollutants to be considered. The meteorological data used in the MARTIK program consist of a set of relative frequencies for 480 meteorological conditions, representing five stability classes, sixteen wind directions, and six wind-speed classes. In addition, information regarding the ambient temperature, ambient pressure, and mixing-layer depth are to be specified.

Once source, receptor, and meteorological data have been input, calculation can proceed. The concentration at any receptor point is the arithmetic sum of the concentrations due to all industrial sources. The contribution of each source is summed for all meteorological conditions weighted by the relative probability of occurrence. Only those conditions corresponding to nonzero probabilities and sources upwind of receptor points are considered. The transfer function describing the relationship between emission at the source point and concentration at the receptor point is the Gifford-Pasquill plume equation, in which the vertical distribution of concentration close to each source-point is represented as a Gaussian function. The following is a diagrammatic representation of how a box and Gaussian plume model represent a discharge. The Gaussian model is clearly preferable for point sources and a more realistic portrayal of line and area sources.

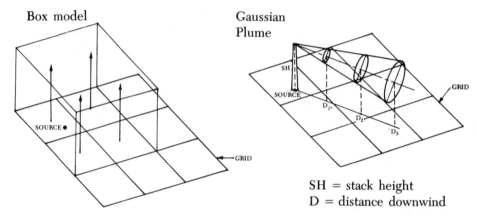

SH = stack height
D = distance downwind

In the determination of the vertical distribution, the effective height of release of the source effluent is used instead of the actual physical stack height. These distribution calculations have a standard deviation which is taken to be a stability-dependent power-law function of the downward distance.

One very convenient feature of the MARTIK model system is that grid data may be used for input but sources and receptors are located in terms of their own geometry, making changes of units and scale possible without the need to alter collected data. The MARTIK program itself is in a general FORTRAN IV name list parameters package, allowing the number, names, and units of pollutants chosen for a study to be entered as data into the program. The program is therefore not restricted to a particular emissions inventory format. The computation parameters which determine the trade-off between accuracy and running time may be specified or default values may be used instead. The program output from MARTIK is in the form of computed total concentrations at each receptor point, presented in tabluar form. The output can include isopleths and can be as small as ½ square mile.

The design philosophy of the MARTIK program centers around developing a method by which changes in data and model structure can be easily performed without the need to redesign the entire system. Achieving this will allow deck setup procedures to be simple and similar for all subprograms and permit straightforward system modifications without the necessity of modifying the programs themselves. A similar data checking procedure setup at the data input phase of each subprogram will help filter out and eliminate any invalid inputs and allow for greater program control and accuracy.

The major pitfalls of MARTIK include the fact that the model fails to account for photochemical reactions and deposition of particles on the ground surface by gravity, both of which are basic parameters in an ideal air pollution model. The only meteorological conditions accounted for and modeled are those assumed to occur on a flat surface with no irregularities. Therefore, the model does not possess the ability to deal with micrometeorological conditions created by valleys, shorelines, and other special surfaces. Another limiting factor deals with extrapolations of wind rose data from one application to another. This inbreeds additional inconsistencies which can adversely affect the accuracy of the model. A third limitation inborn in the MARTIK mathematical formulation is its inability to directly account for decay or transformation of reactive substances in the atmosphere, a basic prerequisite defined in the ideal air pollution model. Two other important disadvantages of MARTIK are high cost to use and initial validation results that were relatively poor.

In the senior author's experience, air dispersion models, such as MARTIK, have not gained as wide acceptance as their water quality counterparts. One reason is that far more is known about water as a receiving medium than is known about air. Second, because water flows in a channel, monitoring sites for water quality studies are selected and justified far more easily than sites for air quality studies.

Channelization of water also means that wind speed and temperature stratification (except in lakes) are not important in water studies. Fourth, water quality standards are only for one or, at the most, two averaging periods. Air quality standards usually require two or more averaging times.

The great complexity of air quality modeling leads us to suggest that consultants be asked the following questions: Is air quality modeling in general, and the model to be used in particular, the most cost-effective means of determining the impact of industrial emitters? Is the model the best available model? If not, why not? If it is not the best available model, is it nevertheless accepted and used by the scientific community? Are the meteorological data and air quality data sets the best available data sets? Does the height at which the meteorological data set was taken approximate the stack height of the proposed facility? Are all the appropriate air quality parameters being modeled? If not, why not? Has terrain been factored into the model? Have coefficients in the model been changed to reflect local conditions? Have all dispersion conditions which would lead the plume over populated areas been modeled? If not, why not?

If you do not receive satisfactory answers to all of the above questions, then EPA or state officials or a court of law may invalidate the impact assessment and call for reevaluation which will be expensive from the financial and credibility perspectives.

Summary and Additional Resources

The impact of industrial emissions on air quality is related to the quantity and quality of pollutants produced by industrial processes, the legal requirement for control equipment, the diffusion of the pollutants which depends upon terrain and atmospheric dynamics, and the location of the receptors. Air pollution impact assessments have become so complex that this chapter can serve only as a general introduction to the variables and parameters. Unique local conditions, such as an already burdened atmosphere or an application from what would be a conspicuous emitter, create the need for flexible research designs and policy-making approaches. If possible, an application from a potentially major discharger ought to be reviewed with the goal of producing a response which offers a variety of alternatives. Producing such a response will require interactions among meteorologists, chemists, engineers, lawyers, politicians, among others, as well as planners.

The complexity of air resources impact studies is mirrored in the literature. At the risk of offending some excellent authors and good journals, we recommend Hesketh's *Understanding and Controlling Air Pollution*[116] and the *Journal of the Air Pollution Control Association* as general follow-ups to this chapter. With respect to industrial air quality management, the following four recently published books are important: Noll, Davis, and Duncan, *Air Pollution Control and Industrial Energy Production;* Noll and Duncan, editors, *Industrial Air Pollution Control;* Cheremisinoff and Young, *Industrial Odor Technology Assessment;* and Cook, *Survey of Modern Industrial Chemistry.*[117]

As in water resources impact analysis, the U.S.EPA and state agencies are valuable sources of information. Consulting firms, likewise, can be of great assistance in establishing the ambient environment and in air quality modeling.

NOTES

1. D.V. Bates, *A Citizen's Guide to Air Pollution* (Montreal: McGill-Queen's University Press, 1972), p.35.

2. U.S.EPA, *Report of Nationwide Survey of Photo-Chemical Smog Using the Morning Glory as an Indicator* (Springfield, Va.: NTIS, 1975).

3. American Industrial Hygiene Association (AIHA), *Air Pollution Manual, Part 1—Evaluation* (Westmont, N.J., 1972), p. 15.

4. American Chemical Society, *Chemistry in the Economy* (Washington, D.C.: American Chemical Society, 1973), pp. 127, 129, 136.

5. *Ibid.*, p. 126.

6. AIHA, Air Pollution Manual, p. 79.

7. Bates, *Citizen's Guide*, p. 40.

8. W. Strauss, *Air Pollution Control, Part 2* (New York: Wiley, 1972), p. 56.

9. *Ibid.*, p. 56.

10. AIHA *Air Pollution Manual*, p. 79.

11. *Ibid.*, p. 77.

12. Battelle Memorial Institute (for U.S.EPA), *Cost of Clean Air 1974* (Springfield, Va.: NTIS, 1974); Council on Environmental Quality, *Sixth Annual Report of the Council on Environmental Quality* (Washington, D.C.: U.S.G.P.O., 1975); T.E. Waddell (for U.S.EPA), *The Economic Damages of Air Pollution* (Springfield, Va.: NTIS, 1974); L. Barrett and T. Waddell, *Cost of Air Pollution Damage: A Status Report* (Springfield, Va.: NTIS, 1973).

13. Barrett and Waddell, *Cost of Air Pollution Damage.*

14. J.A. Jaksch *et al.* (for U.S.EPA), *Outpatient Medical Costs Related to Air Pollution in the Portland, Oregon, Area* (Springfield, Va.: NTIS, 1974).

15. B.W. Carnow, *Chicago Air Pollution Morbidity Studies—SO_2 and Particulate Levels and Acute Illness in Patients with Chronic Broncho-Pulmonary Disease* (Springfield, Va.: NTIS, 1974).

16. A. Rossano, *Air Pollution Control Guidebook for Management* (Stamford, Conn.: ERA, Inc., 1969), p. 90.

17. Barrett and Waddell, *Cost of Air Pollution Damage*, p. 45.

18. *Ibid.*, pp. 5 and 51.

19. AIHA, *Air Pollution Manual*, p. 230.

20. W.E. Bezdek *et al.*, *Professional Appraisers' Judgment of the Effect of Air Pollution on Property Values* (Chicago: University Social Psychology Lab, 1969).

21. Council on Environmental Quality, *Sixth Annual Report*, p. 564.

22. D. Harrison, *Who Pays for Clean Air?* (Cambridge, Mass.: Ballinger, 1975).

23. Council on Environmental Quality, *Sixth Annual Report*, pp. 494-570; Chase Econometric Associates, *The General Economy* (Springfield, Va.: NTIS, 1972); Chase Econometric Associates, *The Economic Impact of Pollution Control: A Summary of Recent Studies; An Overview Prepared for the Council on Environmental Quality, Depart-*

ment of Commerce and the Environmental Protection Agency (Springfield, Va.: NTIS, 1972).

24. H. Hesketh, *Understanding and Controlling Air Pollution* (Ann Arbor, Mich.: Ann Arbor Science, 1974), p.3.

25. M. Gosnell, "*Ozone,* The Trick Is Containing It Where We Need It," *Smithsonian* 6, 3 (June 1974), p. 51.

26. Bates, *Citizen's Guide,* p. 24.

27. Interstate Sanitation Commission, *Preliminary Investigation of the Photochemical Oxidant Problem in the New Jersey-New York-Connecticut Air Quality Control Region* (New York: ISC, 1974).

28. Council on Environmental Quality, *Sixth Annual Report,* pp. 305-6.

29. Council on Environmental Quality, *Fourth Annual Report of the Council on Environmental Quality* (Washington, D.C.: U.S.G.P.O., 1973), p. 267.

30. G. McCutchen, "Stationary Source Emission Control Measures," in J.J. Roberts, ed., *Specialty Conference on Long Term Maintenance of Clean Air Standards* (Chicago: Air Pollution Control Association, U.S. EPA, and others, 1975), pp. 249-274.

31. J. Roberts, E. Croke, and S. Booras, "A Critical Review of the Effect of Air Pollution Control Regulations on Land Use Planning," *Journal of the Air Pollution Control Association* 25,5 (May 1975), p. 507.

32. S.F. Lewin, A.H. Gordon, and C.J. Hartelius, *Law and the Municipal Ecology* (Washington, D.C.: National Institute of Municipal Law Officers, 1970), p.27.

33. AIHA, *Air Pollution Manual,* p. 3.

34. Lewin *et al., Law,* p. 17.

35. N. deNevers, "Enforcing the Clean Air Act of 1970," *Scientific American* 228, 6 (June 1973), p. 15.

36. *Ibid.*

37. Hesketh, *Understanding Air Pollution,* p. 12.

38. Council on Environmental Quality, *Fifth Annual Report of the Council on Environment Quality* (Washington, D.C.: U.S.G.P.O., 1974), p. 118.

39. Council on Environmental Quality, *Sixth Annual Report,* p. 45.

40. G. Leonardos, "A Critical Review of Regulations for the Control of Odors," *Journal of the American Pollution Control Association* 24, 25 (May 1974), p. 456.

41. J. Holmes, J. Horowitz, R. Reid, and P. Stolpman, *The Clean Air Act and Transportation Controls: An EPA White Paper* (Washington, D.C.: U.S.EPA, 1973), p. 42.

42. J. Crossland, "Aerosols," *Environment* 16, 6 (July/August 1974), p. 16.

43. Council on Environmental Quality, *Fifth Annual Report*, p.130.

44. A. Reitze, Jr., and G. Reitze, "Law: The Energy Supply Act," *Environment* 16,10 (December 1974), pp. 3-4.

45. K. Roberts, "The Role to Be Played by the Federal Government," *Proceedings of HEW National Conference on Air Pollution, December 10-12, 1962* (Washington, D.C.: HEW, 1963), p. 328.

46. J. Roberts *et al.*, *A Critical Review*, p. 500.

47. Lewin *et al.*, *Law*, p. 29.

48. Council on Environmental Quality, *Third Annual Report of the Council on Environmental Quality* (Washington, D.C.: U.S.G.P.O., 1972), p.124.

49. N. deNevers, *Enforcing the Clean Air Act*, p.16.

50. Hesketh, *Understanding Air Pollution*, p. 12.

51. *Ibid.*

52. J. Roberts *et al.*, *A Critical Review*, p. 515.

53. Council on Environmental Quality, *Third Annual Report*, p. 162.

54. *Ibid.*, p. 165.

55. Council on Environmental Quality, *Fourth Annual Report*, p. 159.

56. *Ibid.*, p. 159.

57. Hesketh, *Understanding Air Pollution*, p. 12.

58. Lewin *et al.*, *Law*, p. 25.

59. N. deNevers, *Enforcing the Clean Air Act*, p. 20.

60. Lewin *et al.*, *Law*, p. 29.

61. Council on Environmental Quality, *Sixth Annual Report*, pp. 47-49.

62. State of New Jersey, Proposed Regulation: Notice of Public Hearing Docket no. DEP 018-76-07.

63. Lewin *et al.*, *Law*, pp. 25-26.

64. *Ibid.*, p. 26.

65. Interstate Sanitation Commission, *Preliminary Investigation.*

66. *Star Ledger*, August 2, 1976, p.1.

67. Lewin *et al.*, *Law*, pp. 13-14.

68. *Ibid.*, p. 18.

69. AIHA, *Air Pollution Manual*, p. 6.

70. Lewin *et al.*, *Law*, p. 18.

71. *Ibid.*, p. 22.

72. *Ibid.*, p. 43.

73. J. Roberts *et al.*, *A Critical Review*, p. 507.

74. Lewin *et al.*, p. 42, and A. Atkisson and R. Gaines, *Development of Air Quality Standards* (Columbus, Ohio: Charles E. Merrill, 1970), p. 216.

75. Lewin *et al.*, *Law*, p. 40.

76. *Ibid.*, p. 14.

77. *Ibid.*

78. *Ibid.*, p. 15.

79. AIHA, *Air Pollution Manual*, p. 2.

80. *Ibid.*, p. 6.

81. *Ibid.*, p. 5.

82. *Ibid.*

83. *Ibid.*, p. 4.

84. Lewin *et al.*, *Law*, p. 27.

85. *Ibid.*

86. Rossano, p. 189.

87. McCutchen, *Stationary Source Measures.*

88. "Electric Arc Furnaces in the Steel Industry: Standards of Performance," *Federal Register*, vol. 40, no. 185 (September 23, 1975), pp. 43850-43854; *Background Information for Standards of Performance: Electric Arc Furnaces in the Steel Industry* EPA-450/2-74-017a (Washington, D.C.: U.S.EPA, 1974).

89. *Federal Register*, vol. 40, no. 185 (September 23, 1975), p. 43850.

90. U.S.EPA, *Compilation of Air Pollutant Emission Factors*, with supplements (Washington, D.C.: U.S.G.P.O, 1972).

91. We thank the following individuals of the New Jersey Department of Environmental Protection for reviewing the quantity and quality of emission data with us: Althea Thorton and Al Sherry.

92. U.S.EPA, *Growth Effects of Major Land Use Projects: Volume 2–Compilation of Land Use Based Emission Factors*, EPA-450/3-76-012-b (Research Triangle Park, N.C.: The Agency, 1976).

93. U.S. Bureau of the Census, *1972 Census of Manufacturers: Fuels and Electric Energy Consumed* (Washington, D.C.: U.S.G.P.O., 1973).

94. F.E. Littman (for U.S.EPA), *Regional Air Pollution Study — Point Source Methodology and Inventory,*. EPA-450/3-74-054 (Springfield, Va.: NTIS, 1974); T.J. Consroe (for U.S.EPA) *Comparison of Four Methodologies to Project Emissions for the St. Louis Area*, EPA-450/3-75-071 (Springfield, Va.: NTIS, 1975); California State Air Resources Board, *Emission Forecasting Methodologies* (Springfield, Va.: NTIS, 1974).

95. U.S.EPA, *Guidelines for Air Quality Maintenance Planning and Analysis, Vol. 10: Reviewing New Stationary Sources* (Washington, D.C.: U.S.EPA, 1975).

96. McCutchen, *Stationary Source Measures.*

97. Environmental Research and Technology for the Maryland National Capital Park Planning Commision, *Carbon Monoxide and Local Land Use Planning* (Lexington, Mass.: The Commission, 1976).

98. U.S.EPA, *Guidelines for Air Quality Maintenance Planning and*

Analysis, Vol. 9: Evaluating Indirect Sources (Research Triangle Park: N.C.: The Agency, 1975).

99. U.S.EPA, *Guidelines for Air Quality Maintenance Planning and Analysis, Vol. 13: Allocating Projected Emissions to Sub-County Areas* (Research Triangle Park, N.C.: The Agency, 1974).

100. Consroe, *Comparison of Methodologies;* T. Briggs *et al., Air Pollution Considerations in Residential Planning,* 2 vols. (Springfield, Va.: NTIS, 1974); A. Kennedy *et al., Air Pollution Land Use Planning Project,* 2 vols., especially vol. 2, *Methods for Predicting Air Pollution Concentrations from Land Use* (Springfield, Va.: NTIS, 1973); and A. Epstein *et al., A Guide for Considering Air Quality in Urban Planning* (Springfield, Va.: NTIS, 1974).

101. U.S.EPA, EPA-450/3-76-012-b.

102. Council on Environmental Quality, *Sixth Annual Report,* p. 308.

103. D. Doctor, *A Manual Model to Predict Highway Related Carbon Monoxide Concentrations* (Springfield, Va.: NTIS, 1975), and R. Patterson *et al.* (for U.S.EPA), *Monitoring and Analysis of Carbon Monoxide and Traffic Characteristics* (Springfield, Va.: NTIS, 1974).

104. Council on Environmental Quality, *Sixth Annual Report,* p. 312.

105. U.S.EPA, *Guidance for Air Quality Monitoring Network Design and Instrument Siting* (Research Triangle Park, N.C.: U.S.EPA OAQPS No. 1.2-012, 1974); "Approval and Promulgation of Implementation Plans: Review and Indirect Sources," *Federal Register,* July 9, 1974, p. 25292; and U.S.EPA, *Guidelines for Air Quality Maintenance Planning and Analysis, Vol. 11: Air Quality Monitoring and Data Analysis* (Research Triangle Park, N.C.: The Agency, 1974).

106. U.S.EPA, *Guidelines for Air Quality Maintenance Planning and Analysis, Volume 12: Applying Atmospheric Simulation Models to Air Quality Maintenance Areas* (Research Triangle Park, N.C.: The Agency, 1974.

107. Atkisson and Gaines, *Development of Standards,* p.177.

108. T. Smith, "Mathematical Models for Environmental Quality Management." Ph.D. dissertation, Rutgers University, 1974.

109. R. Kohn, "A Linear Programming Model for Air Pollution Control: A Pilot Study of the St. Louis Airshed," *Journal of the Air Pollution Control Association* 22 (1970), pp. 78-82; J. Seinfeld and C. Kyan, "Determination of Optimal Air Pollution Control Strategies," *Socio-Economic Planning Sciences,* vol. 5 (1971), pp. 173-190; E. Werczberger, "A Mixed-Inter Programming Model for the Integration of Air Quality Policy into Land Use Planning," *Papers of the Regional Science Association* 33 (1974), pp. 141-154; A. Teller, "The Use of Linear Programming to Estimate the Cost of Some Air Pollution Abatement Policies," *Proceedings of*

the *IBM Scientific Computing Symposium on Water and Air Resource Management* (White Plains, New York: IBM, 1968), pp. 345-353; W. Miernyk *et al, Air Pollution Abatement and Regional Economic Development: An Input-Output Analysis* (Springfield, Va.: NTIS COM-74-10560, 1973).

110. See R. Brail., "Land Use Planning Strategies for Air Quality Maintenance," in *Specialty Conference,* ed. J. Roberts, for a concise review of emission allocation alternatives. John Robson, of the U.S.EPA, Research Triangle Park, North Carolina, provided a draft copy of the model.

111. See U.S.EPA, *Guidelines, Volumes 12 and 9;* California Air Resources Board, *Introduction to Manual Methods for Estimating Air Quality* (Springfield, Va.: NTIS, 1974);Hesketh, *Understanding Air Pollution;* D. Keyes, *Land Development and the National Environment: Estimating Impacts* (Springfield, Va.: NTIS, 1976), pp. 23-38.

112. Equation derived from data presented in Epstein, *A Guide,* p. 55. Equation (2) slightly (2 percent) underestimates N at the lower values of *L* and slightly overestimates (3 percent) at the higher values of *L.* The original publication contains an arithmetic error in going from *ug* to *g.* We have corrected the error for this presentation.

113. G. Holzworth, *Mixing Heights, Wind Speed, and Potential for Urban Air Pollution throughout the Contiguous United States* (Research Triangle Park, N.C.: U.S.EPA, 1972).

114. Epstein, *A Guide.*

115. E. Reifenstein III, R. Horn III, and M. Keefe, *The Hackensack Meadowlands Air Pollution Study, Task 5 Report: The AQUIP Software System Users Manual* (Lexington, Mass.: Environmental Research and Technology, 1974); B. Willis, *The Hackensack Meadowlands Air Pollution Study* (Lexington, Mass.: Environmental Research and Technology, 1973).

116. Hesketh, *Understanding Air Pollution.*

117. K.E. Noll, W.T. Davis, and J.R. Duncan, *Air Pollution Control and Industrial Energy Production* (Ann Arbor, Mich.: Ann Arbor Science, 1975); K.E. Noll and J. Duncan, eds., *Industrial Air Pollution Control* (Ann Arbor, Mich.: Ann Arbor Science, 1975); P.N. Cheremisinoff and R.A. Young, *Industrial Odor Technology Assessment* (Ann Arbor, Mich.: Ann Arbor Science, 1975); and G.A. Cook, *Survey of Modern Industrial Chemistry* (Ann Arbor, Mich.: Ann Arbor Science, 1975).

Chapter 6
Industrial Solid Waste

INDUSTRY IS RESPONSIBLE for less than 3 percent of the American production of solid waste. Agriculture and mining produce more than 90 percent of the total. Yet industry's solid waste problem is critical. In the past, little attention was paid to industrial solid waste. Now, with strong air and water quality legislation, with ocean and coastal zone legislation, and with the banning of open burning dumps, with the Resource Conservation and Recovery Act, industry's solid waste problem has become at lease as critical as its water and air quality problems.

A brief, but poignant example will help to illustrate this problem. The Kin-Buc landfill is about three miles, as the crow flies, from the author's home. On October 11, 1974, a bulldozer operator was killed at the landfill while trying to compact drums of unknown chemical wastes. Between October, 1974, and late 1976, the author observed three major fires at the site and had water quality samples taken near the site. The water samples registered a dissolved oxygen rate of 0 ppm at a time when sites a few miles away had readings of between 9 and 11 ppm. The Kin-Buc landfill is located on 30 acres of land adjacent to the Raritan River in New Jersey. It has received both municipal and industrial wastes for fourteen years. The industrial wastes, which are no longer accepted, arrived in tank trucks and in containers. Bulk liquids were poured directly onto the landfill. Containers of waste were buried and compacted.

Before the enforcement of the FWPCAA of 1972, the Clean Air Act of 1970, the Solid Waste Disposal Act as amended in 1970, and supporting state of New Jersey legislation, hazardous waste found its way into the air, water, and many landfills. As options for disposing of hazardous waste were eliminated by federal and state enforcement, Kin-Buc began to accept more and more industrial waste. The state of New Jersey had prohibited the acceptance of unidentified chemicals at landfills. However, at the time of the explosion which caused the fatality, a court order had suspended the regulations because New Jersey's industries had no other reasonable disposal options. Following the fatality and continued problems, pressure has forced Kin-Buc to develop closing plans.[1]

Kin-Buc illustrates one implication of not developing comprehensive environmental legislation. At the present time, solid waste managers are feeling the pressure of highly funded air and water programs which have made land disposal of solids and liquids the only viable option for some industries.

This chapter will focus on the growing problem of industrial solid waste management. It begins with an overview of solid waste generation, especially industrial solid waste, follows with a consideration of hazardous industrial waste generation, continues with a discussion of alternative treatment methods for nonhazardous and hazardous industrial waste streams, and concludes with a discussion of the nonexpert's role in siting hazardous waste producing facilities.

An Overview of Solid Waste Generation

The United States produces more than half of the world's solid waste. As previously indicated, more than nine-tenths of the waste comes from agricultural and mining activities. Less than one percent of the waste is collected. Nearly all of the waste that is collected is disposed of in landfills. A summary of types, sources, and per capita amounts of solid waste is presented in Exhibit 1.

INDUSTRIAL SOLID WASTE

Industrial solid waste consists of many different types. The bulk of industrial solid wastes are by-products of manufacturing operations. Some of

EXHIBIT 1
MAJOR SOURCES AND TYPES OF SOLID WASTE

Sources	Pounds Per Capita/Day[a]	Types of Waste
Agricultural	57.5	Manure, rejects, trimmings
Mining	42.5	Slag, dirt, rocks
Residential	3-5	Household rubbish, paper, discarded appliances, greenery trimmings
Commercial and Institutional	1-3	Same as residential, but more food service wastes, boxes and cartons, bottles and cans, hospital wastes, paper
Construction and Demolition	0.5-1.5	Wood, metals, concrete, asphalt, glass, bricks, rocks, sand and gravel, trees and stumps, fencing
Industrial	2.5-3.0	Same as residential and commercial, plus a wide variety of manufacturing process wastes
Total	110	

NOTE: [a]Numbers calculated by the authors from a variety of summaries. Total is based on an annual production of between 4 and 4.5 billion tons per year and a population of 220 million.

the by-products are waste semi-liquids and liquids such as solvents and paints placed in drums. Others are solid by-products such as plastics and wood. Paper, food, boxes, cartons, clean-up refuse, and other residential, commercial, and institutional solid wastes are produced by administrative and cafeteria functions.

Several studies have prepared industrial solid waste generation coefficients. The best of these is by Steiker who presents solid waste generation coefficients for 342 manufacturing industries at the four-digit SIC level of aggregation.[2]   The coefficients are based on information gathered from firms in the Philadelphia area. Coefficients are for thirteen types of refuse materials in tons per employee and solid waste generated per employee. Potential users should approach this study with caution because the author reports that the Philadelphia-based coefficients tended to be higher than other published studies.[3]

INDUSTRIAL SOURCES OF HAZARDOUS SOLID WASTE

The bulk of the industrial solid waste stream is a nuisance, can lead to environmental problems, and is costly to dispose of, but is not a direct hazard to people who handle it and to the public. This section focuses on that portion of the industrial solid waste stream which is hazardous.

EPA studies report that about 10 percent of the 100-110 million tons produced annually by industry is hazardous.[4]   This estimate was developed by judging wastes against a list of criteria which would define a dangerous substance.[5]   If a waste had any one of the following characteristics it was considered to be hazardous: (1) capable of producing an unacceptable dose of radioactivity, (2) bioconcentrate in living organisms, (3) flammable, (4) explosive, (5) lethal to experimental animals and plants, (6) capable of producing a serious skin irritation, and (7) causing genetic changes.

Hazardous wastes are produced throughout the United States, but more than two-thirds are generated in the Mid-Atlantic, Great Lakes, and Gulf Coast regions.[6]   About 90 percent comes to the solid waste system in a liquid or semi-liquid form.[7]   While it costs about $3 per ton to landfill or dump hazardous wastes into the oceans, the cost of treating and disposing of these wastes in an environmentally acceptable manner is estimated to be at least $60 per ton.[8]   In response to rapidly increasing demands, the need for hazardous waste management facilities is critical. Conventional solid waste disposal and specialized treatment technologies for hazardous industrial waste are reviewed in the next section.

Treatment and Disposal Methods

Ninety percent of the solid waste stream has been disposed of in landfills. Incineration, resource recovery and ocean dumping account for a small but important portion of the waste. This section overviews landfilling and other means of disposing, recycling, and treating industrial solid waste. The first part overviews methods for both the nonhazardous and hazardous solid waste streams; the second provides additional information about the hazardous industrial waste portion.

CONVENTIONAL SOLID WASTE
DISPOSAL AND RECOVERY ALTERNATIVES

Sanitary Landfills.[9] Landfills range from open dumps to sophisticated engineering projects. Open, rodent infested, smoldering dumps are an inexpensive means of solving solid waste problems; but they are no longer permitted because they create serious environmental, social, and political problems. The engineering projects are not, as their name "sanitary landfill" implies, completely sanitary; but they do not create a serious nuisance or pose an immediate threat to public health and safety.

Sanitary landfilling consists of placing solid waste in a small open area or a dug out trench, covering the waste with fill, and compacting the waste. Possible additions to a landfill design include shredding and/or baling of the waste to achieve greater compaction, barriers to control wind-blown dust and litter, underground piping systems to divert contaminated water flowing through the landfill, and other technologies which will be described in this section.

Landfills, even sanitary landfills, can create serious environmental problems. The most important of these problems is leachate. Leachate is composed of water and landfill materials. The water comes from surface seepage and from groundwater filtering through the landfill. The composition of the leachate depends upon the composition of the landfill. Landfills which receive only residential waste typically register BOD, COD, chlorides, and nitrates. Landfills which receive hazardous wastes exhibit these contaminants in their leachate. For example, Robertson reports on BOD and COD values in five sites.[10] BOD ranged from 59 to 54,610 ppm and COD from 5,750 to 39,680 ppm. By comparison, human waste was 150 ppm. Not only did he report the finding of BOD, COD, nitrates, and chlorides; but, in addition, pesticides, solvents, phenolic compounds, hazardous industrial chemicals, hospital wastes, and numerous other hazardous products were found in the landfill leachate.

If leachate contamination was confined to the area under the landfill, it would be a troublesome, but not necessarily an extremely serious, problem. Unfortunately, numerous landfills have been located on sites which have a shallow water table. The leachate flows into the water table and can contaminate an aquifer which is an important water supply source. Equally unfortunate is the case of a landfill which is located in a floodplain or marshland. Runoff and flood waters can flow over the landfill, sweeping high concentrations of contaminants into the water body.

Another water pollution problem created by landfills is erosion of stockpiled cover soil. Serious erosion can lead to the covering of the bottom of water bodies, consequently destroying a niche in an ecosystem.

Landfills have been infamous for air pollution. With the elimination of open burning, though, fires associated with landfills should be reduced to a minimum. Another source of air pollution at landfills are noxious odors produced by aerobic and anaerobic decomposition of organic materials in the landfills. Proper venting of landfills should greatly reduce the frequency of this problem. Neighborhood and site noise and dust produced by earth moving equipment and by trucks coming to and operating at the site are problems which defy simple solution. They can, however, be minimized by design features.

A final problem commonly found at landfills are vectors of disease. Flies, rodents, and birds are difficult to completely eliminate. However, they can be controlled by using clean fill and other techniques which we will describe.

During the 1970s, legal, site design, and technological advances have slowly begun to make landfills more sanitary. Spurred by water quality and solid waste legislation, most states prepared landfill design criteria and adopted regulations prohibiting the landfilling of specific industrial chemicals. In order to help the reader understand these technologies, we will briefly review environmental considerations in evaluating landfill sites.

Hydrology is a critical variable. Local hydrology determines the extent to which water will filter through the landfill and potentially produce leachate. Sites with little precipitation, far from a water body, and possessing a deep water table are preferred to sites with a good deal of precipitation, close to a water body, and possessing a high water table.

Terrain is a second important site consideration. Unfavorable topographic features include floodplains, any depressions where water might accumulate, and lower sections of streams which are used for public potable supply and discharge into estuaries which contain rich biological communities. Favorable features for landfills include flat terrain, gullies which no longer carry water, and other dry areas such as abandoned coal mines. This land is, however, valuable for other purposes.

Local geology is a third extremely important variable which can affect the environmental impact of a landfill. In general, impermeable soils and bedrocks are preferred. Clay, silt, and loess are preferred as cover soils because they reduce filtration through the landfill, and reduce uncontrolled venting of gas. Thick deposits of silts, loess, and clay, in addition to serving as cover soil, serve as a bottom seal which block filtration of leachate into groundwater aquifers. Gravels and sands are not preferred as cover soils because they permit relatively easy filtration of leachate. Some gravels and sands, however, are used to permit controlled venting of landfill gases. Sands and gravels are considered to be poor subsurface material because water readily filters through them. Overall, a combination of sands and silts makes the best cover material and subsurface geological base.

The structure as well as composition of the bedrock are important. A preferred bedrock structure is not fractured, not weathered, and shallow. A relatively sound and shallow bedrock will prevent infiltration and allow leachate to be drawn off into a treatment facility.

A landfill design should take advantage of favorable natural hydrologic, terrain, and geologic features, and provide engineered structures to overcome disadvantageous features. Surface waters flowing over the landfill, contaminated by contact with solid waste, are diverted by ditches. Diverting groundwater is considerably more difficult. Sometimes an impermeable bedrock tilted in a favorable direction will suffice. In other places, an expensive piping and pumping system must be installed to draw off subsurface leachate. The leachate is directed to storage tanks for subsequent treatment.

A good deal of control of infiltration, wind-blown litter, infectious agents, dust, odors, fires, and an unsightly appearance may be achieved by using cover materials. Normally, regulations require between 6 and 8 inches of cover soil for every 2 feet of solid waste and a one or two foot layer of cover soil for every lift. Lifts are the layers of solid waste which vary considerably in size. Normally, they are between 12 and 16 feet high.

Compaction of the working area reduces gas buildup. A poor packing density (less than 600 pounds of waste per cubic yard) will lead to gas formation in open pockets, rodent and other infectious agent penetration, and wasted space. Compaction with a bulldozer can achieve densities of 1,000 pounds per cubic yard. Shredding and baling the waste can double the compaction density. A variety of other techniques are required or voluntarily used to reduce landfill problems. One obvious procedure, which only recently has been legally required in most states, is confining the working face of the landfill to a small area. Constructed earthen banks, natural barriers, and sometimes green belts are used to control diverted leachate and dust, and reduce the unsightly appearance of landfills. Vents constructed of coarse gravels are used to control the methane, hydrogen sulfide, CO_2, nitrogen, and other gases. Sprinkling the working area is another widely used means of reducing wind blown litter and dust. Fire problems are minimized by banning open burning and by keeping soil and water ready. Finally, as the landfill is constructed, monitoring wells are used to determine the impact, if any, of leachate, and the landfill is graded in conformance with the plan for the post-landfill use of the site.

Technical solutions to landfill problems have been found largely due to legal prods. With respect to industrial waste, two legal developments are particularly important. First, industry can rarely absolve itself of responsibility for its wastes by giving them to a carter for disposal. The private contractor and industry will probably both be held responsible for environmental damage, such as contamination of an aquifer by unauthorized dumping of chemical wastes. Second, many states have prohibited the landfilling of specific materials. For example, the state of New Jersey used the previously mentioned report to Congress on hazardous waste to prepare a prohibited list of about 200 explosives, carcinogens, toxins, and irritants.[11] If your state has a list, it must immediately be obtained.

In recent years, the cost of landfilling has substantially increased. Meeting environmental regulations and political constraints is and will continue to be increasingly costly. Marginal, vacant, and readily accessible land, which does not draw vociferous complaints from neighbors and environmental agencies, is difficult to find. If it is found, it is expensive.

Overall, the advantages of the sanitary landfill for industrial disposal are many. Where feasible and within economic transport range, landfilling costs less than other alternatives. The disadvantages are that landfills are not designed for hazardous and special, bulky wastes, are aesthetically displeasing, and bury valuable resources. Landfilling will probably continue to be the first choice for waste which is not hazardous and not economically feasible to recover.

Ocean Dumping. Ocean dumping of raw refuse has been banned for more than three decades. However, sludges may continue to be dumped into the oceans through 1980 and some chemical wastes are still dumped. Ninety percent of the dumping occurs in the Atlantic Ocean.[12] Industry dumps almost half of the waste.[13] At the present time, dumping of some materials is absolutely prohibited, particularly radioactive materials; radiological, biological or chemical warfare wastes; and floating materials which are nondegradable.[14] Some materials are not to be dumped in other than minute trace quantities—for example, mercury, cadmium, oil and grease, and organohalogen compounds. Dumping of the overwhelming majority of chemicals is closely regulated and confined to a few sites. A variety of special permits are required from the EPA, Corps of Engineers, Coast Guard, and State Department.[15] These permits, issued under authority of the Marine Protection, Research, and Sanctuaries Act and the FWPCAA of 1972, are becoming more and more difficult to obtain.

Ocean dumping cannot be recommended as a viable alternative. Many firms have discontinued ocean dumping, and it decreased more than 33 percent during 1975.[16] Overall, unless the federal government modifies the existing statutes, ocean dumping will shortly cease to be an option.

Incineration.[17] Industrial incinerators were once fairly common and were used in conjunction with landfilling to deal with industrial solid wastes. The large incinerators are now rarely used and when used are closely regulated. The demise of the large industrial incinerator parallels the demise of municipal incineration. However, specialized incinerators for burning combustible solid and liquid hazardous wastes are still common.

Incineration is the burning of material in an enclosed chamber. This definition includes everything from a barbecue pit to the city of Chicago's 1,600-ton-per-day capacity incinerator and Montreal's 1,200-ton-per-day plant. To be more specific, all incinerators have the following components: (1) receiving and storage areas, (2) a means of delivering the waste into a furnace, (3) fans and related equipment required to push oxygen into the furnace, (4) a means of removing noncombustible materials, (5) a stack, and (6) air pollution control equipment.

When used in conjunction with landfills, incinerators have the advantage of burning nearly all the combustible material, thereby reducing the amount of material which must be landfilled to about 25 percent of the generated waste. With respect to industrial waste, the combustible proportion may greatly diverge from the 75 percent (by weight) assumed for municipal waste. The residue from incineration undergoes little, if any, decomposition which drastically reduces water pollution problems and forms a more suitable base for subsequent building on the landfill site.

An important dichotomy is between refractory and waterwall incinerators. The combustion chamber of the refractory unit is lined with mirror-like refractory walls and ceilings. The rate at which material can be burned in a refractory incinerator is constrained by the rate at which heat can be removed. The combustion chamber of the waterwall unit is lined with metal fins and tubes. The tubes are filled with water which absorbs the radiant energy.

The differences in chamber construction favor the waterwall design. If a nearby customer for steam is available, the waterwall system can produce marketable steam. And the volume of air entering the waterwall furnace is a small fraction of the air delivered to the refractory unit. Therefore, the waterwall technology produces far less in air emissions. Overall, the waterwall incinerator is preferred.

Unfortunately, most incinerators were built more than a decade ago, when the refractory design was dominant in the United States. Accordingly, the legislated need for substantially more air pollution control has virtually eliminated the incineration of conventional wastes and has generally made large incinerators economically infeasible in most cases. The development of new waterwall incinerators may once again make incineration an acceptable technology. Incineration of hazardous wastes is a more complex problem which will be reviewed later in this chapter.

Resource Recovery. Recycling of materials has increasingly become economically feasible in the face of increased landfilling costs, the demise of the refractory incinerator, and the increasing cost of energy and materials. Detailed descriptions of resource recovery technologies are provided in many studies including one by the senior author.[18]   The U.S.EPA and the National Center for Resource Recovery maintain detailed bibliographies and have published the majority of the literature on the topic.[19] This section will very briefly describe selected technologies focusing on their applicability to industrial solid waste.

Source separation involves collecting paper, glass, metal cans, and other materials already segregated by kind from homes, offices, and plants; industrial facilities are not major sources of these wastes. Recovery industries spur these movements by offering a place to bring the waste at a worthwhile price to communities and scavengers.

Materials recovery is the mechanical and chemical extraction of glass, ferrous and nonferrous metals, paper, and other economically valuable materials from the residential, commercial, and industrial waste streams. The recovered materials must meet product specifications set by industries that use the salvaged resources. Many industries have been involved in in-plant materials recovery for decades. Some have greatly enlarged their operations; others have recently entered the field.

Materials recovery consists of different processes sequentially arranged to recover specific resources. In some facilities, hammermills are used to shred materials to a uniform size. Other mills use machines which tear open bags and use personnel to separate large and small pieces. When both light and heavy materials are part of the waste stream, the light and heavy materials are separated by an air classifier—a rapidly moving column of air which blows the light materials along while the heavy materials drop out. The light organic portion can be converted into an energy product. The heavy portion is primarily inorganic. A series of technologies can be used to separate the heavy fraction into its components. The following technologies are commonly used or being tested: magnets for ferrous metals; dry and wet processes for aluminum; froth flotation and optical glass sorters for glass.

Industry produces residential type wastes from cafeteria and sanitary facilities, paper from administrative activities, and a variety of solid wastes from manufacturing operations. Industry should be able to do a better job than households of segregating its waste streams. Accordingly, industry should be able to carefully select the most feasible material recovery technologies and participate in materials recovery projects.

Energy production from the combustible, light fraction of the solid waste stream has potential for industry from two perspectives. First, energy in the form of steam, a dry fuel, or gas can serve as a substitute when some forms of energy are not available to facilities or when energy prices skyrocket.

Second, some of the energy recovery technologies offer the potential of disposing of hazardous and other perplexing waste problems such as tires and plastics. In particular, pyrolysis, the cooking of organic materials in an oxygen deficient atmosphere, is a technology which could theoretically convert plastics, tires, and other problem organic wastes into valuable solids, liquids, and gases.

Presently, tires are an annoying problem because they are difficult to successfully landfill. They often rise out of landfills. When burned they produce high emission levels and noxious odors. Plastics are not degradable. They are dangerous to incinerate because, when polyvinyl chloride is burned, corrosive hydrogen chloride gas and other hazardous products are produced. In contrast to the problems they cause when landfilled or incinerated, tires and plastics have high energy values as a fuel. High temperature pyrolysis presumably could process sludge and perhaps even produce a relatively harmless slag from heavy metal wastes. Pyrolysis has the potential of producing useful energy products with a minimum of air pollution; however, its technological and economic feasibility on a large scale has yet to be demonstrated.

Overall, recycling and materials recovery by industry on a plant by plant basis have a history and are expanding. The operation of large-scale, regional resource recovery facilities requires financial, political, and legal forces to provide stable markets and prices for recovered products, reliable technologies, and enough solid waste. Providing these bases is difficult when the initial capital cost may be three to seven times as great as a landfill of comparable capacity. A new industry's role in this phase of environmental planning might be both as a source of solid waste and as a market for recovered materials and energy products.

TREATMENT AND DISPOSAL OF HAZARDOUS WASTES[20]

One alternative for solving the hazardous waste problem is finding a substitute or banning production so that the waste is not produced. The economic implications of such decisions are far beyond the scope of this volume. Assuming the waste is produced, this section will review the major types of treatment. Some of the methods of disposing of and treating hazardous wastes have been touched on above.

Thermal treatment technologies include incineration and pyrolysis. Incineration has been the normal technology used for destroying solid, liquid, and gaseous wastes, particularly organic chemicals without heavy metals, and biological, flammable, and explosive types. Recently, European firms have incinerated hazardous wastes on special ocean going vessels. The cost is reported to be high ($70 per ton), but it is encouraging from the environmental perspective. As previously noted, pyrolysis is a relatively new thermal degradation process with the potential to convert organic chemical wastes with and without heavy metals and biological wastes.

Biological treatments such as those used in sewage treatment plants are capable of treating dilute organic wastes without heavy metals. All of the biological treatment methods depend on microorganisms which can be easily killed by a waste stream with moderately high salt and metal contents.

A variety of chemical treatment processes is used on liquid inorganic, organic, and radiological wastes. Some wastes are neutralized by reacting bases with acids or vice versa. Some wastes are destroyed or converted to a less hazardous state by oxidation or reduction. For example, cyanide is treated by chlorine oxidation.

Physical treatment methods may be used on liquid and gaseous forms of inorganic and organic, radiological, and biological wastes. The physical processes are used to separate and concentrate the hazardous materials.

Finally, a host of technologies are used to dispose of or store organic, inorganic, radiological, biological, flammable, and explosive solid, liquid, and gaseous wastes. These include landfilling into deep caverns or into landfills with plastic and asphalt linings,[21] burial in steel or concrete tanks, ocean dumping, detonation, and, if necessary, as in the case of high-level radioactive waste, specially engineered storage.

Industrial solid waste is normally processed by thermal techniques and disposed of in landfills, buried, stored, or dumped into the ocean. Semiliquid and liquid wastes are treated and/or disposed of with the full range of above technologies.

In response to the growing industrial hazardous waste problem, the U.S.EPA has commissioned studies to provide alternative management strategies. One set of alternatives pivots around treatment technologies, a second focuses on the location of the treatment facility(ies). The location decision is relevant to planning because dispersed, in contrast to centralized, treatment facilities imply different probabilities and a spatial distribution of potential accidents such as explosions, release of toxic gases, and oil spills.

The location options are three: (1) on-site processing, (2) off-site processing, and (3) on-site pretreatment and off-site final treatment.[22] On-site processing would include some combination of resource recovery, pretreatment, final treatment, and perhaps on-site disposal. A mobile or permanent facility would be used for incineration and effluent disposal. Off-site processing would necessitate the transfer of all hazardous materials to public or private off-site resource recovery and disposal facilities. The third alternative is to combine on-site and off-site options.

Consultants to the U.S.EPA studied these three options from the national perspective.[23] Using economic, environmental, legal, and political criteria, they compared small on-site facilities with small, medium, and large off-site facilities. Economic analyses revealed that on-site treatment was justified only for facilities which produce large amounts of dilute toxic metal wastes in aqueous form. These studies estimated that about 1.5 million tons, or 15 percent of the total waste, fit into this category and would be treated by about fifty facilities. About 85 percent of the hazardous waste would be transported to five large and fifteen medium sized off-site facilities and five disposal sites. The capital cost for the total system is estimated at over $900 million, the annual operating cost at over $600 million. Variations of this system were also developed.

In contrast to what the EPA sponsored studies present as necessary, there exist in the whole country approximately ten regional off-site treatment facilities, mostly in the Middle Atlantic, North Central, and Gulf Coast regions.[24] These private facilities are capable of handling about 25 percent of the nation's hazardous industrial waste load. However, despite the fact that they are generally in, or within 500 miles of, the major industrial centers, they operate at only 25 percent of capacity. None provides the full range of technologies recommended by the EPA studies. Clearly, if national policy dictates that the protection offered by the EPA studies be provided, government incentives and investments will have to be forthcoming to construct and operate the facilities. And government regulations and enforcement will be required to induce industry to use these facilities instead of ocean dumping, landfilling, on-site incinerators, and other less expensive but less environmentally sound options.

Ongoing Decisionmaking Affecting
Hazardous Industrial Waste

While EPA's plans are going through the political decision-making machinery, decisions continue to be forthcoming about hazardous waste facilities and communities worry about plants that already exist. Discussions with U.S.EPA personnel suggest that generally every industrial facility requires a combination of treatment techniques and one or more disposal technologies. For example, an organic chemical plant might use biological treatment for dilute waste, incineration for concentrated waste, a high-energy scrubber to remove hazardous particulates which might escape from the incinerator stack, and a means of disposing of the sludge from the scrubber. EPA has an organic chemicals and products branch with offices in Cincinnati; Washington, D.C.; Research Triangle Park, North Carolina; and Edison, New Jersey, for advising industry and governments on alternative treatment technologies.

In addition to U.S.EPA personnel, a number of extremely useful publications have appeared during the last few years. One surveys *Hazardous Waste Management Facilities in the United States.* It includes types of waste handled, phone numbers, locations, and other critical information.[25] A second advises on how to take a hazardous waste survey.[26] Others report on hazardous substance classification systems,[27] and landfill disposal options,[28] in a form which should be helpful to the nonexpert.

Judging from our experience, those who are interested in the potential hazards from liquid and solid wastes deposited on their lands from existing manufacturing facilities will find little data. Water and air emissions are registered in state and federal permit programs. The record of materials placed in landfills is miniscule in comparison to air and water emission files; and frankly, the air and water records may not be as informative as one would hope because industries normally provide information only about those pollutants which are required. The discharging of most carcinogenic and other harmful agents is not recorded.

To help remedy this and other problems, the Toxic Substances Control Act (TSCA) was passed and became effective on January 1, 1977.[29] Basically, the act has two important implications for hazardous solid waste. It seeks to identify and screen potentially hazardous substances before they are marketed. Second, it seeks to coordinate the numerous laws and agencies that govern the production, distribution, and disposal of toxic substances. The Council on Environmental Quality heads an interagency committee on toxic substances which includes the EPA, OSHA, the Food and Drug Administration, and the Consumer Product Safety Commission.

Three provisions of TSCA are critical. First, the act requires that information about the production, marketing, and environmental effects of chemicals be maintained by the manufacturer or importer and be made available to EPA. This provision should help determine which hazardous chemicals may be deposited on land or emitted into the air and water. Second, mechanisms are established for alerting the EPA to potential risk from the manufacturing, distribution, and disposal of chemicals. Already marketed chemicals will be screened by a committee which will identify those that pose the highest risk. New chemicals and mixtures or new uses of existing chemicals and mixtures must be approved by EPA before the substances are marketed. Third, if a chemical is suspected to be a problem, it can be banned, limited in production to specific amounts and for particular types of uses, and required to carry labels. To manage chemical waste products, Congress passed the Resource Conservation and Recovery Act of 1976 (RCRA). Briefly, this act establishes a permit program to control the treatment, storage, and disposal of hazardous waste.[30] RCRA has received much less attention than TSCA. In our opinion, however, it could be crucial to the management of hazardous industrial solid waste because of its broad definitions of disposal and hazard. For example, standards are to be set for hauling, disposing, and handling hazardous waste and for trucking wastes from generation to disposal.

THE NON-EXPERT'S ROLE

While the nonexpert can find material which will provide an understanding of the problem, few people have the time or inclination to master this extremely complex literature to the extent that they can participate in the decision about which treatment(s) and/or disposal system(s) to use. Understanding some of the alternative strategies can help the nonexpert participate in the siting decision and in contingency planning, if the facility is to be built or allowed to remain in the community.[31]

The first decision is whether to live with hazardous industries and/or their wastes. The siting decision is complex. The benefits to the local and larger regions must somehow be weighed against the potential hazards of normal emissions and accidents. The precise trade-offs of cost and benefits are not known, although spokesmen for both sides provide estimates. The process of accepting or rejecting a hazard is fraught with opportunities for rational and yet hypocritical decision making. Representatives of the local government may gleefully recruit a hazardous industry or waste processing center for jobs and property tax advantages, while the risks are distributed to all the communities in the region. While these representatives seek industries in their town, similar projects in neighboring towns will be greeted with outraged opposition. Latecomers to this game face additional opposition from state and federal agencies which see a new industry and its waste facilities as a threat to nondegradation.

The mirror image problem has also been appearing in hazardous waste siting. A facility with assumed widespread benefits and geographically concentrated costs is located in an "ugly duckling" community/region.

Better regional impact and trade-off assessments are part of the solution to this problem.[32]   Frankly, however, so long as simple semi-autonomous political units are permitted to make crucial decisions in the ecological sphere, the potential for irrational decisions from the regional perspective are highly probable. Tax sharing among communities should reduce the potential for tunneled vision decision making.[33]   A state and/or regional site selection board would help provide better sites.

After a decision to permit hazardous industries and waste processing and disposal centers, decisions should follow on how to live with them as safely as possible. Alternatives include, but are not limited to, the following: special construction standards and back-up, engineered systems in the event of an accident; redundant transportation systems for evacuation and access by emergency equipment; and restrictions on residential activity near the potential impact area.

A community which will benefit from the facility is unlikely to be willing to impose these costly conditions on the industry or assume responsibility for them. Therefore, the locus of decision making must shift from the local government to an agency, perhaps a state hazardous waste siting board, to control development and, if necessary, to compensate affected municipalities.

Finally, contingency plans should be developed on the assumption that a possible accident is a highly probable accident. Indeed, while this chapter was being revised a hazardous waste recovery facility in New Jersey had a serious accident in which workers were killed and the area around the facility possibly contaminated. Also a petroleum refinery had a blow-out which sprayed petroleum product over many square miles. Such steps as alerts, evacuation, moving emergency equipment, resettling people, decontamination, restoration, and liability must be planned for. For this purpose, a special land use and transportation plan would be prepared as an adjunct to the master plan.

Are not federal agencies such as the EPA, the Nuclear Regulatory Commission, the Army Corps of Engineers, and the Office of Emergency Preparedness already doing all or part of this job? In the case of industrial solid waste, does not the RCRA call for contingency plans? Are not state departments of environmental protection and Civil Defense involved in these activities? And does not the insurance industry work with local, county, and state agencies to provide services in the event of an emergency? The answer in each case, fortunately, is yes. Yet, so many agencies are involved that none is really in charge. In order for there to be consistency among siting, environmental adaptation, and disturbance and recovery plans these fragmented agency powers should be integrated under the auspices of a single agency. At whatever government level proposed agency may be, we believe that studies to develop hazardous facility planning boards are as necessary as the economic and environmental studies which have been prepared. Since many of the citizens who are likely to accommodate the hazardous industry and waste processing center are part of the general public, representatives of these citizens as well as planners, engineers, chemists, and other technical people should be part of the agency.

Summary and Additional Resources

This chapter overviewed the industrial solid waste management problem. It began with a characterization of the municipal and industrial waste streams. Second, the serious industrial hazardous waste problem was considered. Hazardous wastes were defined and their regional distribution presented. Next, conventional and unconventional treatment and disposal methods were reviewed. Landfilling is the primary disposal method. Environmental problems caused by poor landfilling practices were presented, and methods of reducing these problems were considered. Other methods which were discussed include ocean dumping, incineration, and resource recovery.

Special attention was paid to the treatment and disposal of hazardous wastes. Thermal, biological, chemical, and physical methods and on-site and off-site treatment options were overviewed. While U.S.EPA-sponsored studies have suggested means of dealing with the hazardous waste management problem, decisions are ongoing. Accordingly, sources of information were reviewed, and a role for the local government in hazardous waste mangement siting was suggested.

The solid waste literature may, in essence, be dichotomized into that major portion dealing with the municipal waste stream and that small fraction focusing on hazardous waste. The most comprehensive set of books dealing with solid waste management are EPA's *Decision-Makers Guide to Solid Waste Management* and Baum and Parker's two volumes on *Solid Waste Disposal*.[34] EPA's 1974 *Report to Congress, Disposal of Hazardous Wastes* and the *State Decision-Makers Guide for Hazardous Waste Management* are the best sources on the hazardous waste options.[35] Historically, the journal *Public Works* has had quite a few articles on solid waste management. The *Bulletin* of the National Center for Resource Recovery is the best up-to-date journal about resource recovery.

Government and private sources of information are those noted in the previous chapters. If the problem is hazardous industrial waste, EPA maintains a special hazardous waste group located in Cincinnati.

NOTES

1. See U.S.EPA, *Hazardous Waste Disposal Damage Reports* (Cincinnati: U.S.EPA, 1975), pp. 6-8 for a brief review of the Kin-Buc case.

2. G. Steiker, *Solid Waste Generation Coefficients: Manufacturing Sectors*, Regional Science Research Institute series no. 70 (Philadelphia: The Institute, 1973).

3. *Ibid.*

4. U.S.EPA, *Report to Congress, Disposal of Hazardous Wastes* (Washington, D.C.: U.S.G.P.O., 1974), Table 1, p. 4.

5. *Ibid.*, Appendix C, pp. 55-58.

6. *Ibid.*, Table 1, p. 4.

7. *Ibid.*, Table 1, p. 4.

8. *Ibid.*, p. ix.

9. Four useful general publications are: National Center for Resource Recovery, *Sanitary Landfill* (Toronto: Lexington Books, 1974); D.R. Brunner and D.J. Keller, *Sanitary Landfill Design and Operation*, Report SW-65TS (Washington, D.C.: U.S.EPA, 1971); U.S.EPA Office of Solid Waste Management, *Decision-Makers Guide to Solid Waste Management* (Washington, D.C.: U.S.EPA, 1975); and W.J. Graff and J.R. Rogers, *The Economic and Social Aspects of Sanitary Landfill Site Selection* (Springfield, Va., NTIS, 1972).

10. J. Robertson, *Organic Compounds Entering Ground Water From a Landfill* (Springfield, Va.: NTIS, 1974).

11. State of New Jersey, Department of Environmental Protection, Bureau of Solid Waste Management, *List of Prohibited Materials* (Trenton, N.J., 1975).

12. See *Environmental Quality: The Fifth Annual Report of the Council on Environmental Quality* (Washington, D.C.: U.S.G.P.O., 1974), p. 150.

13. *Ibid.*, p. 150.

14. The federal responsibility in ocean dumping is established in the Marine Protection, Research and Sanctuaries Act, Public Law 92-532, 86 Stat. 1052, October, 1972.

15. *Federal Register*, vol. 38, 1973, pp. 8725 and 12872.

16. *The Fifth Annual Report of the Council on Environmental Quality*, 1974, p. 150; S. Smith and R. Brown for U.S.EPA, *Ocean Disposal of Barge-Delivered Liquid and Solid Wastes from U.S. Coastal Cities* (Washington, D.C.: U.S.G.P.O., 1971); and conversation with Herb Skovronek of U.S.EPA, Edison, N.J., January 4, 1977.

17. A good general treatment is: National Center for Resource Recovery, *Incineration* (Toronto: Lexington Books, 1974).

18. M. Greenberg and others, *Solid Waste Planning in Metropolitan Regions* (New Brunswick, N.J.: Center for Urban Policy Research, Rutgers University, 1976).

19. EPA publishes numerous reports. Its *Decision-Makers Guide to Solid Waste Management* is a must for all persons interested in solid waste management. The National Center for Resource Recovery, a private organization located at 1211 Connecticut Ave. N.W., Washington, D.C. 20036, publishes a monthly bulletin, maintains a bibliography, and has written many books and reports.

20. U.S.EPA, *Report to Congress, Disposal of Hazardous Wastes*, Appendix D, pp. 59-64, briefly reviews the technologies.

21. A.J. Geswein, *Liners for Land Disposal Sites* (Cincinnati: U.S.EPA, 1975); and U.S.EPA, *Landfill Disposal of Hazardous Wastes: A Review of Literature and Approaches* (Washington, D.C.: The Agency, 1975).

22. See U.S.EPA, *Report to Congress, Disposal of Hazardous Wastes*, Appendix F, pp. 71-81, and Table 8, p. 27.

23. The following are particularly interesting: W.M. Swift, *Feasibility Study for Development of a System of Hazardous Waste National Disposal Sites*, 2 volumes (Richland, Wash.: Battelle, 1973); J. Funkhouser, *Alternatives to the Management of Hazardous Wastes at National Disposal Sites*, 2 volumes (Cambridge, Mass.: Arthur D. Little, 1973); and Booz-Allen Applied Research, Inc., *A Study of Hazardous Waste Materials, Hazardous Effects and Disposal Methods*, 3 volumes (Bethesda, Md.: Booz-Allen, 1972).

24. U.S.EPA, *Report to Congress, Disposal of Hazardous Wastes*, p. 11.

25. T. Leshendok, *Hazardous Waste Management Facilities in the United States* (Cincinnati: U.S.EPA, 1976).

26. H. Porter, *State Program Implementation Guide: Hazardous Waste Surveys* (Cincinnati: U.S.EPA, 1975).

27. A.M. Kohan, *A Summary of Hazardous Substance Classification Systems* (Cincinnati: U.S.EPA, 1975).

28. T. Fields, Jr., and A.W. Lindsay, *Landfill Disposal of Hazardous Wastes: A Review of Literature and Known Approaches* (Cincinnati: U.S.EPA, 1975).

29. Toxic Substances Control Act, Public Law 94-469, 90 Stat. 2003, October 11, 1976.

30. Resource Conservation and Recovery Act, Public Law 94-580, 90 Stat. 2808, October 21, 1976.

31. I would like to thank my two colleagues, Professors Donald Krueckeberg and George Carey of Rutgers University, for helping me

formulate my ideas about this issue. See G.W. Carey and M. Greenberg, "Toward a Geographical Theory of Hypocritical Decision-Making," *Human Ecology* 2,4, pp. 243-57, and D. Krueckeberg and M. Greenberg, "Land Use Plans and All Hazards Planning," paper prepared for the Council of State Governments, Lexington, Kentucky, November 28, 1973.

32. For example, Battelle-Columbus Labs, *Development of the Arizona Environmental and Economic Trade-Off Model* (Columbus, Ohio: The Labs, 1973).

33. K.C. Lyall, "Tax Base Sharing: A Fiscal Aid Towards More Rational Land Use Planning," *Journal of the American Institute of Planners* 41, 2, pp. 90-100.

34. B. Baum and C.H. Parker, *Solid Waste Disposal*, 2 vols. (Ann Arbor, Mich.: Ann Arbor Science, 1973 and 1974; U.S.EPA, 1975).

35. U.S.EPA, *Report to Congress*, and U.S.EPA, *State Decision-Maker's Guide for Hazardous Waste Management* (Washington, D.C.: U.S.G.P.O., 1977).

NECESSARY WEIGHTS AND MEASURES

Length

1 foot	= 0.3048 Meter
1 meter	= 3.280 Feet = 39.37 inches
1 statute mile	= 1.609 Kilometers
1 kilometer	= 0.621 Statute Mile

Area

1 square mile	= 640 acres = 2.59 square kilometers
1 acre	= A square with sides of 209 feet
	= 43,560 square feet = 0.00156 mile^2
	= 0.405 hectare

Volume

1 cubic foot	= 0.028 cubic meter = 1,728 cubic inches
	= 7.481 U.S. gal.
1 cubic meter	= 35.3 cubic feet
1 cubic yard	= 0.765 cubic meter
1 cubic meter	= 1.3 cubic yards
4 quarts	= 1 gallon = 231 cubic inches = 3.79 liters
	= 0.14 cubic feet
1 barrel	= 31½ gallons
1 acre foot	= 325,851 gallons = 43,560 cubic feet
1 million gals.	= 3.07 acre feet

Weight

1 grain	= 0.0648 gram
1 gram	= 15.43 grains
1 pound	= 16 ounces = 453.6 grams = 7,000 grains
1 ton	= 2,000 pounds
1 gram	= 1 million micrograms
	= 1 thousand milligrams
10 grams	= 0.3527 ounce (avoirdupois)
1 gal. of water	= 8.34 pounds
1 acre ft. water	= 2,722,500 pounds

Flow

1 cubic ft. per second = 7.48 gallons per second
1 cubic ft. per second = 1.98 acre feet per day

APPENDIX A (Continued)
NECESSARY WEIGHTS AND MEASURES

Other

1 grain/ft.^{3}	= 2.29 g/m^3
natural logarithm, e	= 2.7183
π	= 3.14159
1 ton/mi^2	= 3.125 lb/acre
1 g/m^3	= 0.0283 g/ft.^{3}
1 lb/hr	= 0.126 g/sec
1 degree Fahrenheit	= 32 + 9/5 degrees Centigrade

APPENDIX B
UNITED STATES ENVIRONMENTAL PROTECTION
AGENCY REGIONAL OFFICES

Region	States	Address
1	Connecticut, Maine, Massachusetts, New Hampshire, Rhode Island, Vermont	J.F. Kennedy Federal Bldg. Room 2203 Boston, Massachusetts 02203 617-223-7210
2	New York, New Jersey, Puerto Rico, Virgin Islands	26 Federal Plaza Room 1009 New York, N.Y. 10007 212-264-2525
3	Delaware, District of Columbia, Maryland, Pennsylvania, Virginia, West Virginia	Curtis Building 6th and Walnut Streets Philadelphia, Pa. 19106 215-597-9814
4	Alabama, Florida, Georgia, Kentucky, Mississippi, Tennessee, North Carolina, South Carolina	1421 Peachtree Street, N.E. Atlanta, Georgia 30309 404-526-5727
5	Illinois, Indiana, Minnesota, Ohio, Michigan, Wisconsin	230 S. Dearborn Street Chicago, Illinois 60604 312-353-5250
6	Arkansas, Louisiana, New Mexico, Oklahoma, Texas	1600 Patterson Street Suite 1100 Dallas, Texas 75201 214-749-1962
7	Iowa, Kansas, Missouri, Nebraska	1735 Baltimore Avenue Kansas City, Missouri 64108 816-374-5493
8	Colorado, Montana, North Dakota, Utah, South Dakota, Wyoming	1860 Lincoln Street Suite 900 Denver, Colorado 80203 303-837-3895
9	Arizona, California, Hawaii, Nevada, Guam, American Samoa	100 California Street San Francisco, Calif. 94111 415-556-2320

APPENDIX B (Continued)
UNITED STATES ENVIRONMENTAL PROTECTION
AGENCY REGIONAL OFFICES

Region	States	Address
10	Alaska, Idaho, Oregon, Washington	1200 6th Avenue Seattle, Washington 98101 206-442-1220

Selected Bibliography

Chapter 2—Screening Questions for Industrial Environmental Impact Analysis

J.L. Moore, D.E. Manty, P.B. Cheney, and J.L. Rhuman, *A Methodology for Evaluating Manufacturing Environment Impact Statements for Delaware's Coastal Zone.* Columbus, Ohio: Battelle-Columbus, 1973.

Chapter 3—Noise Impacts of Industrial Development

American Industrial Hygiene Association, *Industrial Noise Manual*, 2nd ed. Detroit: The Association, 1966.

L.L. Beranek, *Noise and Vibration Control.* New York: McGraw Hill, 1971.

Bolt, Beranek, and Newman, Inc., *The Technical Feasiblity of Noise Control in Industry.* Springfield, Va.: NTIS, 1976.

Center for the Study of Science Policy, Pennsylvania State University, *The Effects of Mobile-Source Air and Noise Pollution on Residential Property Values.* Springfield, Va.: NTIS, 1975.

P.N. Cheremisinoff and P.P. Cheremisinoff, *Industrial Noise Control Handbook.* Ann Arbor, Mich.: Ann Arbor Science, 1977.

C. Duerden, *Noise Abatement.* London: Butterworths, 1970.

T.J. Schultz and N.M. McMahon, *Noise Assessment Guidelines.* Washington, D.C.: HUD, 1971.

U.S.EPA, *Noise from Construction Equipment*, NTID 300.1. Washington, D.C.: U.S.EPA, 1971.

———, *Noise from Industrial Plants*, NTID 300.2, Washington, D.C.: The Agency, 1971.

———, *Information on Levels of Noise Requisite to Protect Public Health and Welfare with an Adequate Margin of Safety*, Document 550/9-74-004. Washington, D.C.: The Agency, 1974.

———, *Federal Machinery Noise Research, Development and Demonstration Program: FY73-FY75*, Document 600/2-75-008. Washington, D.C.: The Agency, 1975.

———, *Model Community Noise Control Ordinance*, Document 550/9-76-003. Washington, D.C.: The Agency, 1975.

H.E. von Gierke, *Noise—How Much Is Too Much?* Springfield, Va.: NTIS, 1975.

M.A. Whitcomb, *Effects of Long Duration Noise Exposure on Hearing and Health.* Springfield, Va.: NTIS, 1975.

Chapter 4—Water Resources

Battelle-Columbus, *Water Quality Criteria Data Book, Effects of Chemicals on Aquatic Life*, PB-213-210. Springfield, Va.: NTIS, 1971.

J.B. Berkowitz et al., *Water Pollution Potential of Manufactured Products*, PB-222-249. Springfield, Va.: NTIS, 1973.

H.C. Bramer, *Economic Feasibility of Minimum Industrial Waste Load Discharge Requirements*, PB-221-490. Springfield, Va.: NTIS, 1973.

R. Eisler, *Annotated Bibliography on Biological Effects of Metals in Aquatic Environments*, PB-228-211. Springfield, Va.: NTIS, 1973.

Environmental Information Center, Inc., *Environmental Regulations Handbook*. New York: 1973 and updates.

G. Fair, J. Geyer, and D.A. Okun, *Elements of Water Supply and Waste Water Disposal*. New York: Wiley, 1971.

M. Greenberg and R. Hordon, *Water Supply Planning*. New Brunswick, N.J.: Center for Urban Policy Research, Rutgers University, 1976.

Hittman Associates, Inc. *Forecasting Municipal Water Requirements*, 2 vols., HIT-43. Columbia, Md.: Hittman, 1969.

E. Odum, *Fundamentals of Ecology*. Philadelphia: University of Toronto Press, 1963.

J.W. Patterson, *Wastewater Treatment Technology*. Ann Arbor, Mich.: Ann Arbor Science, 1975.

R.P. Pikul, *Fixed vs. Variable Environmental Standards*. Washington, D.C.: Mitre Corp., 1973.

G.K. Reid, *Ecology of Inland Waters and Estuaries*. New York: Van Nostrand Reinhold, 1961.

C. S. Russell, D.G. Arey, and R.W. Kates, *Drought and Water Supply*. Baltimore: John Hopkins Press, 1970.

R. Sanks and T. Asano, *Land Treatment and Disposal of Municipal and Industrial Wastewater*. Ann Arbor, Mich.: Ann Arbor Science, 1976.

R.F. Schneider, *The Impact of Various Heavy Metals on the Aquatic Environment*, PB-214-562. Springfield, Va.: NTIS, 1971.

S. Schultz, *Design of USAF Water Quality Monitoring Programs*, AD-756-504. Springfield, Va.: NTIS, 1972.

U.S. Bureau of the Census, *Census of Manufacturers, 1972, Subject Statistics: Water Use in Manufacturing*. Washington, D.C.: U.S.G.P.O., 1975.

U.S.EPA, *A Primer on Waste Water Treatment*. Washington, D.C.: The Agency, 1971.

R.C. Ward, *Data Acquisition Systems in Water Quality Management*, PB-222-622. Springfield, Va.: NTIS, 1973.

Water Resources Engineers, Inc., *Future Direction of Urban Water Models*, PB-249-049. Springfield, Va.: NTIS, 1976.

Chapter 5—Air Resources

American Industrial Hygiene Association, *Air Pollution Manual, Part 1–Evaluation*. Westmont, N.J.: The Association, 1972.

L. Barrett and T. Waddell, *Cost of Air Pollution Damage: A Status Report*. Springfield, Va.: NTIS, 1973.

D.V. Bates, *A Citizen's Guide to Air Pollution*. Montreal: McGill-Queen's University Press, 1972.

Battelle Memorial Institute (for U.S.EPA), *Cost of Clean Air 1974*. Springfield, Va.: NTIS, 1974.

P.N. Cheremisinoff and R.A. Young, *Industrial Odor Technology Assessment*. Ann Arbor, Mich.: Ann Arbor Science, 1975.

G.A. Cook, *Survey of Modern Industrial Chemistry*. Ann Arbor, Mich.: Ann Arbor Science, 1975.

D. Harrison, *Who Pays for Clean Air?* Cambridge, Mass.: Ballinger, 1975.

H. Hesketh, *Understanding and Controlling Air Pollution*. Ann Arbor, Mich.: Ann Arbor Science, 1974.

S.F. Lewin, A.H. Gordon, and C.J. Hartelius, *Law and the Municipal Ecology*. Washington, D.C.: National Institute of Municipal Law Officers, 1970.

G. McCutchen, "Stationary Source Emission Control Measures," in *Specialty Conference on Long Term Maintenance of Clean Air Standards*, ed. J.J. Roberts. Chicago: Air Pollution Control Association, U.S.EPA and others, 1975.

K.E. Noll, W.T. Davis, and J.R. Duncan, *Air Pollution Control and Industrial Energy Production*. Ann Arbor, Mich.: Ann Arbor Science, 1975.

K.E. Noll, and J. Duncan, eds., *Industrial Air Pollution Control*. Ann Arbor, Mich.: Ann Arbor Science, 1975.

E. Reifenstein III, R. Horn III, and M. Keefe, *The Hackensack Meadowlands Air Pollution Study, Task 5 Report: The AQUIP Software System Users Manual*. Lexington, Mass.: Environmental Research and Technology, 1974.

U.S.EPA, *Compilation of Air Pollutant Emission Factors*, with supplements. Washington, D.C.: U.S.G.P.O., 1972.

———, *Guidelines for Air Quality Maintenance Planning and Analysis, Volume 9: Evaluating Indirect Sources*. Research Triangle Park, N.C.: The Agency, 1975.

———, *Guidelines for Air Quality Maintenance Planning and Analysis, Volume 10: Reviewing New Stationary Sources*. Washington, D.C.: The Agency, 1975.

———, *Guidelines for Air Quality Maintenance Planning and Analysis,*

Volume 13: Allocating Projected Emissions to Sub-County Areas. Research Triangle Park, N.C.: The Agency, 1974.

————, Growth Effects of Major Land Use Projects, Volume 2: Compilation of Land Use Based Emission Factors, EPA 450/3-76-012-b. Research Triangle Park, N.C.: The Agency, 1976.

T.E. Waddell, (for U.S.EPA), The Economic Damages of Air Pollution. Springfield, Va.: NTIS, 1974.

Chapter 6—Industrial Solid Waste

B. Baum and C.H. Packer, Solid Waste Disposal, 2 vols. Ann Arbor, Mich.: Ann Arbor Science, 1973 and 1974.

Booz-Allen Applied Research, Inc., A Study of Hazardous Waste Materials, Hazardous Effects and Disposal Methods, 3 volumes. Bethesda, Md.: Booz-Allen, 1972.

D.R. Brunner and D.J. Keller, Sanitary Landfill Design and Operation, Report SW-65TS. Washington, D.C.: U.S.EPA, 1971.

T. Fields Jr., and A.W. Lindsey, Landfill Disposal of Hazardous Wastes: A Review of Literature and Known Approaches. Cincinnati: U.S.EPA, 1975.

J. Funkhouser, Alternatives to the Management of Hazardous Wastes at National Disposal Sites, 2 vols. Cambridge, Mass.: Arthur D. Little, 1973.

W.J. Graff and J.R. Rogers, The Economic and Social Aspects of Sanitary and Landfill Site Selection. Springfield, Va., NTIS, 1972.

M. Greenberg et al., Solid Waste Planning in Metropolitan Regions. New Brunswick, N.J.: Center for Urban Policy Research, Rutgers University, 1976.

A.M. Kohan, A Summary of Hazardous Substance Classification Systems. Cincinnati: U.S.EPA, 1975.

T. Leshendok, Hazardous Waste Management Facilities in the United States. Cincinnati: U.S.EPA, 1976.

National Center for Resource Recovery, Incineration. Toronto: Lexington Books, 1974.

————, Sanitary Landfill. Toronto: Lexington Books, 1974.

H. Porter, State Program Implementation Guide: Hazardous Waste Surveys, Cincinnati: U.S.EPA, 1975.

G. Steiker, "Solid Waste Generation Coefficients: Manufacturing Sectors," Paper Series no. 70. Philadelphia: Regional Science Research Institute Paper Series, 1973.

W.M. Swift, Feasibility Study for Development of a System of Hazardous Waste National Disposal Sites, 2 vols. Richland, Wash.: Battelle, 1973.

U.S.EPA, *Report to Congress, Disposal of Hazardous Wastes.* Washington, D.C.: U.S.G.P.O., 1974.
————, *Decision-Makers Guide to Solid Waste Management.* Washington, D.C.: U.S.EPA, 1975.
————*;State Decision-Makers Guide for Hazardous Waste Management,* Washington, D.C.: U.S.G.P.O., 1977.

GLOSSARY

ABSORPTION: process by which one material is chemically captured by another or goes into solution; important in pollution control equipment.

ACID: a compound having a high hydrogen ion concentration and low pH; forms a salt upon reaction with a base.

ACRE: 43,560 square feet.

ACRE FOOT: volume of water required to cover an acre to a depth of one foot; 325,851 gallons.

ADIABATIC LAPSE RATE: change in temperature with elevation and air pressure; in dry air is 5.4°F/1000 feet.

ADSORPTION: attach through adhesion; positive charged particles become attached to negatively charged surfaces; important in air pollution control devices.

AEROBIC: an environment in which oxygen is present.

AEROSOL: fine particles suspended in gas; can damage the respiratory system.

ALDEHYDE: volatile, colorless liquid produced by oxidation of alcohol.

ALGAE: one-celled aquatic plants which grow and release oxygen when light, nutrients, and CO_2 are present.

AMBIENT ENVIRONMENT: the environment to which the general public is exposed; distinguished from the occupational environment.

AMPLITUDE: in noise control, a measure of the magnitude of pressure vibrations.

ANAEROBIC: an environment in which oxygen is not present.

APPROPRIATION DOCTRINE: basis for water supply law in the arid western United States.

AQUIFER: an underground body through which groundwater flows.

AREA SOURCE: many indistinguishable air emission sources (e.g., home heating).

ASTHMA: chronic breathing problem characterized by coughing, wheezing, shortness of breath.

ATMOSPHERE: gaseous envelope surrounding the earth; consists predominantly of nitrogen (78 percent) and oxygen (21 percent).

BACTERIA: one-celled, microscopic organisms some of which are beneficial, others of which cause disease.

BAFFLE: a device to control and dampen noise.

BAG FILTER: a system of filters which remove particulates.

BAROMETRIC PRESSURE: atmospheric pressure, force per unit area exerted by the atmosphere.

Benthos: species that live along the bottom of water bodies and feed upon organic materials which fall from above.

Bioassay: a method of evaluating water quality by testing the ability of different species to reproduce and survive.

Biochemical oxygen demand: amount of oxygen used by organisms in oxidation of organic material at a specific temperature and time.

Bioconcentrate: process by which harmful substances are passed along and accumulate in higher levels of the food chain; a serious problem with pesticides, insecticides, and other chemicals widely used in the environment.

Biodegradable: organic substances that are broken down when released into the environment.

Biomass: the living part of the ecosystem.

Brackish water: water which contains dissolved minerals in excess of limits for normal potable use.

British standard: method of establishing the ambient noise level.

Bronchitis: inflammation of the bronchial membrane.

Calcination: process of reducing to a powder through the application of heat.

Carbohydrates: substances produced by photosynthesis (e.g., sugar, cellulose, starch).

Carbon Monoxide: colorless, poisonous, stable, relatively odorless gas formed by combustion in an oxygen deficient atmosphere.

Carcinogenic: compound capable of causing cancer.

Carnivores: consumers which feed upon species lower in the food chain.

Catalytic converter: equipment designed to reduce auto pollution by causing a chemical reaction between exhaust and a catalyst.

Chemical oxygen demand: test for oxygen in water in which organic material is chemically oxidized.

Chlorophyll: green pigment in plants.

Coefficient of haze (COH): general indicator of visibility and air quality.

Coliforms: species of bacteria, some of which are associated with feces of humans and other warm-bodied animals; used as an indicator of water quality.

Community: groups of different species who occupy the same area.

Condensation: change to a denser form (e.g., gas to liquid, liquid to solid).

Consumptive water use: water removed from a water body and not returned because it has been incorporated into a product or lost through evaporation and transpiration.

Consumers: members of the food chain, opposite of those which are producers.

DECOMPOSERS: members of the food chain (e.g., bacteria, fungi) which convert dead organic matter back into nutrients.

DECIBEL: unit of sound measurement in a logarithmic scale; normal conversation is about 60-65 decibels.

DISSOLVED OXYGEN: amount of free oxygen (not chemically combined) in water, measured in parts per million (ppm) or in milligrams per liter (mgl).

DISSOLVED SOLID: vital elements of the ecosystem (e.g., nutrients); include carbonates, sulfates, calcium, iron, magnesium, nitrates, and phosphates.

DISTILLATION: process of producing refined substances by heating to separate volatile and less volatile substances, then cooling and condensing vapor to produce desired substance.

DRY FUEL: fuel made from municipal solid waste.

ECOSYSTEM: groups of communities interacting with one another and their environment.

EFFLUENT LIMITED: water bodies which will meet water quality standards if the effluent limitations of the FWPCAA of 1972 are met.

ELECTROSTATIC PRECIPITATOR: device for removing particulates by giving them an electrical charge, then collecting them in a device with the opposite charge.

EMPHYSEMA: swelling of the alveoli or the tissue connecting the alveoli in the lungs.

ESTUARY: a water body lying between a stream and an ocean which is affected by the tides.

EUTROPHICATION: process by which a water body becomes clogged with nutrients and plants, often ends in serious degradation of water body.

EVAPORATION: process by which a liquid changes to a gas.

FOOD WEB: a series of energy and matter transformations in the ecosystem.

FROTH FLOTATION: liquid process for sorting glass.

FUNDAMENTAL: lowest frequency in a sound.

FUNGUS: plant life having no chlorophyll and living on organic waste.

GROUNDWATER: water found below the land surface in the zone of saturation which originated in seepage from the surface.

HABITUATION: process by which people become accustomed to a degraded environment.

HARDNESS: the relative presence of dissolved calcium and magnesium salts in water.

HARMONICS: tones that are multiples of the fundamental frequency.

HAZARDOUS: dangerous to health because of toxicity, flammability, explosiveness, or other characteristics.

HERBIVORES: consumers which feed directly upon producers.

HERZ (Hz): number of vibrations per second; humans can sense between 20 and 20,000 Hz.

HYDROCARBONS: compound containing only hydrogen and carbon (e.g., benzene, methane).

HYDROGEN SULFIDE: a smelly (rotten eggs), toxic gas (H_2S).

HYDROLOGIC CYCLE: never-ending circulation of water and water vapor between the land, the atmosphere, and the seas.

HYDROSPHERE: the water portion of the earth.

HYDROXYL: a chemical consisting of the attachment of one hydrogen and one oxygen atom.

INCINERATION: reducing materials to ashes by combustion.

INFILTRATION: movement of water through the surface of the earth into the ground.

IMPACT LEVEL: time when sound level is at a maximum.

IMPERMEABLE: material through which water cannot pass, important in landfill management.

INTERCEPTION: objects on the surface of the earth, particularly vegetation, which prevent precipitation from reaching the soil.

INVERSION: atmospheric condition when temperature increases with altitude rather than decreases; when this condition occurs, serious air pollution can result.

IONIZE: process of adding or subtracting electrons from atoms.

LAKE: a large body of water surrounded by land.

LDN: weighted formula which produces an average daily decibel measurement, penalizes night noises.

LEACHATE: substance produced by water filtering through a landfill.

LEEWARD: side of a body of water protected from the wind.

LIFT: section of landfill, usually 2 to 16 feet in height.

LEQ: weighted average decibel measurement.

LIMNOLOGY: the study of lakes.

LINE SOURCE: an extended source of pollution (e.g. road, railroad line).

LITHOSPHERE: the solid portion of the earth.

LOUDNESS: human response to sound frequency and amplitude.

MAJOR DISCHARGER: a facility discharging toxic substances or more than 50,000 gallons each day into a water body.

METABOLISM: chemical change in living cells which provides energy for work, removes waste products, and repairs injured cells.

METHANE: an odorless, colorless, flammable gas (CH_4), often called marsh gas.

MICROORGANISMS: a life form which cannot be seen or can barely be seen with the naked eye; are nevertheless critical to the aquatic and terrestrial ecosystems.

MUTAGENIC: a substance capable of causing genetic changes.

NATIONAL POLLUTANT DISCHARGE ELIMINATION SYSTEM: water pollution abatement program under the FWPCAA of 1972.

NITROGEN: a critical element in the ecosystem; accounts for about 79 percent of the volume of air.

NITROGEN OXIDES: oxygen and nitrogen combinations as nitrates and nitrites; some like fertilizers are useful, others are petroleum combustion products and harmful; major component of reddish brown photochemical smog.

OCTAVE: interval between one tone and another tone having twice as many vibrations per second.

ORGANIC: substances composed of carbon; all other substances are called inorganic, including carbonates.

OXIDANTS: substances in the Air (PAN, ozone and NO_2) capable of oxidizing other chemicals.

OXIDATION: addition of oxygen to a substance.

PARTICULATES: solid or liquid particles discharged into the atmosphere.

PATHOGEN: a substance or organism which can cause disease.

PEROXYACETYL NITRATE (PAN): compound that is formed in photochemical smog; causes eye irritation and injures plants.

PESTICIDE: chemical used to kill pests, including mice, rodents, and bacteria; may cause serious pollution and health problems.

pH: stands for potential hydrogen, an index which ranges from 1 (acid) to 14 (base), 7 is neutral in hydrogen.

PHENOL: product produced by distillation of organic substances; in some forms as an antiseptic it is useful, in other forms as carbonic acid in water it produces a bad taste.

PHOTOCHEMICAL SMOG: air pollution caused by the reaction of sunlight, hydrocarbons, and nitrogen oxides; includes PAN and ozone.

PHOTOSYNTHESIS: process requiring light, water, CO_2, and chlorophyll by which sugar is manufactured in living cells.

PLANKTON: microscopic animals which are consumed by fish and other water species.

POINT SOURCE: facilities that emit an important amount of air pollutants from a stack (e.g., factory).

POLLUTION: physical, chemical, or biological changes in atmosphere, lithosphere, or hydrosphere which limit their use.

POPULATION: groups of similar species which occupy the same geographical area.

POTABLE WATER: water judged safe for human consumption according to national public health standards.

PRECIPITATION: all forms of falling moisture including rain, snow, and their variations.

Primary treatment: in water pollution, the removal of large solids by screens and settling tanks.

Producers: members of the food chain which are capable of producing organic matter (e.g., green plants, phytoplankton, sopme bacteria).

Protein: essential food substance composed of compounds containing nitrogen, carbon, hydrogen, and oxygen.

Pyrolysis: combustion in an oxygen deficient atmosphere.

Relative humidity: relative amount of water vapor in the atmosphere.

Residual level: time when sound level is at a minimum.

Respiration: process by which organism takes in oxygen, uses it in oxidation, and gives off carbon dioxide and other products.

Ringelmann's chart: a series of charts which are a measure of smoke density.

Riparian doctrine: basis for water supply law in the eastern United States where water is relatively abundant.

Root-mean-square error: square root of the average value of the square of the errors.

Runoff: precipitation which strikes the earth and/or vegetation and moves along the ground into water bodies.

Safe yield: amount of water that may be withdrawn indefinitely from a water body without depleting the resource; also known as permissive yield, long-term yield, cumulative yield, dependable yield, and maximum possible yield.

Salinity: concentration of salts, usually sodium chloride in water.

Scrubber: device that removes gaseous and aerosol air pollutants by contact with water.

Secondary treatment: removal of oxygen demanding materials from water through biological and other treatment processes.

Secondary yield: amount of water which is in excess of safe yield and can be obtained from a watershed during high flow conditions.

Seepage: movement of water through the soil.

Sling psychrometer: instrument used to measure atmospheric moisture.

Soluble: a substance (solute) which is dissolvable in a solvent.

Sound level meter: device for measuring sound in decibels (dB), in A, B, C, or D scales.

Species: a group of individuals which share common inherited traits.

Spill: the amount of water which cannot be stored in a reservoir when it is full and may therefore be lost.

Standard industrial code: a classification of economic activity according to product types (e.g., food, paper, chemicals).

Storage: water detained in a surface or underground water body.

STRATOSPHERE: upper part of the atmosphere; begins at about seven miles, fairly constant temperature throughout.

STREAM: a body of water flowing from the upland in a channel and emptying into an estuary or ocean.

SUBLIMATION: process of purifying or refining.

SULFUR DIOXIDE: nonflammable, colorless gas formed when sulfur burns.

SUSPENDED SOLIDS: fine particles that remain suspended in water and air for a long period of time.

SYNERGISM: action of two or more substances or species such that the combined effect is greater than the sum of all taken independently, opposite of antagonism.

TERTIARY TREATMENT: in water pollution, the removal of particular constituents of sewage with chemicals.

TINNITUS: ringing of the ears caused by prolonged exposure to high level noises.

TOTAL ORGANIC CARBON: test for oxygen in water in which organic material is combusted and then measured.

TRANSPIRATION: process by which water vapor passes from the leaves of plants to the atmosphere.

TROPOSPHERE: lower part of the earth's atmosphere where weather occurs.

WATER QUALITY LIMITED: water bodies which require more stringent effluent limitations than those imposed by the FWPCAA of 1972 to meet water quality standards.

Index

Filtration (at landfills), 254-255
Finite difference models (of pollutant diffusion), 231
Fire(s), 180, 187-188, 197, 249, 254-255
Fish, 133-134, 138-140, 154, 156
Flammable (or combustible wastes), 252, 257, 259, 260
Flies, 254
Floating solids (oil and grease), 129, 133, 135
Floodplain, 14, 253, 254
Floods, 128, 253
Flora. *See* Plants; Vegetation
Fluoride, 209
Fly ash, 181
Fog, 176, 228
Food chain, 137-138, 174
Food processing industry, 115, 140
Fossil fuels, 189, 207, 214, 217
Fourth Amendment, 206
Frequency (of sound), 20, 23, 28, 82-83
Fresh water, 102, 130, 165
Front-end operation (of resource recovery), 90, 92, 94
Fuel oil. *See* Fossil fuels; Petroleum
Fumes (in air), 188-189, 204
Fundamental (of sound), defined, 20
Fungi, 137

Garbage compactor truck noise. *See* Solid waste truck noise
Gases (as landfills), 254-255
Gases (in air), monitoring of, 186-191, 221, 223, 227
Gases (in air), pollution from, 174, 177, 179-182, 209
Gasoline. *See* Petroleum; Rationing (of gasoline)
Gaussian plume model (of pollutant diffusion), 231, 239-240
General Radio Corporation, 96
Geology, 126, 132, 162, 254-255
Geyer, J., 166
Gifford-Pasquill plume equation, 239
Glass, 181, 186, 202-203, 210, 258
Glass recovery operation, noise from, 90
Glossary of Geology, 1972 edition of, 125
Global view (of air pollution), 174
Greenberg, M. (senior author), 135, 156-157, 241, 249, 258
Ground water, 117, 121, 125-126, 156, 165, 253-255
Guidelines for Air Quality Maintenance Planning and Analysis, 212, 220, 226, 228
Gulf Coast (region), 252, 261
Gypsum, 179

HEW, Department of. *See* United States Department of Health, Education, and Welfare (HEW)
HUD Department of. *See* United States Department of Housing and Urban Development (HUD)
HUD method (of noise monitoring), 51-62, 70-71
HUSH computer model, 51, 70-71
Harmonics (of sound), defined, 20
Havighurst study, 185
Hazardous substances, decision-making affecting, 261-265
Hazardous substances, impacts of, 177, 252, 253, 264
Hazardous substances, management of, 145-146, 191, 250, 256, 257, 259-261
Hazardous substances, standards for, 148, 196, 198
Hazardous Waste Management Facilities in the United States, 262
Health (of people), impacts of pollution on, 174-178, 181-184, 253
Health (of people), protection of, 202, 204, 206-207
Health (of people), standards for, 27, 28, 50, 192, 195, 200
Health, Education, and Welfare, Department of. *See* United States Department of Health, Education, and Welfare (HEW)
Hearing damage or loss (from noise), 24-25, 28, 81
Heart disease, 178, 183
Heat loss, 214-217
Heavy metals, 135, 145, 259, 260. *See also* Metals
Herbivores (in food chain), 137
Hertz (measurement of sound), defined, 20
Hesketh, H. 242
Highway noise. *See* Truck noise; Automobile noise
Histogram (of sound), 22-23, 46, 47, 48, 66-67
Historic structures, 15
Hittman Associates, 113
Holding lagoons (for effluents), 151
Holmes, J., 197
Horowitz, J., 140
Hospitals, 192, 221, 253
Housing and Urban Development Act of 1974, 200
Housing and Urban Development, Department of. *See* United States Department of Housing and Urban Development (HUD)
Human health. *See* Health (of people)
Human waste, 153, 253

Loess, 254
Long-term yield (of reservoirs), 126
Loudness (of sound), defined, 20, 28
Low frequency noises, 22

MARTIK model (Martin-Tikvart diffusion
modeling program), 239-241
Maggots (Tubifera), 154
Magnesium, 133, 134, 137
Major dischargers (of pollutants), 142, 148,
150, 242
Major users (of water), 115-116
Mammals, 139. *See also* Animals
Man-made pollutants, 187-191
Marble, 179, 186
Marine Protection, Research, and Sanctuaries
Act of 1972, 256
Marsh gas. *See* Methane (CH$_4$)
Marshland. *See* Swamps
Mass-balance relationship (of rivers), 157
Mass transit, 74, 201, 205
Materials handling equipment noise, 78
Materials recovery. *See* Resource recovery
Mathematical programming, 232
Mathematical models (for air pollutants),
230-241
Maximum possible yield (of reservoirs), 122
McCutchen, G., 191, 208
Mean speed (of trucks), noise associated with,
51, 53, 57-59
Meaning. *See* Infromation content (of sound)
Meinzer, O.E., 125
Mercaptans, 180
Mercury, 196, 256
Metabolism, 131, 133, 134
Metal(s), 85, 90, 179-181, 185, 258-261
Metal dust, 197
Meteorological conditions, 179, 182, 226-230,
239, 241
Meteorological factors (in noise monitoring),
46, 47
Meteorology, 153, 223
Methane (CH$_4$), 131, 133, 189, 255
Microfilm, 180, 184
Microorganisms, 131, 260
Microphone (in noise monitoring), 33, 40, 41,
47
Middle Atlantic (region), 109-111, 252, 261
Midwest (region), 154, 190, 203
Midwest Research Institute study, 186
Mini-computer (in noise monitoring), 46, 47
Mining, 3, 187, 200, 249, 250
Mini-steel mill, noise from, 91, 92, 94
Mist, 188
Mobile sources (of pollution), 204-205, 223,
238

Mollusks, 138
Monitoring, air, 180; emissions information,
192-203; ambient air, 203-209; noise
methods, British Standards, 24-27;
composite method, 28-30; computer
method, 30-33; New Jersey method,
27-28; site selection, 22-25; solid waste,
232-234; water data, 126-129, 129-131;
goals of, 127; 128 parameters, 122-126,
129-131; sources of 136-137; testing
methods, 129-130, 131-135
Moore, J.L., 6
Motorcycle noise, 29, 50
Motor vehicles, 174, 184, 188, 189, 204
Motor vehicles. *See also* Automobiles
Motor vehicle emissions, 179, 181, 191,
199-201, 202, 213
Motor vehicle emission standards, 194, 195,
220-221
Mountain (region), 149
Municipal noise control ordinances, 87-88
Municipal water treatment plants, 142, 144,
146, 146-147

National Bureau of Standards, 28
National Center for Resource Recovery, 258,
265
National Environmental Policy Act of 1969,
197
National Institute for Occupational Safety and
Health (NIOSH), 197
National Pollutant Discharge Elimination
System (NPDES), 141
National Technical Information Service
(NTIS), 96, 144, 166
Natural pollutants, 187-188, 197
New England (region), 149
New Jersey (state), air monitoring in, 190,
202-203, 210-212, 214-215
New Jersey (state), noise monitoring in,
35-36, 45-46
New Jersey (state), solid waste monitoring in,
250, 256, 264
New Jersey (state), water monitoring in, 107,
121-124, 149, 164
New Jersey Department of Environmental
Protection N.J.DEP), 202-203, 210
New source performance standards (NSPS)
(for air pollution), 207-209, 212
New source technology (for effluent
limitations), 143, 144, 145, 151-152
Newsprint mill, 90-92, 94
New York City, 27, 123-125, 135, 203-204
New York State, 46, 107, 190, 203
Nighttime noise, monitoring of, 41, 46, 63,
72, 74

United States Bureau of Mines, 194, 212
United States Bureau of the Census, 212
United States Census of Manufacturing, 102
United States Coast Guard, 256
United States Congress, 193, 195, 203, 256, 263, 265
United States Consumer Product Safety Commission, 262
United States Department of Commerce, 200
United States Department of Health, Education, and Welfare (HEW), 194, 195, 197, 199, 200, 202
United States Department of Housing and Urban Development (HUD), 51-62, 78, 200
United States Department of State, 256
United States Department of the Interior, 194, 198
United States Environmental Protection Agency (U.S. EPA), air monitoring by, 182, 187, 195-200, 202, 207-227, 232, 242
United States Environmental Protection Agency (U.S. EPA), noise monitoring by, 32, 37, 46-47, 63-71, 81
United States Environment Protection Agency (U.S. EPA), noise research done by, 27-29, 50, 83, 87-88, 96
United States Environmental Protection Agency (U.S. EPA), noise standards set by, 21-24, 45, 62, 78, 84, 95
United States Environmental Protection Agency (U.S. EPA), solid waste monitoring by, 252, 256, 258, 260-265
United States Environmental Protection Agency (U.S. EAP), water monitoring by, 134-136, 141-151, 154, 166
United States Environmental Protection Agency (U.S. EPA), Office of Noise Abatement and Control, 37
United States Environmental Protection Agency (U.S. EPA), National Aerometric Data Bank, 221
United States Food and Drug Administration, 262
United States Geological Survey (U.S.G.S.), 126, 135, 136
United States Nuclear Regulatory Commission, 264
United States Office of Emergency Preparedness, 264
United States Public Health Service, 194
United States Public Health Service Drinking Water Standards, 135-136
United States Supreme Court, 198, 202
United States Weather Service, 229-230
Urban areas, 182, 197, 198, 204, 229
Urban population, 183, 185

Valleys, 241
Vectors of disease, 254
Vegetation, 139, 176-177, 184, 230
Vehicle mix (in noise monitoring), 70
Vehicle volume (in noise monitoring), 70
Velz, C.J., 136
Venting (of landfills), 254, 255
Vinyl chloride (in air), 196
Visibility, 176, 184, 190
Volatile organic chemicals, 210
Volcanoes, 132, 187, 197

Waco, Texas, 23, 36-42. See also EPA-Waco composite (noise monitoring procedure)
Waddell, T.E., 183-186
Walsh-Healey Public Contracts Act, 25
Ward, R.C., 134
Waste Water Treatment Technology, 166
Wastler, T.A., 159
Water, color of, 129, 135, 148, 152
Water, currents in, 134, 137, 138, 153, 161
Water, discoloration of, 12, 129
Water, eutrophication of, 12
Water, light penetration of, 12, 129, 130, 152, 156
Water, odor of, 129, 133, 135, 152
Water, taste of, 135
Water cooling systems, 102, 109-110
Water cycle, 117-122, 125
Water demand, by electric utilities, 102
Water demand, commercial/institutional, 101, 113-115
Water demand, industrial public potable, 115-117
Water demand, industrial self-supplied, 101-112
Water demand, long-term planning for, 103-112, 117
Water demand, regional planning for, 103-112, 117
Water demand, residential, 101, 113
Water demand, short-term impacts on, 102-103, 117
Water imports and exports, 125
Water Information Center, 154
Water intake coefficients, 103, 107-116
Water monitoring, by aquatic and terrestrial surveys, 136-139
Water monitoring, by biological and chemical analyses, 134-136
Water monitoring, establishing the ambient environment in, 129-134
Water monitoring, federal, 96, 102-103, 135, 139-152
Water monitoring, sampling sites for, 136, 156-165, 227, 249